OTHER TITLES IN THE SERIES

Alternative Kilns
Ian Gregory

Ceramics with Mixed Media
Joy Bosworth

Ceramics and Print
Paul Scott

Coiling
Michael Hardy

Colouring Clay
Jo Connell

Crystalline Glazes
Diane Creber

The Electric Kiln
Harry Fraser

Glazes Cone 6
Michael Bailey

Handbuilding
Michael Hardy

Impressed and Incised Ceramics
Coll Minogue

Kiln Building
Ian Gregory

Large-scale Ceramics
Jim Robison

Lettering on Ceramics
Mary White

Low Firing and Burnishing
Sumi von Dassow

Oriental Glazes
Michael Bailey

Paper Clay
Rosette Gault

Porcelain
Jack Doherty

Raku
John Mathieson

Resist and Masking Techniques
Peter Beard

Setting Up a Pottery Workshop
Alistair Young

Single Firing
Fran Tristram

Slipcasting
Sasha Wardell

Stoneware
Richard Dewar

Soda Glazing
Ruthanne Tudball

Throwing Pots
Phil Rogers

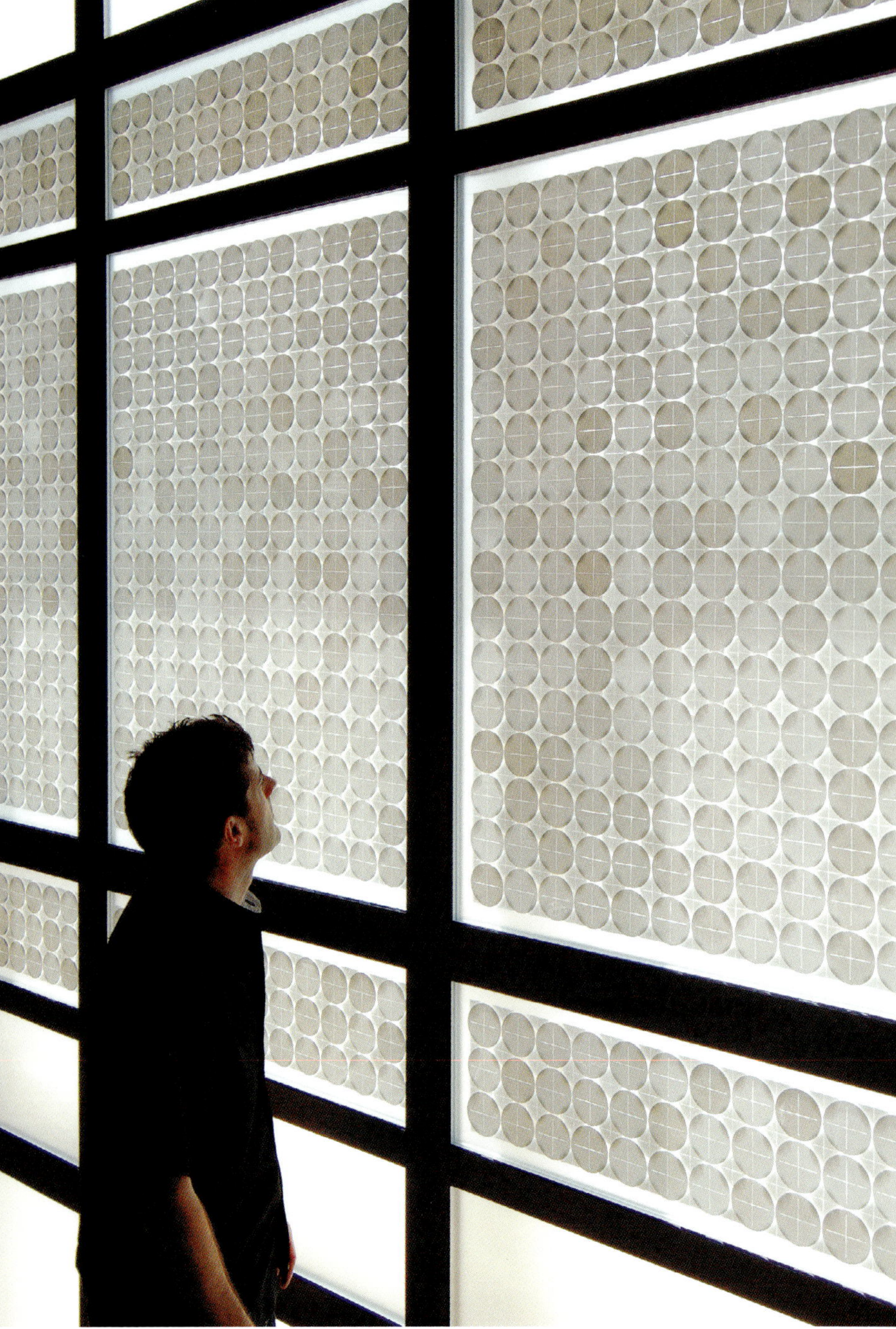

WALL PIECES

Dominique Bivar Segurado

A & C Black • London

The American Ceramic Society • Ohio

COVER (FRONT) *Power of Running Water* by Jeanne Opgenhaffen. 95 × 95 cm (37 × 37 in.). White porcelain mounted on zinc. *Photo courtesy of the artist.*
COVER (BACK) *Flock*, by John Butler, Jonna Behrens, Anne Jamison, Debbie Metherell, 2003. University of Westminster, Regent Street Campus, London. Size: 40.21m^2 (433 sq. ft). *Photo by Andy Golding.*

FRONTISPIECE *Chapel Doors* by Chris Wight, 2008. Commissioned for The Minster School, Southwell. Each door: Ht: 4 m (13 ft); W: 3 m (9 ft 10 in.). Discs: 15.5 x 7 x 4.5 cm (6 x 2¾ in. x 1¾ in.). 'Cross-hair' bone china discs; toughened glass held within an aluminium framework. *Photo courtesy of the artist.*

First published in Great Britain in 2009
A & C Black Publishers Limited
36 Soho Square
London W1D 3QY
www.acblack.com

ISBN 978-1-408-10407-1

Published simultaneously in the USA by
The American Ceramic Society
600 N.Cleveland Ave., Suite 210
Westerville, Ohio 43082, USA
www.ceramicartsdaily.org

ISBN 978-1-57498-292-3

CIP Catalogue records for this book are available from the British Library and the US Library of Congress.

Typeset in 10 on 12pt Photina
Book design by Susan McIntyre
Cover design by Sutchinda Thompson

Printed and bound in China

This book is produced using paper that is made from wood grown in managed, sustainable forests. It is natural, renewable and recyclable. The logging and manufacturing processes conform to the environmental regulations of the country of origin.

Contents

Acknowledgements

This book has been a very interesting journey for me as both a maker and a person who has struggled with dyslexia over the years, but one that would not have been possible without the support of those involved in the project, both personal and professional, and I would like to take this opportunity to thank them.

Thanks to my family for all their support and encouragement over the years, and to my husband Edward for his patience, new-found love of cooking and help while writing the book. Thanks to Dot Pennycot and Rick Smith who first inspired me to work with clay: your encouragement and energy in the subject does live on! Thank-you also to John Burrell and John Harrison for their specialist subject knowledge, and Jan Wells and Emily Peters at the Henry Moore Foundation. I would also like to thank Anne Mercedes for her involvement and energy given to chapter one. Without the help, kindness and guidance of my editor Alison Stace this book would not be a reality, so thanks.

But most of all, I would like to thank all the artists, institutions, organisations and suppliers who have contributed to this book, as it would not be possible without their fantastic work.

Introduction

Over the last decade, the innovation and determination of ceramicists to push the boundaries of clay as well as people's perceptions of the material has surprised and excited me.

I hope this book will offer inspiration for a material that is extremely versatile, natural and beautiful. The chapters give an insight into how makers from all over the world are working with clay and the wall space in an exciting and dynamic manner. The book also provides some technical information and guidelines to help get you started in designing, creating and hanging your own wall piece.

The wall piece

The fascination with the decoration of a wall's surface is not a recent concept but can be traced as far back as Ancient Egypt, where they decorated their walls with stories of the gods using oxides painted directly on a surface and in some cases using ceramic tiles. Although ceramic wall pieces have evolved and changed from the use of the tile, the concept of decorating and expanding an idea, pattern and visual relief across a surface or a whole room is present throughout history and continues to this day (*see* p. 17, The Gamble Room at the V&A). The traditional tile still has a good relationship with our environment and architecture, as people continue to crave the functional, hardwearing, bespoke and the new for their surroundings. However, it still is important to have a creative approach to space, whether this is within our homes, offices or urban environment. A more recent awareness of the spaces we occupy could be attributed to the successful presence of designers, architects and artists continuing to exert an influence on us through our surroundings and the media. Over the years, demand on space has become greater, due to a number of factors, one of which is an increasing population, so the spaces we now occupy are generally smaller. There is a need to ensure these spaces are therefore more inviting, and this is why a creative approach is essential. These various influences have provoked many ceramicists, both consciously and subconsciously to respond by creating innovative new pieces of work which vary in scale and no longer purely focus on three-dimensional objects which exist independently. Instead they have begun to create forms that interact with our environments, and use otherwise 'wasted' space such as the wall.

The current move towards the wall as an area for creative ideas should now be described as a new 'movement', from the three-dimensional crafted object into a new art form which crosses the boundaries of two-dimensional into three-dimensional.

The original source of this movement is routed not only with the tile but also the framed canvas, as the framed picture has always been a reliable and traditional form of decoration. It has offered an opportunity to convey an artist's idea or vision, or document a certain location which we might respond to.

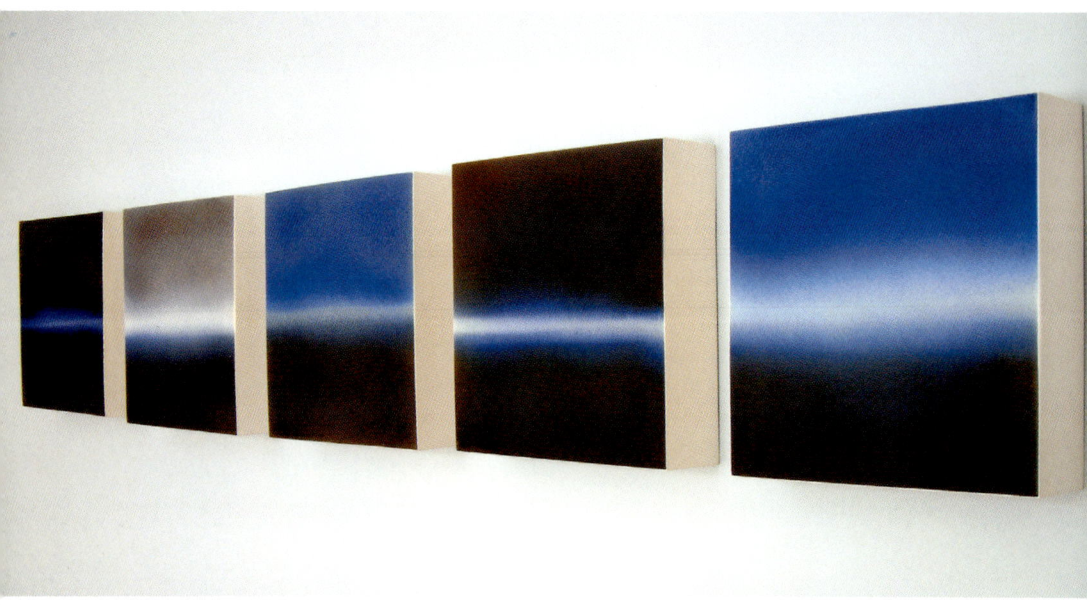

Large Landscape Horizon by Karin Schösser, 2005. 27 × 27 × 6.5 cm (10½ × 10½ × 2½ in.). Glazed white earthenware. *Photo courtesy of the artist.*

More people are now making a conscious decision to hang contemporary wall pieces in spaces where they might have once opted for a painting. Some believe that one reason for this is down to the fact that 'crafted' ceramics are becoming more accessible, collectable, approachable and affordable than the fine art market.

It has become apparent in recent times that ceramicists have become aware of how open and approachable the three-dimensional form can be when placed in different spaces. Through ceramic wall pieces, three-dimensional forms are entering the realm of the painting and hung canvas. One maker who engages in this is Karin Schösser (*see above*). One could say this is the evolution of the humble tile and a reflection on contemporary approaches to the use of clay; taking a simple idea and interpreting it in a new and exciting way.

Many of the projects presented throughout the book mention the artist's connection to the space, and how they have used it or responded to it, whether through a commission, exhibition, or personal initiative. On larger-scale projects this can involve the architect, owner or commissioning body, with the aim of collaborating to transform a wall, (an example of this is Henry Moore's *Bouwcentrum Wall*, Rotterdam, *see* p. 13). This integrated wall piece was created after a conversation between the artist and the architect J.W.C. Boks who was an admirer of Moore's work. He felt the extension to the existing building would be an ideal opportunity to incorporate sculptural forms with architecture.

Another contemporary artist whose work engages in the concept and successful marriage of ceramics, wall pieces and architecture is Pieter Stockman (*see* p. 9). The continuing presentation of ceramics on wall spaces has given him the opportunity to engage with a new audience who have perhaps not considered clay

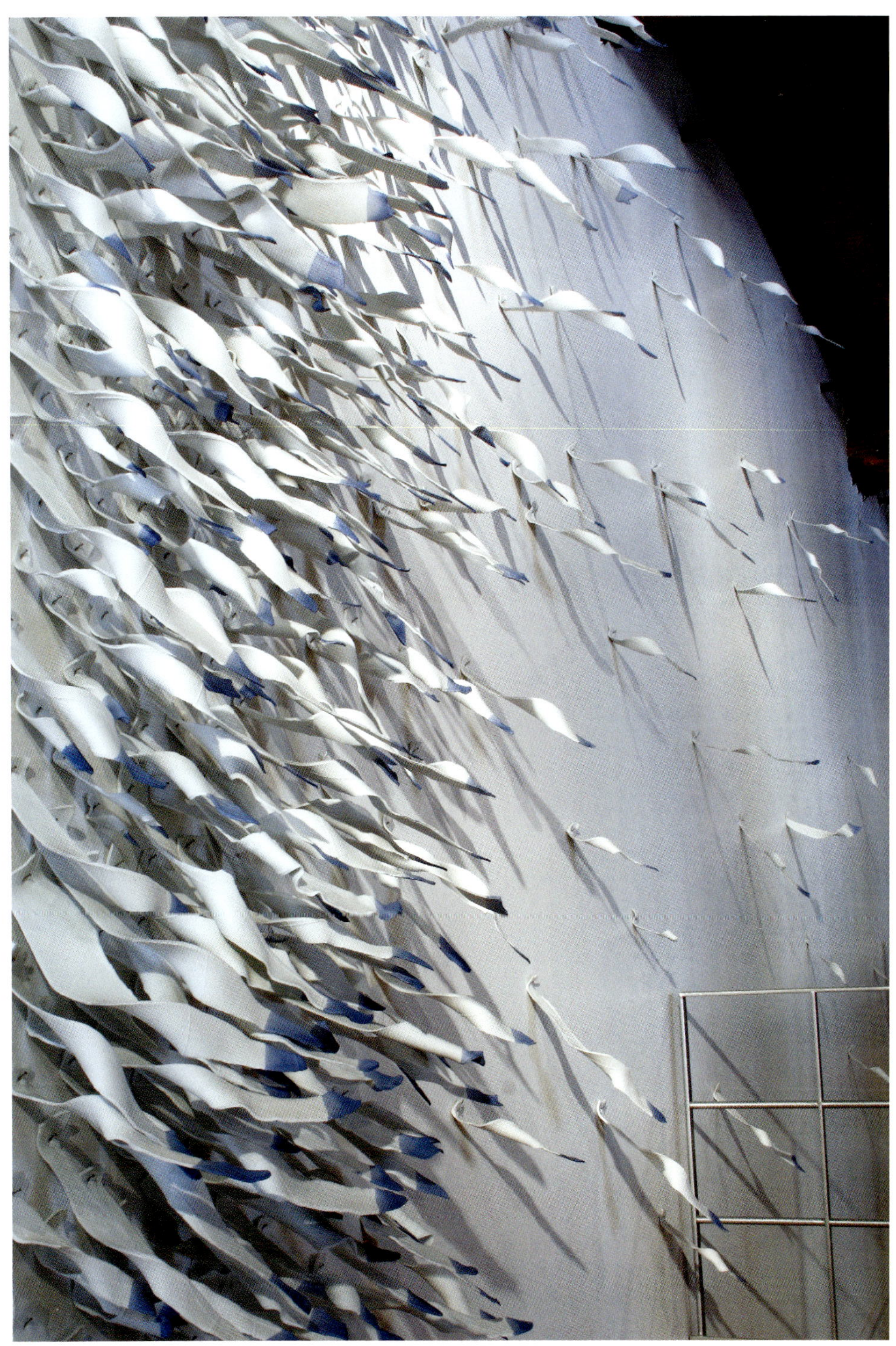

Untitled, by Pieter Stockmans. 2006. Luminaire, Chicago, USA.

before. Its tactile qualities and multiple uses are becoming more apparent to the public, which in turn makes it more approachable to the viewer, maker, client and commissioning agent. His innovative projects raise the public's awareness of the space they are placed in, as much as the work itself.

It could be argued that 21st century artists have been strongly influenced by elements of design and architecture, the result being an increasing tendency to use innovative materials alongside the clay. Along with this is our continuing need to develop and evolve our creative efforts, which is driving us forward as makers, artists and studio ceramicists to achieve larger-scale and grander projects.

The possibilities for creating wall pieces remain open, to be shaped through the individual artist's style, material and use of space. Wall pieces can provide a focus, regenerate and transform an ugly space or corridor, or unify a space by covering several walls. They can conceal or exploit a wall or space, and can even be combined with a use of light, as with Margaret O'Rorke and Chris Wight's work. The boundaries on placing wall pieces remain open, and works have been sited in chapels, museums, bars, subways and law courts, and it currently remains for modern artists to continue this development to find out what can be achieved.

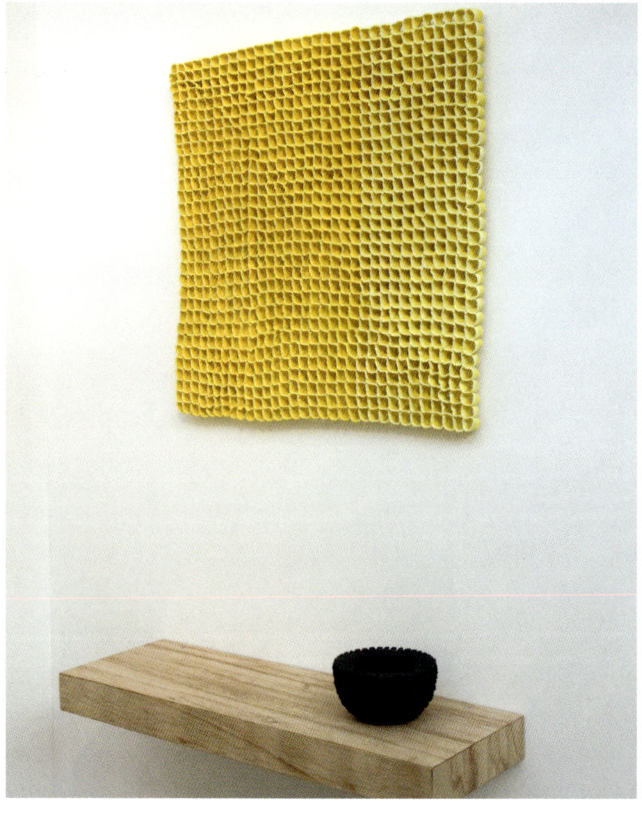

Clay Knit, Glossy Yellow by Stine Jesperson, 2008. 62 × 62 × 2 cm (24½ × 24½ × ¾ in.). Earthenware. *Photograph by Sylvain Dele.*

Chapter 1

Wall pieces from past to present

This chapter provides an overview of what wall pieces are, and how they fit into the contemporary scene, with a look at their historical origins in other forms, and how they have evolved. More and more artists and designers working with ceramics are showing an interest in making wall pieces, and finding ways of producing large-scale work for which they may not have been trained. Achieving these projects often involves working in collaboration, so this chapter briefly examines the practical and economic factors influencing the different forms of collaboration.

The projects that this chapter examines provide examples of different types of wall pieces, and highlight the social and economic developments relevant to anyone wishing to undertake projects of this kind.

Walls; structuring space and life

A wall is a vertical solid structure which divides or encloses, and by doing so defines two areas: as soon as a wall is erected, two discrete spaces or territories are created. When a single wall, even though it does not enclose a space, is erected outdoors or stands as a ruin, it nevertheless affects the space around it. A wall thus plays an important role in

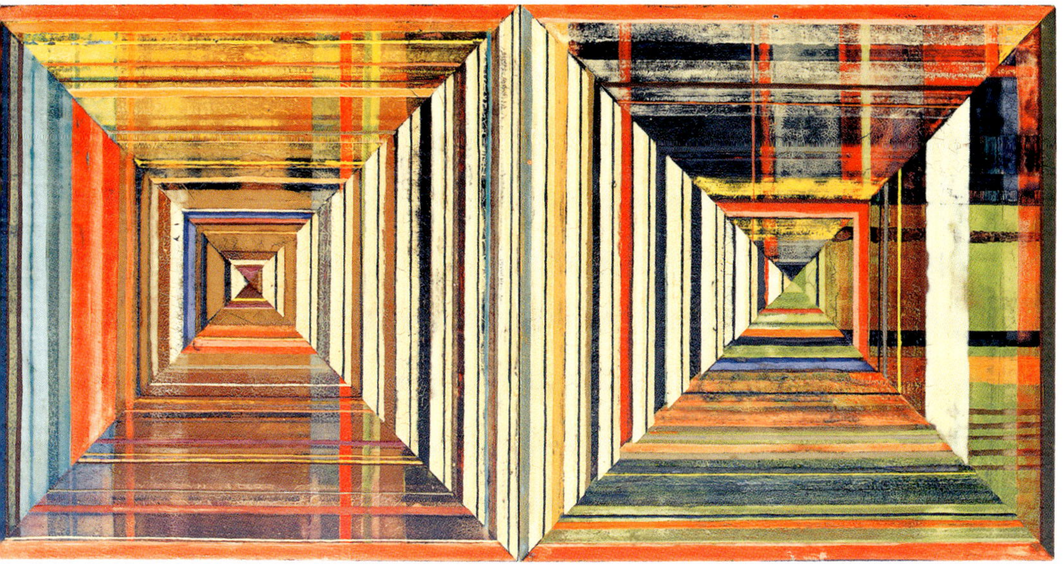

Fired Painting by Shin Sang Ho, 2005. Glazed ceramics, 50 x 50 cm (19¾ x 19¾ in.) and 50 x 50 cm (19¾ x 19¾ in.). *Photo by Hyungduk Shin.*

shaping the identity of different areas, as when delineating public and private space, or the various activities catered for in different rooms in a building. It also helps to demarcate the limits of a property.

A wall can, then, protect one or more of the areas which have been delineated, and thus meet one of the most fundamental needs of human beings: to be safe and feel safe.

Conversely, walls can be used to lock people up or to prevent them from circulating or escaping. Many walls, though not specifically erected to lock up, nevertheless have this effect, at least symbolically, as when preventing the light from coming into a room, blocking the view or being dark and imposing. Walls can be reassuring or threatening, depending on their function, history and appearance. Walls thus bear within them the fundamental contradiction of human beings: the need for both security and freedom.

The final basic function of a wall is to support the superstructure of a building and, nowadays, to house various types of electrical wiring or plumbing. In spite of innovations made in the middle of the 19th century, which allow large loads to be supported by columns inside the building rather than by the external walls and façades, this role is still important in many constructions and is emphasised by the symbolic presentation of the face (façade) of the building. Walls that play a role in supporting the superstructure of a building are called 'building' or 'load-bearing' walls.

Through their different roles and the ways they are perceived, walls seem to play a vital part in the complex relation that human beings weave with space; they even contribute to making life possible, in that they delineate, canalise, concentrate and accompany all forms of human activities, whether physical, psychological or spiritual. Indeed, beyond the fundamental needs they meet, walls make it possible for people to gather together and communicate, or to isolate themselves and dream. This is why walls have from the start been a support for human expression and memory, and a sign of cultural and social identity.

Ceramics became involved in this process from the moment that brick was invented (bricks being ceramic themselves). By 'ceramic wall pieces' we can understand different things that all have a long tradition behind them, as well as a strong presence on the contemporary scene.

Four main categories of wall pieces

1. Any ceramic load-bearing wall (which supports the structure of the building), and which has a distinctive ornamental dimension or has been created as a work of art in itself. In this case the ceramic components are part of the building structure. They can be unglazed or glazed bricks, terracotta building blocks (distinguished from bricks by their relatively large size and finer quality of clay)[1], and faience building blocks, which are glazed terracotta.
2. Any ceramic composition added to a wall built of other material, to act as a protective and decorative skin or to make an artistic statement. It usually involves many components such as tiles and is meant to be permanent; however, it can be removed without affecting the structure of the wall.
3. Any removable ceramic composition hung onto a wall. It can be made of one or several parts of various dimensions,

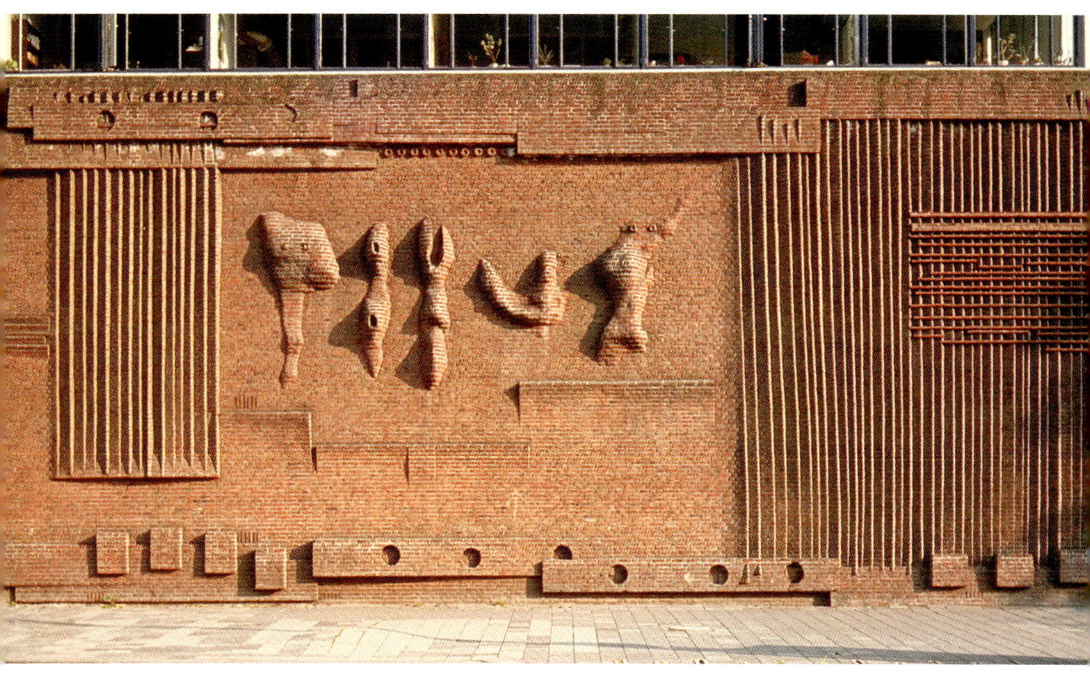

Bouwcentrum Wall by Henry Moore, 1955. Commissioned for the Building Centre, Rotterdam, by architect J.W.C. Boks. Ht: 8.5 m (28 ft.), W: 19.2 m (63 ft.). Brick. Rotterdam's Building Centre, Rotterdam. The project was designed to integrate sculpture and architecture by making the wall a work of art. *Photo courtesy of the Henry Moore Foundation.*

and varies in size from domestic pieces to monumental work.

4. Any temporary ceramic installation that uses a wall or several walls as a support for creating a spatial experience and that 'by consuming the entire visual field of the viewer becomes three-dimensional even if it is flat'[2].

Ceramics has been used as a construction or decorative architectural component for thousands of years. The Egyptians used small greenish-blue glazed tiles to decorate the subterranean chambers of the great Step Pyramid of Saqqara, built of stone between BC2630–2611. At about the same time, the builders of the Harappan Civilisation were using fired bricks for the construction of the city of Mohenjo-Daro in the Indus Valley (Pakistan). In the 6th century BC, the Babylonians used glazed bricks as a decorative medium for the Gate of Ishtar, and their skills were employed in Persia when Darius created a new royal complex at Susa at the end of the same century.

These instances were followed by many more in every civilisation throughout world history. Altogether, they form a continuous but ever-evolving tradition, proving that ceramics can play a role as a structural component of a wall, or as its skin, or even as a decorative effect integrated into the structure. Indeed, in a brick wall, a linear grid pattern appears automatically as a result of its structural system; it is possible to lay bricks in such a way that pleasing geometrical patterns appear. If the bricks are relief-moulded or even glazed, the grid pattern is undermined by the image or form that the relief and colours create, as in the Gate of Ishtar. With this kind of brick, the creative possibilities are endless.

The wall as work of art

A masterly example is provided by Henry Moore's *Bouwcentrum Wall* in Rotterdam, the Netherlands (*see* p.13). Built in 1955 on the side of a new extension of this Building Centre, the huge red-brick wall is 8.5 m high and 19.2 m long (28 x 63 ft). It was designed to integrate sculpture and architecture and was commissioned by the architect J.W.C. Boks. Framed by vertically ribbed lines, the five organic shapes that stand out of the wall suggest animal and human forms, but they seem to emerge from the surface or disappear under it. This evanescent quality is obtained thanks to elements of raised decoration on the surface of the brick, the technique known as bas-relief. Moore produced 10 relief motifs in plaster and bronze, and the brick clay was then press-moulded to produce the patterns. By suggesting there is something beyond the façade, this piece highlights the ambiguity which is inherent in any wall: it creates a limit but entices beyond it. Moreover this heavy structure, whose stability relies on the downpull of gravity, reveals uplifting forms which change and take the viewer on a journey through different worlds, depending on the position of the sun and the shadows it produces.

Moore was an internationally renowned artist when Boks contacted him, but this wall piece would not have existed had an architect not commissioned it. The need for an independent artist to be able to afford the materials and facilities or to be commissioned or sponsored, cannot be ignored. This may explain not only why certain materials seem to be popular at certain times and then fall from favour, but also how some large-scale work is achieved.

In *Brickworks*[3], Gwen Heeney examines and illustrates in depth the rich tradition in which Moore was working. She shows that in the second half of the 20th century, after a period of decline, artistic brickworks underwent a renewal. In tracing the ups and downs of this medium in the UK, she explains the role the 'specials' departments in factories played in promoting one-off projects, how their closure in most factories in the 1960s accelerated the decline of these projects, and how the 1980s building boom prompted some factories, which no longer had any craftsmen, to ask artists to design 'specials' instead.

The decorative skin or artistic statement

The collaboration between at least two kinds of protagonists, architects and manufacturers, or architects and craftsmen/artists, has also been decisive in the development of the second category of wall pieces: those which are permanently added to an existing wall, or built concomitantly with the wall as a decorative skin, or an artistic statement.

From a rich body of work developed over three decades and represented in dozens of public collections around the world, I have selected *Lex Portalis* (the Portal of the Law) by the Norwegian artist Ole Lislerud. This was commissioned for the Oslo Court Building designed by Østgaard Arkitekter, and created in 1994 with architect Terje Grønmo. Lislerud has etched in handwriting the 1814 Norwegian Constitution and the Penal Code, as well as Viking laws, on

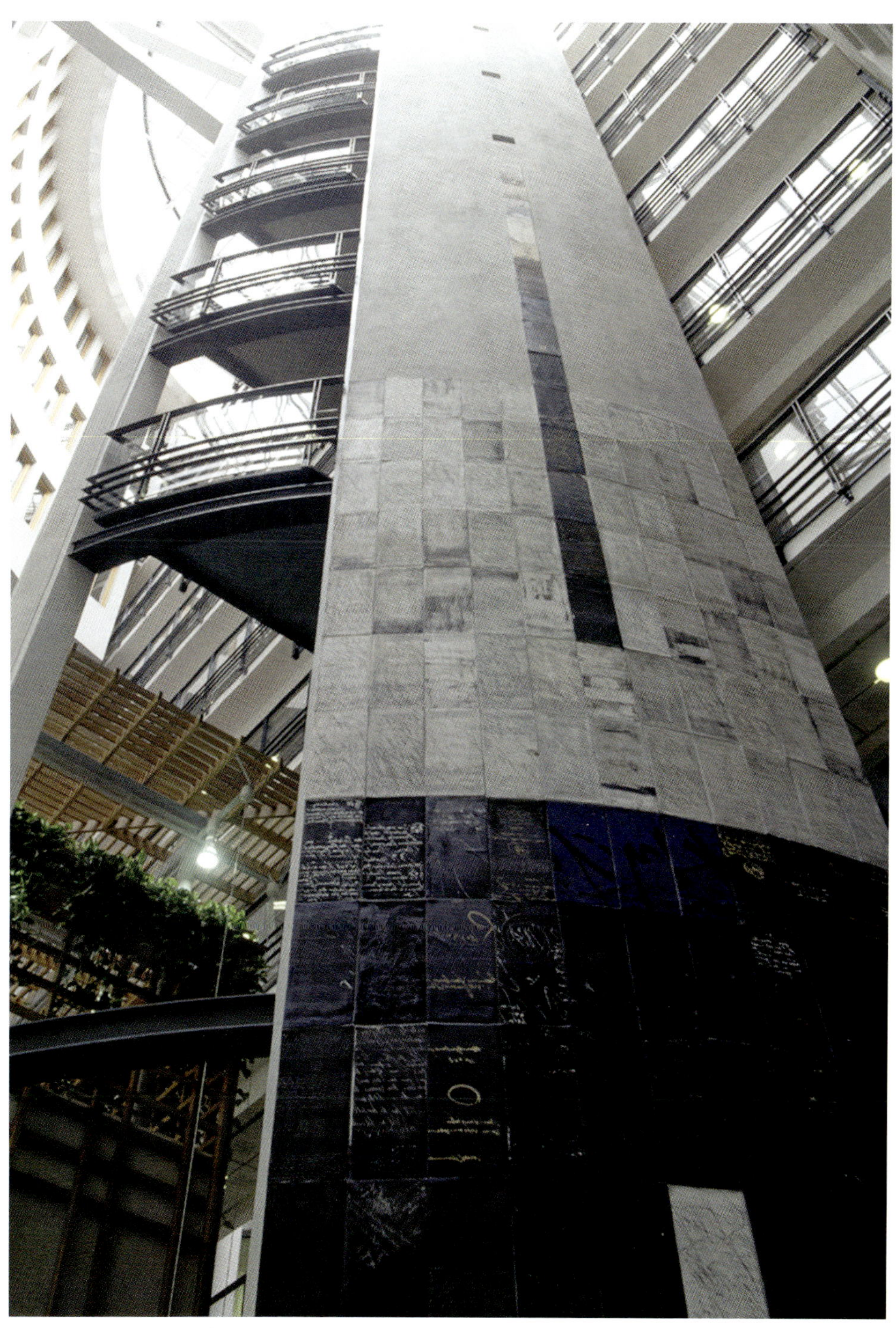

Lex Portalis by Ole Lislerud, 1994. Commissioned for the Oslo Court Building by Østgaard Arkitekter. Ht: 32 m (105 ft). Porcelain tiles. *Photo by Glenn Hagbru.*

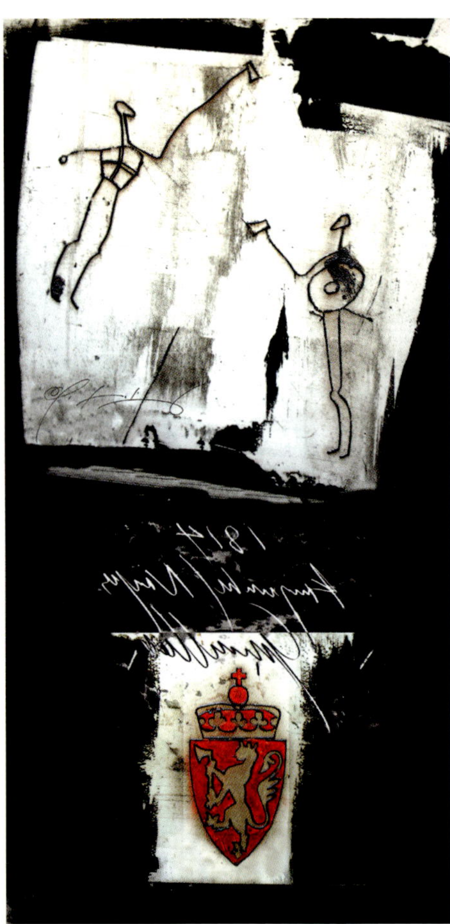

Lex Portalis, detail, by Ole Lislerud, 1994. *Photo by Glenn Hagbru.*

2 mm (1/16 in.) thin porcelain tiles that cover 400 m² (4305 sq. ft). This porcelain skin covers the surface of the 32 m (105 ft) high arch erected in the luminous space of the atrium, where the central staircase is positioned.[4] Before this public and physical affirmation of the law, one cannot help thinking of the 2.25 m (7.38 ft) stone on which Hammurabi, King of Babylon (*c.*1795-1750BC), had the laws of his kingdom engraved (this stone is now in the Louvre, Paris). But, apart from being much taller, Lislerud's contemporary echo of this royal enterprise reflects how much our relation to the law has changed: by reversing the handwriting when transferring it onto the porcelain tiles, Lislerud deliberately renders it illegible.

Though visible from the windows of the surrounding courtrooms, the text yields no answer until the different interpreters of the law bring it to life. The arch itself and the stairs running along it symbolize a society in transformation, constantly assessing its system of values. Lislerud writes: 'In this site-specific work, art and architecture combine to create an integrated statement that gives identity and meaning not only for those who work in the court building but also for society at large.' Concern for identity runs consistently through Lislerud's great variety of projects. He acknowledges how modern life has evolved 'from local social integration, with generation households, to mass culture, small nuclear family households and web communication.'[5] These relations develop in the constantly changing urban space: his aim is to promote landmarks around which exchanges and openness to the world are facilitated. By using walls as an opportunity to create a specific atmosphere, art and architecture become the means by which people appropriate the space and weave their identity. Professor Ole Lislerud teaches students how to work with architectural plans to render three-dimensional proposals.[6]

As already mentioned, Lislerud's use of tiles participates in a tradition with ancient origins. Ceramic tiles are durable, waterproof and easy to clean; they protect buildings from the heat of the day but also provide good insulation after sundown. Tiles can be any shape, and the diversity of colours that can be obtained from different clays and glazes allows for a great variety of decorative possibilities that has been extensively explored world-wide. As anthropomorphic representation is forbidden by Islam, geometric patterns and calligraphy became central to the visual arts of its realm. From the 9th century tiles of different shapes were developed in Baghdad, showing seemingly endless possibilities. This tradition greatly influenced architectural ceramic design and manufacture, and in the Middle Ages it gradually spread via contact with Islam to the whole of Europe, with especially innovative centres in Spain, Portugal, Holland and England. Until the 19th century, tile-making was a craft-based industry of small workshops, despite enormous demand, which had to meet the needs of huge mosques and palaces in Persia, Morocco and Spain (Alcazar in Seville and Alhambra in Grenada), private houses and English churches. In Europe, mass-production of both bricks and tiles developed as the Industrial Revolution modified production techniques, and these ceramics components became used across Europe and America on a very large scale. Designers and architects benefited from the opportunity to work in collaboration with ceramic manufacturers and to produce one-off projects.

The central café at the Victoria and Albert Museum in London, known as the Gamble Room, is the result of such a collaboration between 1865 and 1877.[7] It was designed by Godfrey Sykes, whose ideas were developed after his death by

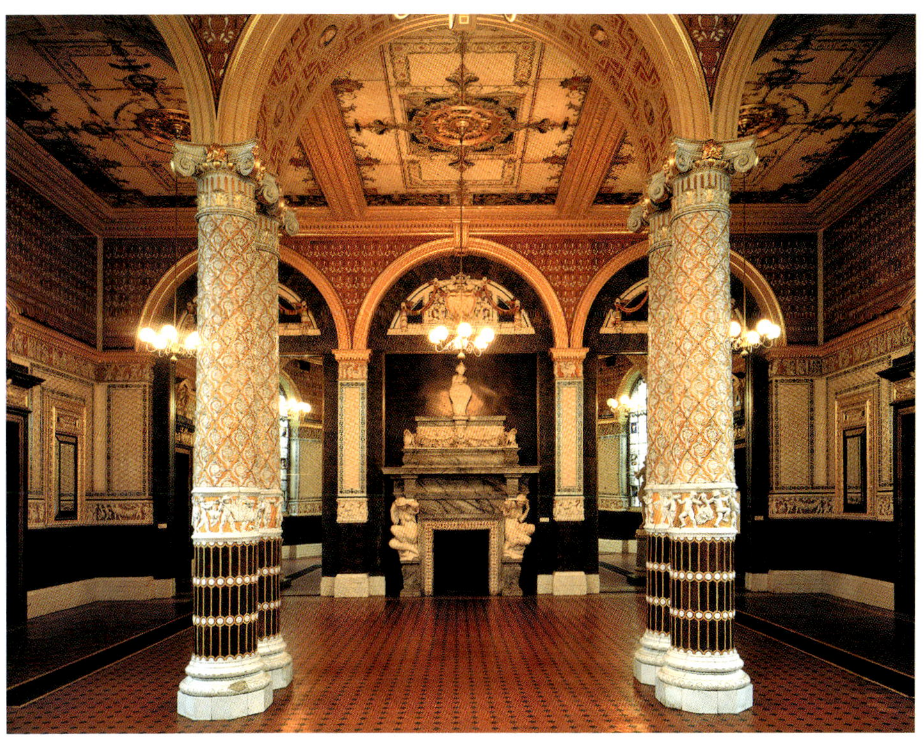

The Gamble Room, Victoria & Albert Museum, by James Gamble, Godfrey Sykes and Reuben Townroc, 1865–77. Tiles and glazed, moulded terracotta. *Photo © V&A Images/Victoria & Albert Museum.*

James Gamble and Reuben Townroe. The tiles, glazed moulded terracotta and the central columns were produced by Minton Hollins of Stoke-on-Trent. The frieze reads: 'There is nothing better for a man than that he should eat and drink, and that he should make his soul enjoy good in his labour.' (Ecclesiastes, 2.24.)

Other famous projects deserve to be mentioned: the Majolica House in Vienna, designed by Otto Wagner 1898–1899, Michelin House in London, designed by François Espinasse in 1911, the Park Güell in Barcelona, designed by Antoni Gaudí 1900–1914 and named after the rich builder who supported his work, and several entrances to the Paris Metro, designed by Hector Guimard in 1900. All these projects were designed by architects, some, like Gaudí, leaving the ceramicist assisting him to take the initiative; others, like Guimard, making sure to be in control of every detail.

This ornamental trend developed to such an extent that it was perceived as excessive. Under the combined influence of an ongoing revolution in building techniques, new architectural theories and the economic crisis of the 1930s, it started to decline before the Second World War.

Here a point needs to be made, which should also help to explain the progressive lack of interest not only in tiles, but also in brickwork. As previously mentioned, up to the middle of the 19th century, buildings were constructed with the exterior walls supporting the load of the entire structure. This affected the choice of materials. But thanks to the development and widespread use of structural steel and reinforced concrete, the exterior walls are no longer always required for structural support: large loads can be supported by columns inside the

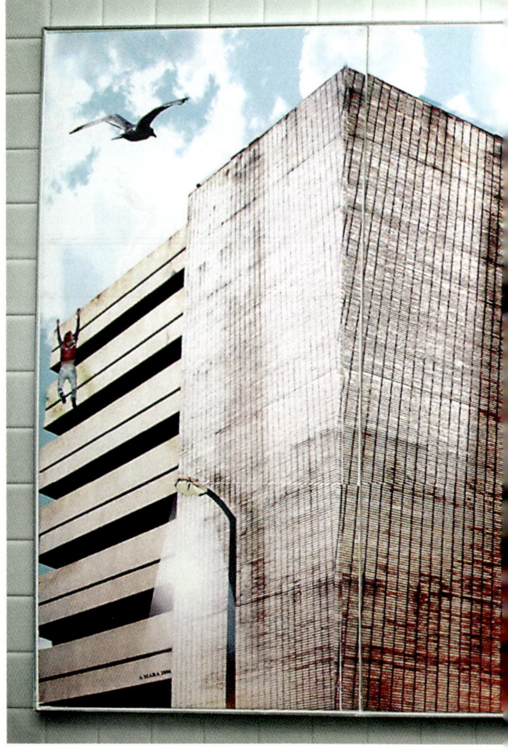

building. This allows the use of lighter materials on the exterior façade, which can be hung onto the building like a curtain, hence the name: curtain wall. This definitive change has had a negative impact on the use of ceramics for façades, because architects have become fascinated by the possibility of using other exciting materials that could not be used before, such as glass.

But ceramics have much to offer as a material for façade cladding, especially now that the tile industry is able to produce extraordinary large-scale tiles, up to 3 x 1.5 m (10 x 5 ft), as in Jingdezhen, China, or at the Otsuka Ohmi factory in Osaka, Japan, where digital photography and computer processing with ceramic silkscreen also offer new possibilities.

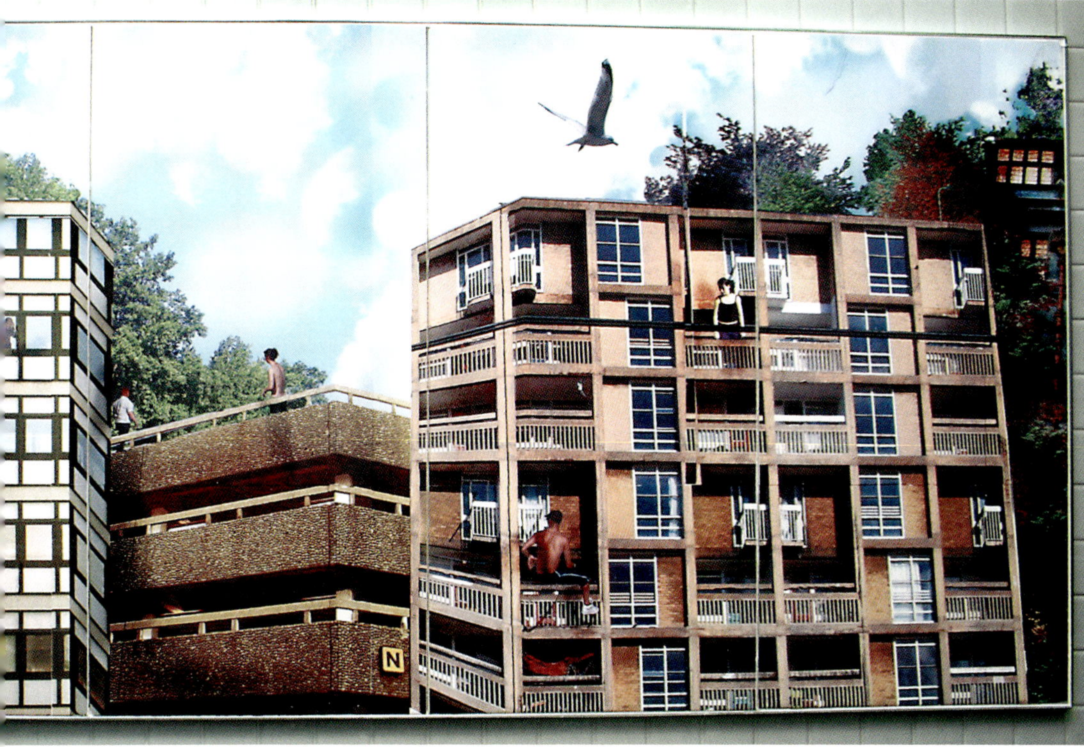

Industrial Tiles, by Alice Mara. Commissioned by Western Parks Museum, Sheffield. 100 x 30 cm (39½ x 11¾ in.) Digitally printed tiles. *Photo by Tom Glendining.*

Lislerud's work reveals his capacity to integrate these technological improvements and opportunities. With the right initiative other artists can also exploit these opportunities, coming up with projects which can create a special ambiance, thus appealing to architects and patrons who want buildings to do more than simply perform a function – to intrigue people and invite them to engage with the space that surrounds them.

Alice Mara's work provides another example of the use of new technological possibilities associated with tiles. She is interested in urban landscape, and documents her own city with her digital camera. She then manipulates the photos on her computer to give them a fantastical, surreal appeal. In 2006 she was commissioned to produce several series of tiles for the Western Parks Museum in Sheffield. The city's famous steel industry suffered a deep crisis in the last quarter of the 20th century, and local government subsequently sought to regenerate this area through projects involving the community. In this context, Mara's wall pieces, *Industrial Tiles* (above), *Bird Man on Building (p.20)* and *Penguin Industrial Tile*, portray the Sheffield environment while weaving into it humorous, colourful elements likely to appeal to a young public and to transport the viewer beyond the bleak aspect it once presented. The images produced by Mara are printed on a photocopier machine using ceramic pigment as toner. The printed image is

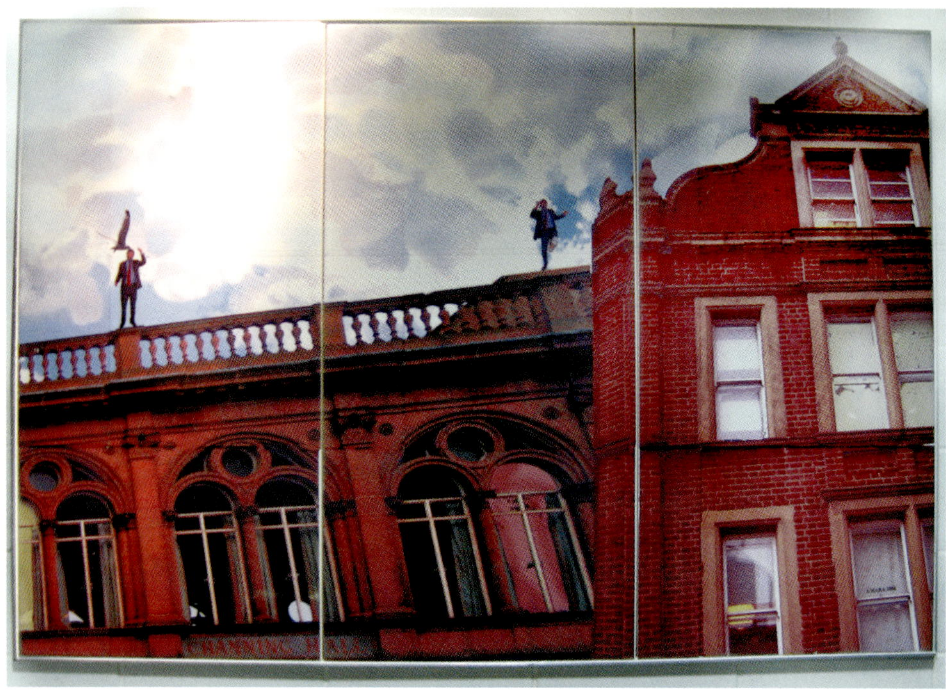

Bird Man on Building by Alice Mara. 90 × 60 cm (35½ × 23½ in.). Digitally printed tiles. Commissioned by Western Parks Museum, Sheffield. *Photo byTom Glendining.*

then coated with a cover coat film which enables the image to be transferred onto the tile. The cover-coated image is put into water and the image slides off the backing paper. The image is then positioned on the tile, any excess water wiped off, and the tile is fired at 850°C (1562°F). The image sinks into the glaze of the tile and does not erode over time.

Another instance of the potential of ceramic tiles as an artistic medium is provided by Shin Sang Ho's *Fired Painting* series (*see* p. 11 and opposite). They magnificently enhance the Clayarch Gimhae Museum, South Korea, opened in 2006 with the aim of strengthening the mutual development of art and architecture: 'ceramics will broaden its possibilities through architecture, while architecture will secure its artistic and material diversity through ceramics'.[8] The building is circular, embellished with 5000 large, hand-made ceramic panels on the second floor of the exhibition foyer and the façades, where Shin Sang Ho proves to be a master of clay-as-painting. The abstract lines of different colours build up patterns reminiscent of textile, and echo the early geometric abstracts of European artists such as Paul Klee and Vassily Kandinsky, as well as the American painters Mark Rothko and Sean Scully.[9] Trained in the tradition of both Korean and Chinese ceramics, Shin developed dark vessels whose surfaces were animated by dynamic abstract strokes remarkable for their tension and liveliness. However, these strokes seemed imprisoned in the shapes of the vessels. He went on to explore the

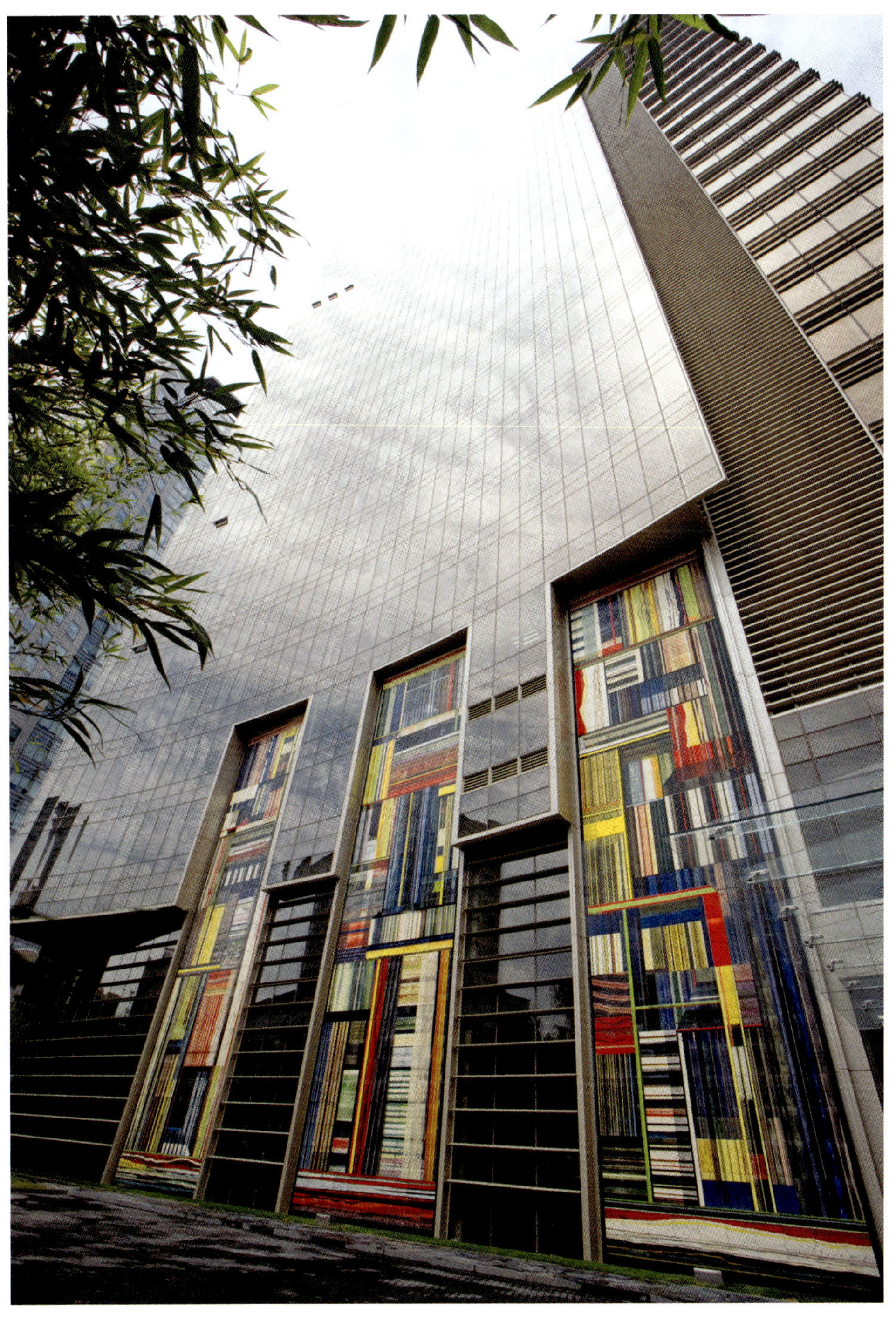

Dream of Africa by Shin Sang Ho, 2005. Hwasung, Kyungkido, South Korea. 300 x 300 cm (118 x 118 in). *Photo by Hyungduk Shin.*

world of the Palaeolithic caves, more specifically sculpting heads of animals, and transferring to three dimensions the dynamic that was previously visible on the surface of his vessels. Shin then decided to paint on large supports (walls), to develop the prodigious vitality and strength we can see at work in the *Fired Painting* series, and which exploit the potential of colours as autonomous realities, freed from the boundaries of any outline.

In 2006, the Clayarch Gimhae Museum hosted a symposium called New Way of Architectural Ceramics, featuring 16 artists from several continents. It also acts as a centre for artists in residence that helps, like other events supported by the Korean government, to foster artistic projects in the realm of architecture. In 2005 the Third World Ceramic Biennale, organised by WOCEF (World Ceramic Exposition Foundation) in South Korea, presented a special exhibition dedicated to Ceramics and Architecture. In 2009 the Fifth Biennale Conference will focus on Ceramics, Architecture and Environment. Like other recently created institutions across the world, Clayarch Gimhae Museum and WOCEF testify to a profound change in the link between ceramics and architecture, as the artists are given help to produce large-scale work and thus become more visible to possible patrons. In Europe, the spearhead of such an alliance is the European Ceramic Work Centre, which opened in 1992 in the Netherlands, and expanded its sphere of work by introducing architecture as one of its subjects.

Ceramic compositions hung on a wall

For the purposes of discussion, these have been divided into four main subcategories which can overlap in twos: monumental or non-monumental work, and site-specific or non-specific work.

Wall pieces where size is relative to domestic space and dimensions

In contrast to paintings, to which they can be related, these are 3D pieces, but often of a thickness negligible in comparison to their width and length. This means that they do not encroach upon the space available in the room: this is sometimes a driving force in the decision to make wall pieces or to acquire a wall piece. In urban areas the domestic space available has generally shrunk over the last 30 years. This is certainly a reality in the UK. These wall pieces offer the possibility of a sculptural approach, and enhance a space while not 'occupying it'. They are often conceived as an autonomous entity, independent of a specific site, and do not always require specific attention to planning regulations. However, unless they are small, they should be attached to a wall with caution. Some pieces include a complex device at the back, which allows for hanging. In spite of their aesthetic unity, the wall pieces in this first category can in fact be comprised of several elements, as in the following example by Marie-Ruth Oda, modest in size though commissioned for a temporary outdoor public project.

During her stay as artist in residence in Shigaraki Ceramic Cultural Park, Japan, Mari-Ruth Oda saw an exhibition of newly excavated dinosaur fossils from China: 'I was overwhelmed by the amazing forms of the dinosaur bones, and how fundamentally similar they

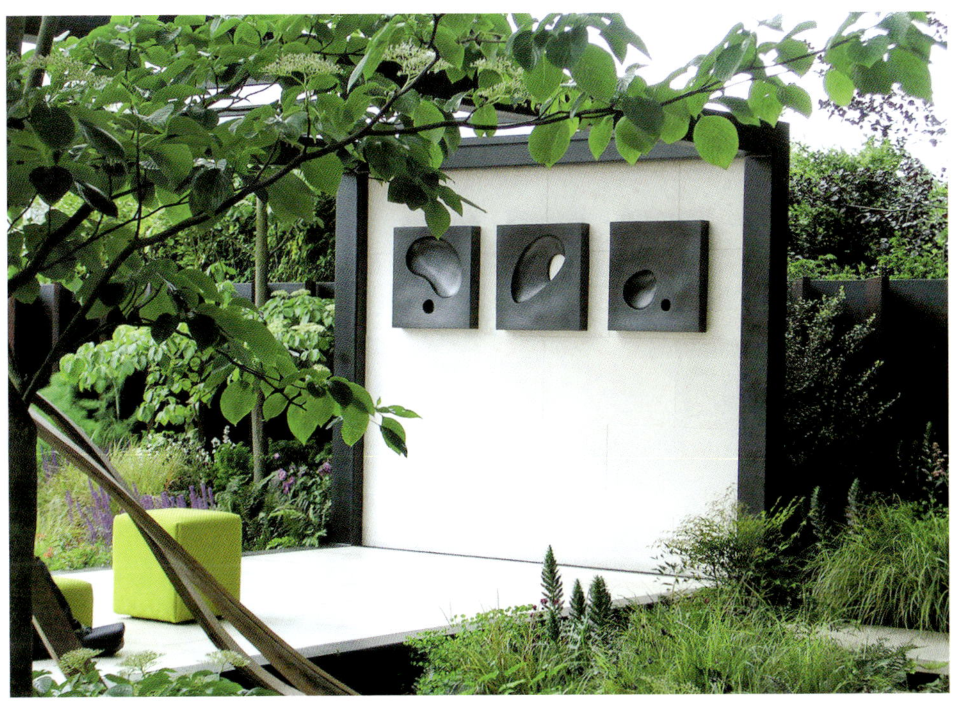

Black Wall Sculpture with Rock Pool Holes by Mari-Ruth Oda, 2007. Commissioned by Anthony Sturgeon, garden designer, for Chelsea Flower Show. Approx. 60 x 60 x 10 cm (24 x 24 x 4 in.). Black stoneware clay (earthstone). *Photo by M. Oda.*

are to ours. And it compelled me to think of our existence in the wider context.'[10] The sober organic abstract forms of *Black Wall Sculptures with Rock Pool Holes*, (see above) made on commission for the Cancer Research UK Garden at the Chelsea Flower Show in 2007, convey a sense of space, peace, time and sensuality that echoes the surrounding nature, and leads the viewer to forget that this nature is a domesticated one, trapped in a busy city. This encapsulates in relatively small pieces – each is approx. 60 x 60 x 10 cm (24 x 24 x 4 in.) – a profound awareness of the way we, as human beings, are connected to the infinite chain of living creatures.

Numerous well-known contemporary artists have produced wall pieces similar in size: Fernand Léger, Marc Chagall, Asger Jorn, Karel Appel, Erik Nyhom, Joan Miró, Claude Champy, Bernard Dejonghe, Haguiko, Claudi Casanovas, Angel Garraza, Wayne Higby – the list is long. The following chapters examine some examples from many other contemporary artists.

Whereas ornamental or artistic ceramic walls and ceramic claddings belong to long traditions that can clearly be identified (as previously mentioned), smaller ceramic wall pieces which are hung to a wall do not form such a tradition, but are the result of many different influences, which cannot all be systematically traced. However, two kinds of influence are broad enough to be pointed out, which still influence contemporary projects:

Decorative plates In many countries functional plates and dishes have been adorned with such skilfully refined patterns that they are not (or not only) used as functional objects; they are considered as ornamental and displayed on walls. Separately, the vessel has become a source of inspiration for some artists who make sculptures derived from plates – though they can by no means be used. 'Containing ... is an expressive idea as well as a function ...'[11] The Robert and Lisa Sainsbury's Collection on display at the Sainsbury Foundation for Visual Arts in Norwich presents astonishing large wall dishes by Claudi Casanovas that explore this expressive idea while displaying exceptional density and strength.

Terracotta There are other important sources of inspiration, which actually worked for both small and monumental-scale work. From the Middle Ages, terracotta has been extensively used in the production of wall reliefs, often meant to adorn churches or to be used as models for marble pieces. Florentine sculptor Andrea Della Robbia (1435–1525) used glazed terracotta (*terracotta invetriata*) to make altars, panels, medallions and large coats of arms for the churches and palaces of Tuscany.[12]

Wall pieces of monumental scale

These are site-specific and necessarily composed of several parts. They require a careful and strong hanging system.

In *Glaciated Mass* Brad Evan Taylor explores the changes that matter goes through in the course of geological time, and suggests the differences that speed makes to this process by orchestrating huge masses of clay. He is interested in how different matter changes at different speeds. The overall composition and size combine to reveal how intimate, monumental and environmental scales form an indestructible cycle.[13]

In 2000 Taylor was commissioned to make a wall piece for the Southtowne Exposition Center in Sandy Utah, USA, designed by architect Jonathan Bradshaw. The members of the selection committee were interested in finding artists to produce works that would interact with the site as well as the architecture. The finalists were invited to submit revised proposals and models, which were scrutinized by a panel of community leaders, engineers, artists and the architect.

This particular site, located at the base of the terminal moraine from the glacier that formed Little Cottonwood Canyon in the Wasatch Range, provided Taylor with the opportunity to propose a large-scale work directly related to his sculptural work (the Compressed Mass series and Compression/Levitation series). He was given complete artistic freedom, which is rare: the issue of artistic freedom was mentioned by all the artists in this chapter working on large-scale commissions.

Glaciated Mass is a 10 x 8 x 1 m (33 x 26 x 3.3 ft) porcelain wall piece that explores the landscape, density, texture and embodied geological time-scale of the Little Cottonwood Canyon. It allowed the artist to take a step further in his own development and provides the community with an exceptional environment. The architect had chosen to echo the angular geometry of the Wasatch Mountains that clearly shows on the photo; Taylor in turn decided to focus on a geometric relationship between his work and the angular architecture. Architect and artist worked separately, but with a shared vision

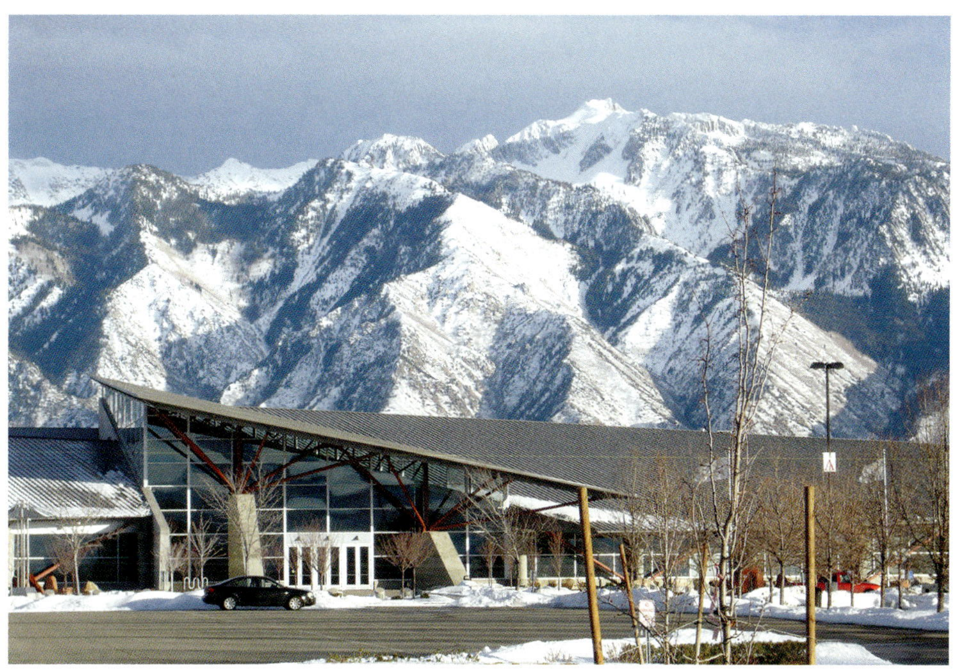

Southtowne Exposition Center in Sandy, Utah, looking to the east, 2000–2003. Architect Jonathan Bradshaw. Behind the center: the glaciated canyon 'Little Cottonwood', in the Wasatch mountains. *Photo by Kerri Buxton.*

discussed from the moment that Taylor handed in his first sketches. Both wall piece and building have a dialogue with each other and with the surrounding environment. This in turn conveys the sense that *Glaciated Mass*, Southtowne Center and Little Cottonwood Canyon, as well as what contains them and what is surrounded by them, form a continuous cycle.

This masterpiece deserves its own richly illustrated book; chapter 4 reveals some aspects of the making and hanging process (*see* pp.107–109). Here, the conditions that made this project possible should be highlighted as they show why such creations are so rare in the history of ceramic wall pieces, and how they could become more frequent, provided that makers have a similarly acute artistic vision. These conditions are:

- ***Access to large facilities***, whether owned by the maker, or not. Taylor made the parts of his work in his studio, but fired them at the University of Utah, which let him use their facilities in exchange for some equipment repairs in the ceramics department where he used to teach. Some ceramics factories invite artists to do a residency on their premises to research and produce ambitious projects. Several ceramics research centres have been created during the last five decades, which provide visual artists and designers with the means to experiment and research.[14]
- ***Funds***. The material costs are enormous, as well as expenses such as insurance, outside contractors, and engineering. Months and years can be dedicated to research, prepare

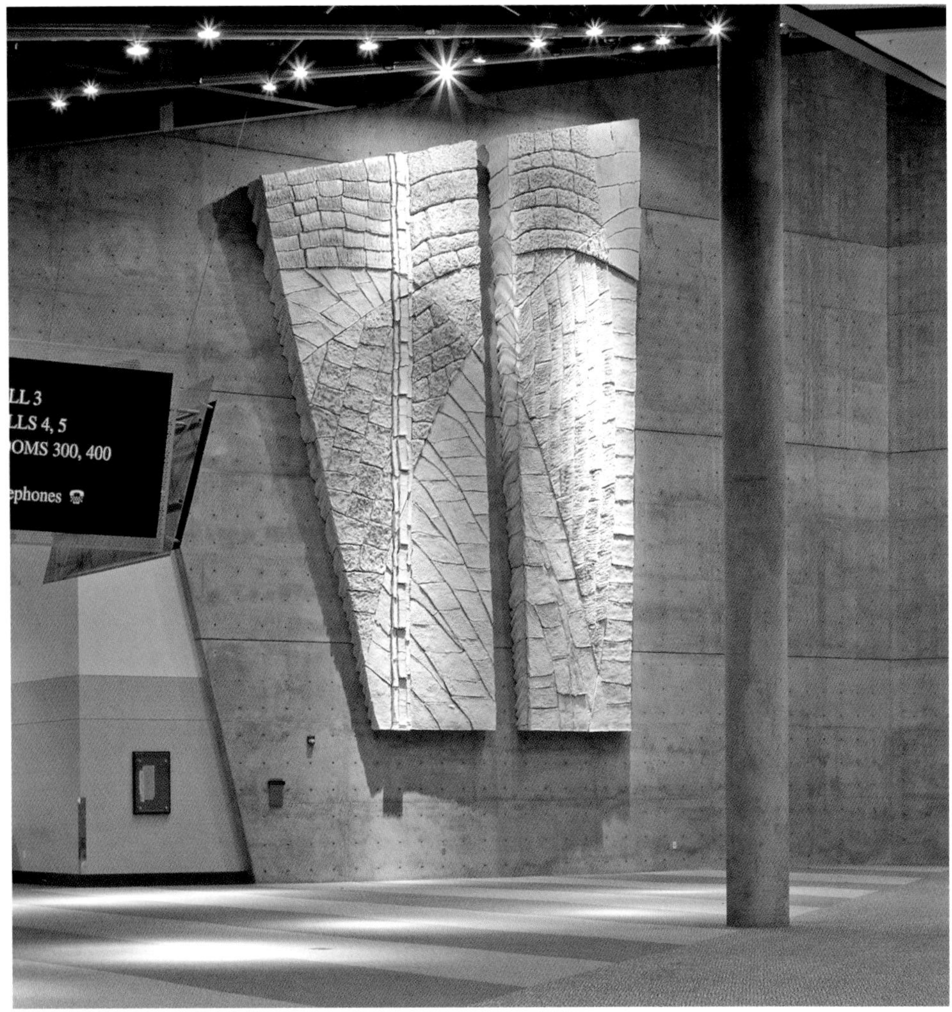

Glaciated Mass, by Brad Evan Taylor, 2000–3. North-east Concourse View. Ht: 10 × 8 × 1 m (33 × 26 × 3.3 ft). Porcelain. *Photo by Trevor Muhler.*

and realise the project; and the maker needs to make a fair amount to live on.

- ***Collaboration with architects and/or engineers.*** In order to get the opportunity to work with architects, the artists must be able to promote their work and make it known to architects, as often they are the commissioners of projects. Help is also required at nearly every stage of the making process.
- ***Ability of the artist to write a proposal.*** That is, to work with architectural tools (drawings and models), to assess the funds required, to deal with issues related to urbanism and a complex matrix of rules and regulations. This is conditioned by access to information. Artists also need to be patient and good at negotiating.
- ***Commissions.*** Large-scale work is bound to be site-specific and depends

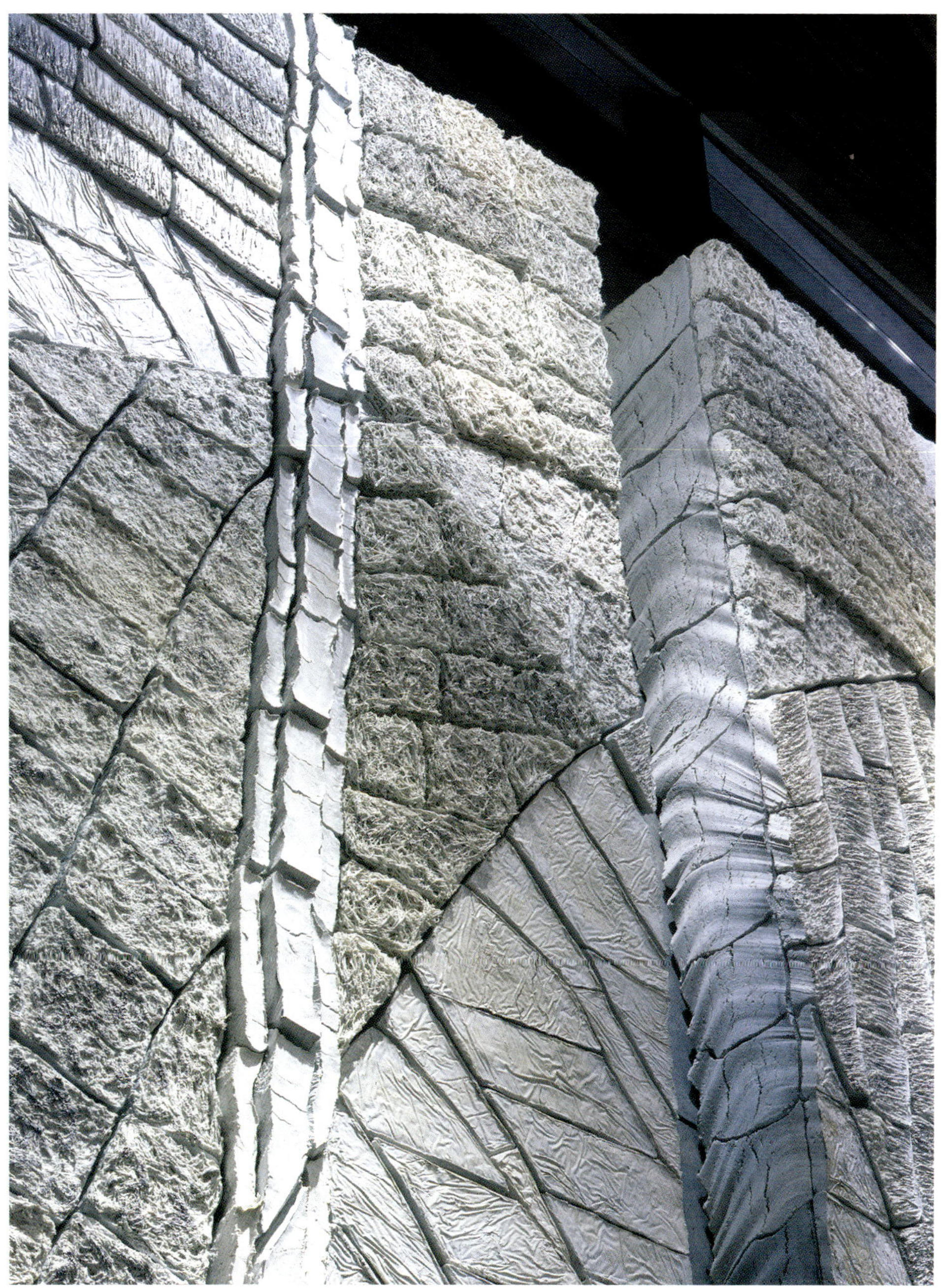

Glaciated Mass by Brad Evan Taylor. North East Concourse View, detail. *Glaciated Mass* was made possible by the Percent-for-Arts Fund, Salt Lake County, Utah, and assistance from The University of Utah, Salt Lake City, Utah, USA. (Documentation and related research for this project, published by *Ceramics Art and Perception* was made possible by KonKuk University in Seoul, Korea.) *Photo by Trevor Muhler.*

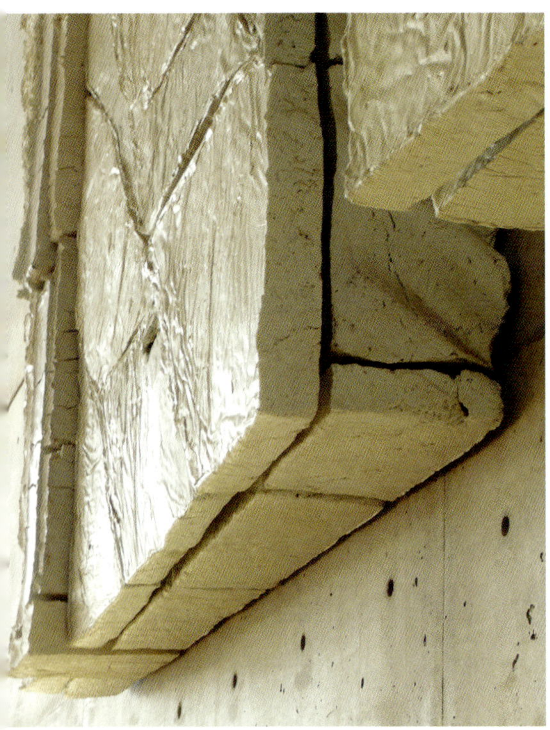

Glaciated Mass by Brad Evan Taylor. Detail illustrating the thickness of the individual porcelain blocks and the way that they interlock. *Photo by Kerri Buxton.*

on patrons commissioning it. Throughout history wealthy patrons, organisations and states have made working on a large scale a reality for artists. Because of the difficulty involved in assessing whether an artist is able to carry out a whole project, patrons (or the committees they employ) tend to select artists who have proven ability.

- ***'Percent' policies.*** Some governments have implemented policies whereby a certain percentage is systematically allotted to the commissioning of art work when a public building is erected. For the artists, the opportunities of making public art always follow the ups and downs of these policies. This fact explains why, depending on the country where they live, artists are more or less likely to find commissions. In France, for instance, the '1% policy' was implemented in 1951 and several ambitious ceramic wall pieces were subsequently constructed in the following decades.[15] Scandinavian countries massively promote public art and more generally support artists through a dense network of grants and art programmes.
- ***Time and freedom*** to document ideas, draw, research materials and techniques, work for some periods without the pressure of making commercial work, so that innovative smaller projects which have already been achieved can be used to show architects and patrons one's potential abilities for larger works. This condition brings us back to the need for funding and facilities.

This list itself helps us to understand why, in spite of several thousand years of collaboration between ceramicists and architects, there are fewer large-scale artistic ceramic wall pieces than might be expected. Indoors, there are many more painted wall pieces (paintings, murals and frescoes) than artistic ceramic wall pieces. Outdoors, ceramics has hardly been exploited artistically in contemporary architecture. This may be because tiles suffer from their association with the stigmatized category of crafts, or with commercial production and its aesthetics.[16] A close study of the history of ceramics courses would throw more light on this paradox, but this is well beyond the scope of this chapter. In broad outline: historically, ceramics courses originated either in training orientated towards functional, small-scale work which progressively integrated sculpture, or in industry-oriented training which turned out designers for the factory rather than autonomous artists. In today's world, this has now completely changed, Pieter Stockmans' career is exemplary in highlighting this complex evolution.

The growth of large artistic ceramic wall pieces is linked to the emergence of a new type of protagonist: the freelance designer or artist who applies for a commission in the way that craftsmen and architects have previously done.

Installation wall pieces

Human beings live in an evolving world. In the words of Venezuelan-born artist Carlos Cruz-Diez: 'We are not the artists-craftsmen of the 12th century, artists of the single space, the unchangeable, of the myth of eternity. . . We are the artists of the dawn of the third millennium. . . It is a society of the moment, of the event, of mutation and of the ephemeral.'[17]

Nothing in the arts, except perhaps cinema and video, shows this better than installation-based work which, by its very nature, always ends up being un-installed. The fact that ceramics, which 'freezes' its material, should participate in this form of art, reveals how powerful a medium it is for testifying to the evolution of humankind. At the moment, humankind is set on the irreversible consumption of many natural resources. To consume means to eat, drink, use up and completely destroy. Trained as an architect, Canadian artist Ian Johnston explores 'the bizarre relationship we have by way of consumption to the material world that sustains us'.[18] He uses different materials depending upon the context, and shows the contradictions of *homo consumens* by installing a series of objects that suggest and relate to everyday life: objects that epitomize the absurd choices we are sometimes forced to make. In fact, instead of showing anything literally, he immerses the viewers in an atmosphere aimed to unsettle them 'enough to allow for alternative thought, speculation and reflection on the contemporary consumption paradigm'.

In *Swimming Upstream Through the Looking Glass*, an installation whose component parts were made during a residency at the Pottery Workshop[19] in Jingdezhen, China, Johnston's destabilising concept is achieved by fixing 80

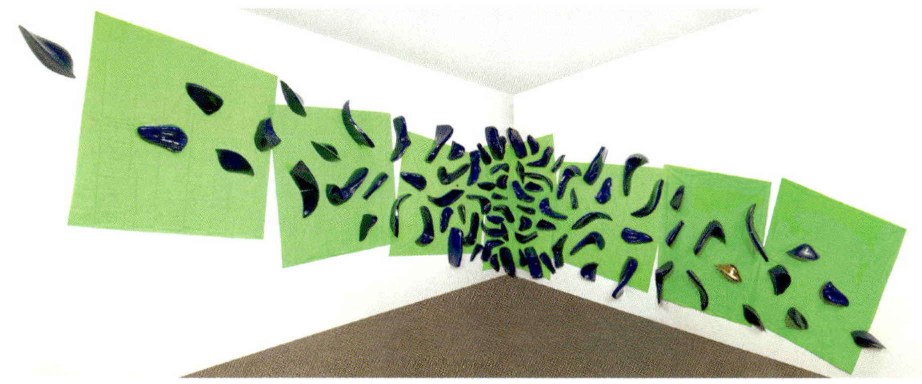

Swimming Upstream Through the Looking Glass, by Ian Johnston, 2007–8. Porcelain, vinyl sheets, 12.8 x 3 x 0.41 m (42 x 10 x 1⅓ ft). *Photo by Jeremy Addington.*

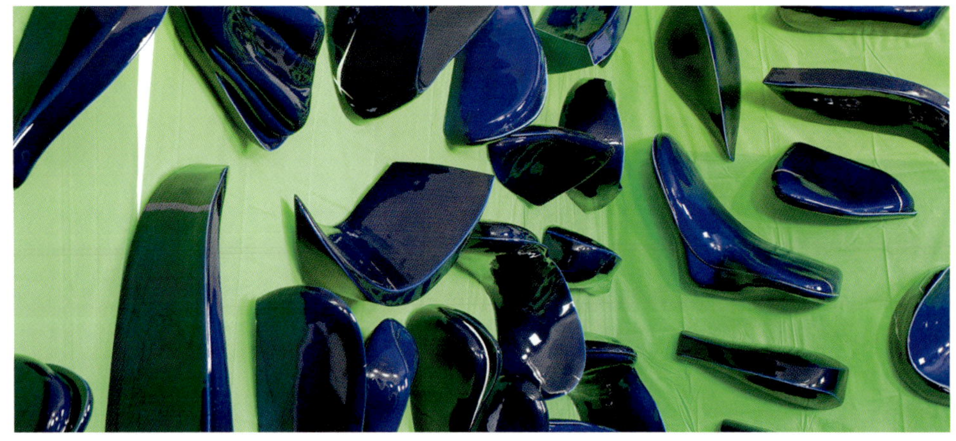

Swimming Upstream Through the Looking Glass, by Ian Johnston, detail. Porcelain, vinyl sheets. 12.8 x 3 x 0.41 m (42 x 10 x 1⅓ ft.). *Photo by Jeremy Addington.*

ceramic pieces on to the entire surface of a corner formed by two walls. The wall installation presents its viewers with both a visual vanishing point and a real cul-de-sac, and elicits a response at a visceral level: they feel drawn to the mysterious blue forms, possibly to touch their soft and shiny surface, until they are entirely engulfed by the cold colours as if drowned in a whirlpool. They cannot swim further, but it is also too late to escape. The spatial experience created by the scale and material nature of the installation engages its audience at a physical level. The ceramics refer to the form of the Chinese broom, 'the epitome of an entire class dedicated to make China appear orderly. They become droplets and waves in a sea like the legions of broom wielding workers who keep order and calm in a storm of activity'. By combining ceramics and plastic, one of the oldest and one of the most recent materials created by human technology, Johnston puts the viewers' resilience to the test: he forces them – especially those nostalgic lovers of antique ceramics who will at once recognise the Meissen blue glaze – to acknowledge that we live in a changing world where China, with all its contradictions, stands as both the cradle of many innovations in ceramics and the spearhead of major economic and social upheavals.

Anne Mercedes

Notes to Chapter One

[1] See: Stratton, Michael, *The Terracotta Revival*, Victor Gollancz, London, 1993. McErlain, Alex, 'Rediscovered Beauty', *Ceramic Review*, 211, Jan–Feb 2005.
http://www.buildingconservation.com/articles/terracot/terracot.htm

[2] Johnston Ian, *Thoughts on Ceramic Wall Installation, Architecture and Sculpture*, 2008, unpublished.

[3] Heeney, Gwen, *Brickworks*, A & C Black, London, 2003, p.174.

[4] His methods for casting and decorating these slabs are fully described and illustrated in *Contemporary Porcelain: Materials, Techniques and Expressions*, Peter Lane, A & C Black, London, University of Pennsylvania Press, 2003.

[5] Lislerud, Ole, *The Potential of Ceramics in Architecture*, Metaphorical Signs, Beijing Today Art Museum, 2008.

[6] Bright, Erik, 'An Alternative Approach to Teaching Ceramics', *Ceramics Monthly*, December 1998, pp.46–50.

[7] Physick, John, *The Victoria and Albert Museum: The History of Its Building*, V&A, London, 1982.

[8] Clayarch Gimhae Museum website: www.clayarch.org

[9] Kuchta, Ronald Andrew, 'Shin's Fired Painting series and the Korean artist's evolution from potter to painter of clay or ceramist/painter', The Shin Sang Ho exhibition, catalogue, Clayarch Gimhae Museum, 2007.

[10] *Uptown Magazine*, see her website: www.mari-ruthoda.com

[11] Shadbolt, Doris, 'The Transparency of Clay', in Ceramic Millennium, 2006, edited by Garth Clark, The Press of the Nova Scotia College of Art and Design, p.31.

[12] In Italy, Andrea Della Robbia (1435–1525) developed a unique body of glazed terracotta sculptures, mainly in blue and white, that stands out in the ceramic wall pieces of the early Renaissance.

[13] 'Glaciated Mass', *Ceramics Art and Perception*, issue 57, 2004, pp.15–19.

[14] Among the most important ones where large scale work can be achieved: The European Ceramics Work Center (EKWC), the Netherlands, The Shigaraki Ceramic Sculptural Park, Japan, The International Ceramics Studio in Kecskemet, Hungary, The Archie Bray Foundation for the Ceramic Arts, USA, The CRAFT Limoges (Centre de Recherche sur les Arts du Feu), France, the World Ceramic Exposition Foundation of Korea (WOCEF) and the Clayarch Gimhae Museum, Korea. There are many more places, such as private or state factories, which promote residency programs.

[15] Vallet, Albert, *La Céramique Architecturale*, Dessain et Tolra 1982, p.87. This book provides many illustrations of interesting projects.

[16] Kuchta, Ronald Andrew, 'Shin's Fired Painting series and the Korean artist's evolution from potter to painter of clay or ceramist/painter', The Shin Sang Ho Exhibition, catalogue of exhibition, p.167: By naming his wall pieces 'Fired Painting', Shin Sang Ho has dismissed 'the possible pejorative utilitarian sound of the words "glazed tiles" or "ceramic plaques", as if to avoid relating them to the stigma of belonging to the category of crafts.'

[17] Cruz-Diez, Carlos, *My reflections on color*, (Reflexion Sobre el Color, Fabriart Ediciones. Caracas, 1989). www.cruz-diez.com/Reflexioneng.pdf

[18] Johnston Ian, *Thoughts on Ceramic Wall Installation, Architecture and Sculpture* 2008, unpublished. All following quotes in this subsection from the same article.

[19] www.potteryworkshop.org

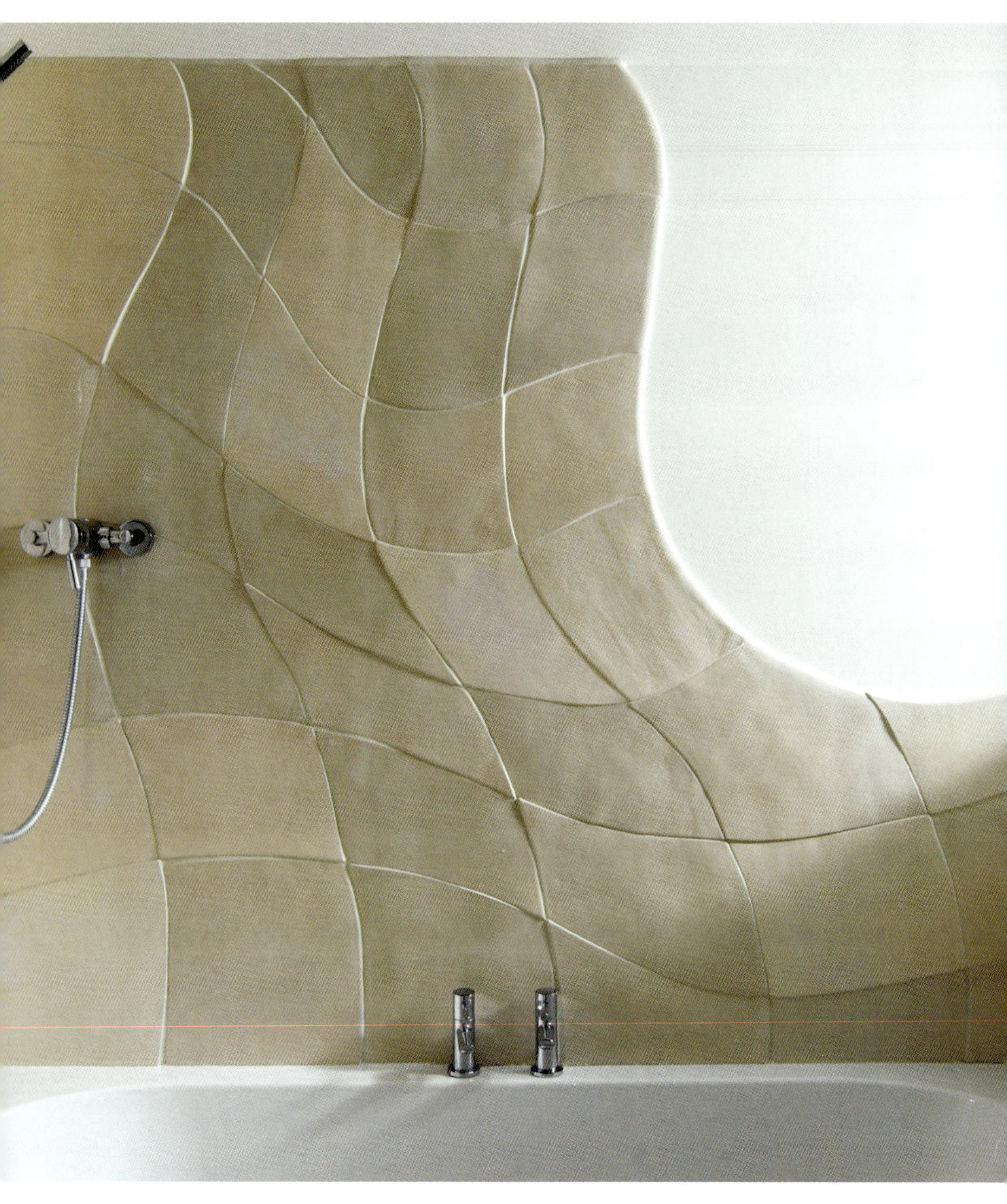

Wave by Victoria Ellis, 2006. 165 × 190 cm (65 × 75 in.). Stoneware tiles in bathroom. *Photo by David Goulding.*

Chapter 2

Designing and planning

Before embarking on the making of a wall piece it is essential to take time to plan and design your idea. In this chapter you will find some pointers to help you consider design issues and think about planning, as well as information on how other makers have used design planning to create a number of successful wall pieces.

One of the first and most important steps is to take time to consider the location, as this could have a strong influence on the starting points of the design, scale, weight and overall aesthetic. This will then influence your choice of materials and methods suitable to create your piece of work. In this way, making wall pieces involves a reversal of the usual approach, where an artist will often create a piece, and then consider how and where to display it. Wall pieces, at least for the larger works, are often location-led, and where they are to be located may dictate their design, style and atmosphere.

One advantage of creating a wall piece for a specific location, exhibition or event is that this does help to support

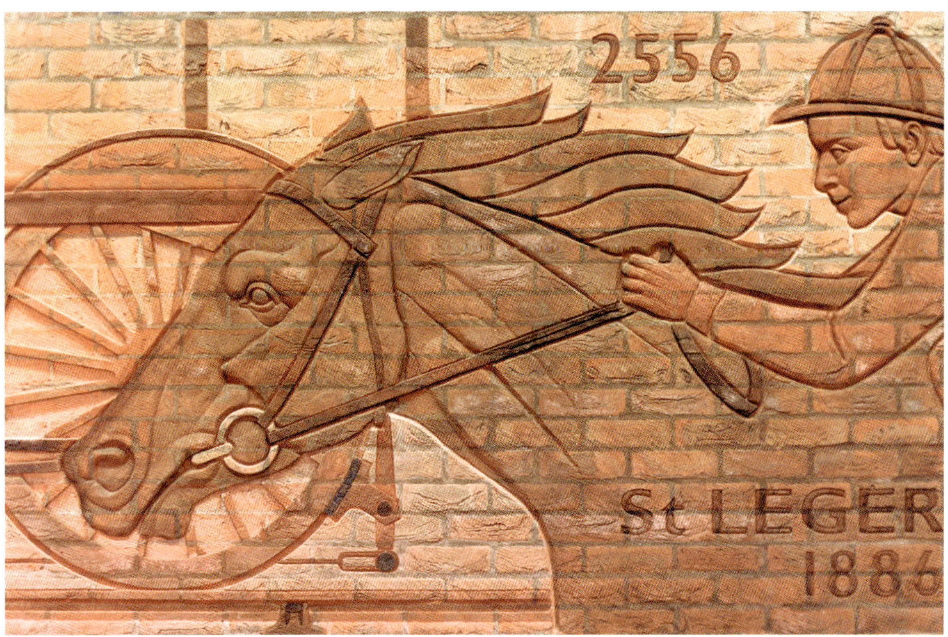

Doncaster St Leger by Richard Kindersley, 1990. 4.05 x 1.5 m (15.4 x 4.9 ft). Commissioned for Doncaster retail complex, England. Brick carving with proprietary brick dye. *Photo by Richard Kindersley.*

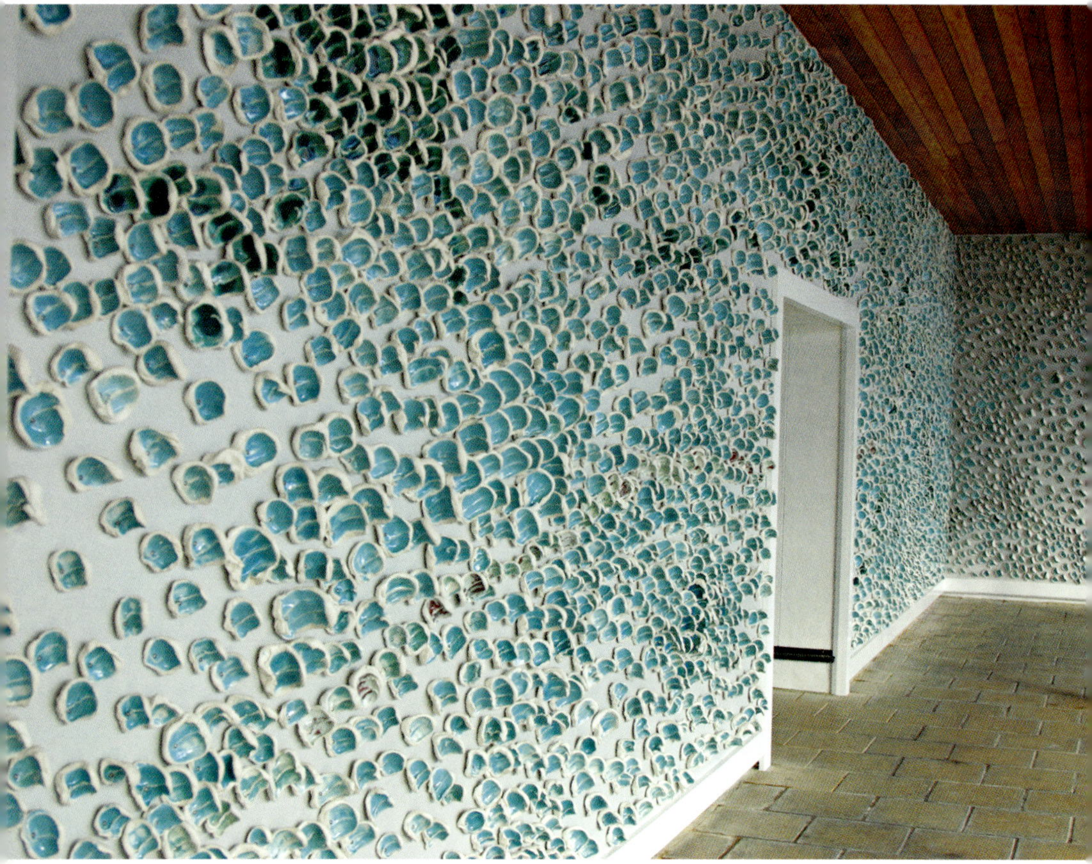

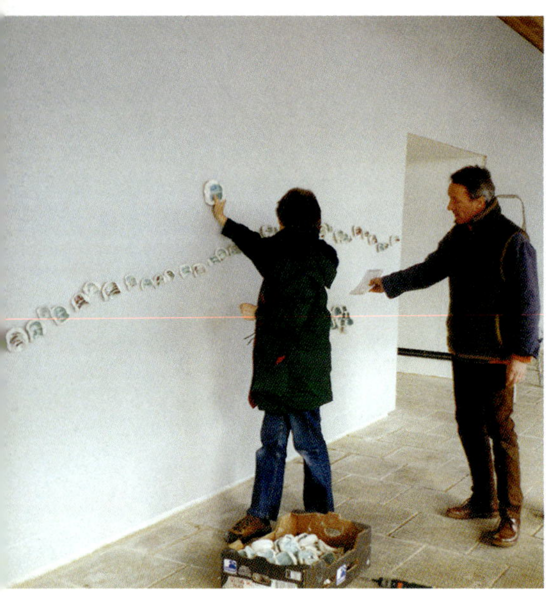

Flock, by John Butler, Jonna Behrens, Anne Jamison, Debbie Metherell, 2003. (Detail of planning installation, left.) Commissioned for the University of Westminster, Regent Street Campus, London. Size: 40.21m^2 (433 sq. ft). Valentine's special porcelain with glaze. *Photos by Andy Golding.*

and inform the design process: it offers the chance to visit the space and/or to be provided with the measurements, dimensions and the needs of the space. These aspects are all serious considerations in the planning and design process.

Nevertheless, there are some great advantages to searching out a new, exciting and different space for which to design and make a wall piece. This should and can give the opportunity to display ceramics in a space in need of visual regeneration, so it is important to remain open-minded as you might also find the piece takes a journey of its own. The space itself may suggest a very different approach from the work you had in mind.

As part of good design practice, it can be a very useful exercise to create some designs or concepts that might also show your wall pieces in different locations. The process might begin by taking photographs of several locations or creating a virtual location with computer software. The images can be scanned in and the project superimposed on top. With the aid of a number of design packages such as Illustrator (a graphics package), InDesign (desktop publishing and image manipulation), Adobe Photoshop (photographic manipulation package) and CAD, Computer Aided Design (architectural and engineering software) on the computer, more and more makers are using this approach to develop designs. Adobe Photoshop is the preferred package used by some of the makers (such as Chris Wight, Alice Mara, Tulla Elieson and Rafael Perez for example), to place their work in virtual new locations.

This method of working at the design stage can ensure a focused approach to the making; by looking carefully at the concept first, it can save weeks of potentially wasted work in the studio. Chris Wight has created several design concepts with the aid of design software to give people the opportunity to see the breadth and scale he is able to create from his ceramics. This enables him to

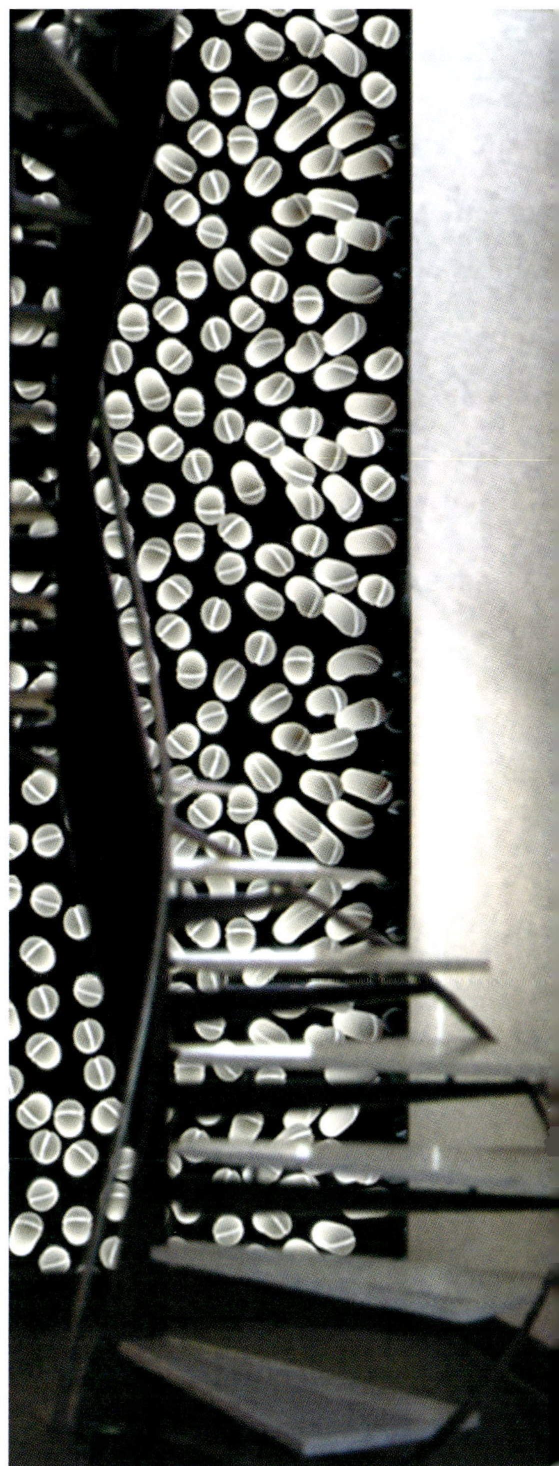

Staircase Feature Concept – a virtual design, not yet made, of glass-encased slipcast, hand-carved bone china forms, by Chris Wight. Ht: 10 cm (4 in.), dia: 2.5 cm (1 in.). Bone china, Perspex and toughened glass. *Photo by Chris Wight.*

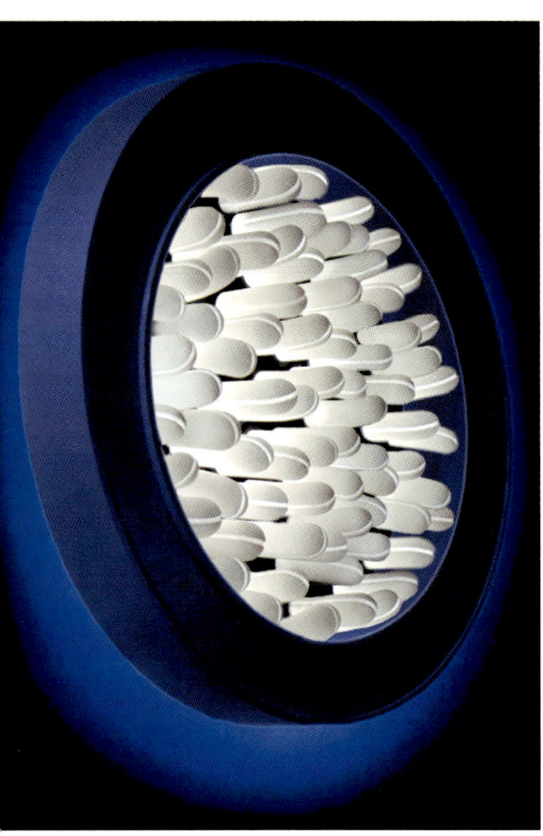

Wall Light Concept by Chris Wight. This is a virtual construction, not yet made. Proposed work: Ht:10 cm (4 in.), dia: 2.5 cm (1 in.). Glass encased slip-cast hand-carved bone china forms. Bone china, Perspex and toughened glass. *Photo by Chris Wight.*

play with scale, layout, pattern, structure and the overall concept for the design. If computer graphics are beyond you, there is nothing to stop you from making alternative forms of models using photographs, drawings, cardboard or wood models, or simply taking a few ceramic maquettes to the site in advance. Planning ahead is a crucial part of making large-scale work, and it will save a great deal of time and effort if you can resolve your design issues before getting too far with making the work.

Most of all, wall pieces offer the chance to push and develop design if this is the first time you are considering using this approach. This chapter aims to guide you through the process of creating, planning and designing, all of which suit a variety of approaches to clay. The following key points should help you in your planning;

1. Choosing and assessing the location
2. Space restrictions and other considerations
3. Considerations for hanging and mounting
4. Making your piece
5. Budgeting

Location

The location of a work can and should play an essential role in the design process as it will naturally dictate elements such as scale, fixings and material choice. While there are obviously a few exceptions to this, as in the case of smaller-scale works, which can be hung almost as a picture would be, the majority of larger works will interact completely with their surroundings.

It is important to review the purpose of the space you will be designing for. If it is a public space, you need to consider who will be using it, and its function. For example, if you are creating a project for a school it might be wise to think about creating pieces that are not sharp to touch, which are durable, safely attached and possibly out of reach of the ground, so that children are not tempted to climb on them. You will probably want to make the piece more fun, colourful and lively. If the work is to be in a museum or library, it can be more fragile, and have a quieter presence. The work may be in a busy corridor or thoroughfare, as with *Flock* (*see* p.34), or it may echo the reflections of a swimming pool, as in Henk Wolver's *Swimming Pool* (*see* p.114). Whatever the location, it will certainly influence the final piece.

There are a number of ways that a wall piece can be installed in a large area. Ceramicists may be approached by a client and commissioned to make a piece for a very specific area, or the maker may find a space that would be fantastic for a piece of work, and then go about making it possible. Then again, the idea for the work might come first, until a suitable space is found for it. Choosing a space for work can be an exciting task as this might involve approaching a gallery with an idea, or approaching a council for a public space, or a company, bar or office with private space. You may want to submit a collection of designs and a proposal for a space to be regenerated by your work. The clearer you are about your design, vision and space requirements, the more open the client will be to considering the project. If you are asked to come up with ideas, it is important to gather as much information on the project as possible to ensure your proposal fits the project outlines. Alice Mara's tile project (*see* pp.19–20) was commissioned by Western Parks Museum in Sheffield, and is a good example of a maker successfully following the client's brief.

Wall pieces vary widely in their locations. There is no set formula for where a wall piece should or can be placed, and pieces have been installed in chapels, museums, cultural centres, bars, private homes, law courts and even subways (*see* Piet Stockmans, p.115), so it is important to remain open-minded and consider where your work is best suited. The aim could be to liven up an unused or drab area, to provide a focal point, to disguise and cover up an otherwise ugly wall or area, or to simply have a fantastic piece of work in a way that does not take up further space, but uses an already existing surface.

Every part of architecture and buildings can be considered as possible locations. The sculptors Richard Kindersley and the late Walter Ritchie shared an interest in brick. By working with brick in its fired state Kindersley was able to produce carvings with a limited depth of 18–24 mm ($^{3}/_{4}$–1 in.) (*see* p.33), giving an interesting surface but also an exciting approach to incorporating ideas into architecture. Kindersley continues to use the wall as a blank canvas by directly carving into brick and creating a façade. For him, working directly on the wall, the planning, design and drawing are essential as mistakes are hard to correct. It is worth noting that both sculptors ensured the bricks they used were suitable; in some cases a solid brick was used in the construction and precautions were taken to ensure the structure could withstand this method of work. In another example (*see* pp.51–53) Walter Ritchie has created large brick panels which are then joined or incorporated into or onto the facing of walls afterwards.

If the location is in an office, bar, home, degree show or gallery it is important to remember that people will always be tempted touch. And why not? It shows an interest in the work. So remember, especially if your design involves a number of sections, that each piece must be secured safely as it is liable to be touched. Think, for example, of Satoru Hoshino's *Birth of Bubbles, Ancient Woodland and Peat Deposits* (*see* p. 40).

When creating the project *Flock* the team knew it would be essential to consider the surface of the clay they would

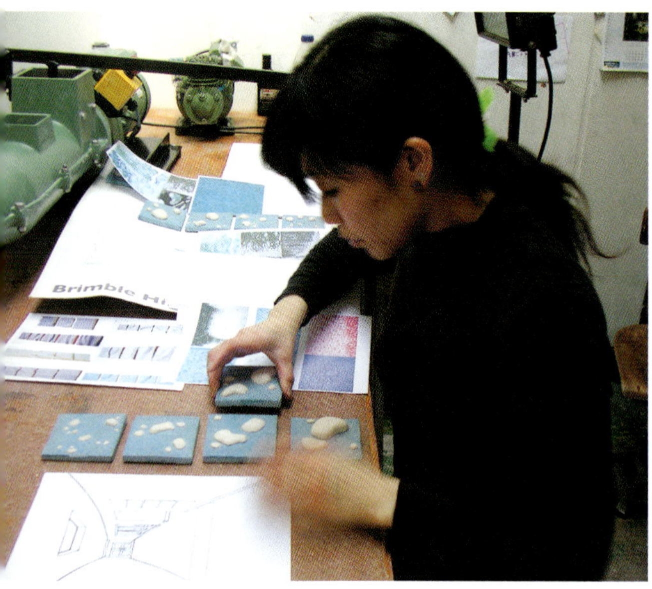

LEFT, FROM TOP

Mari-Ruth Oda planning the design process for Brimble Hill School project in her studio with maquettes and designs, 2008.

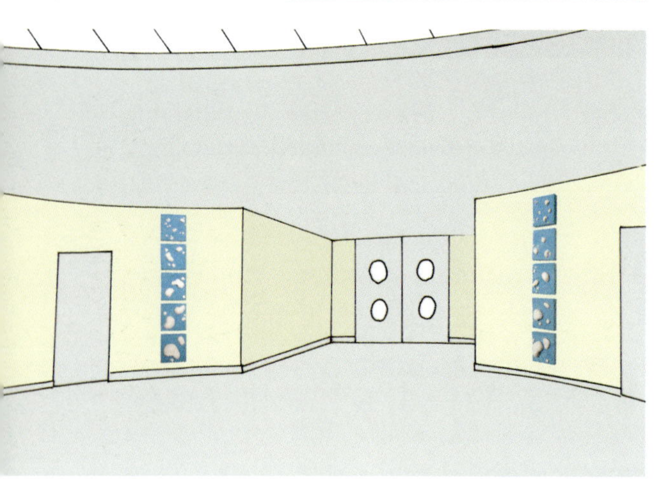

Brimble Hill Main Hall design, by Mari-Ruth Oda.

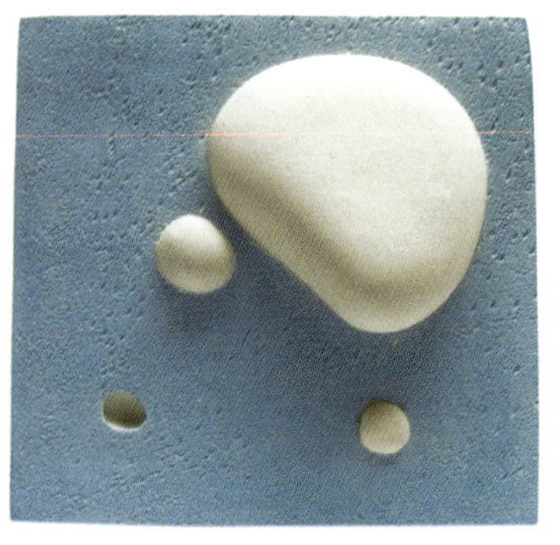

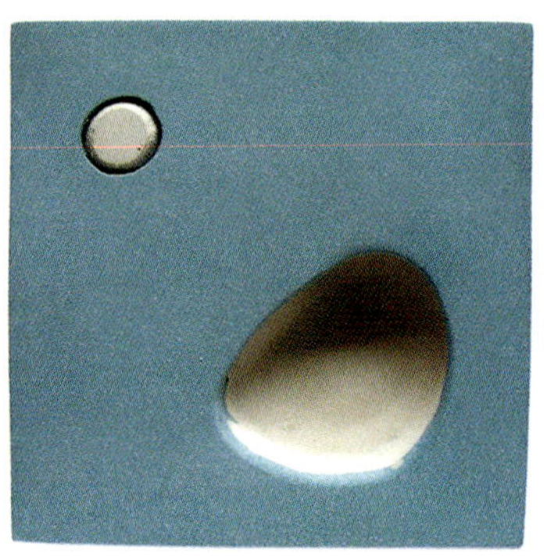

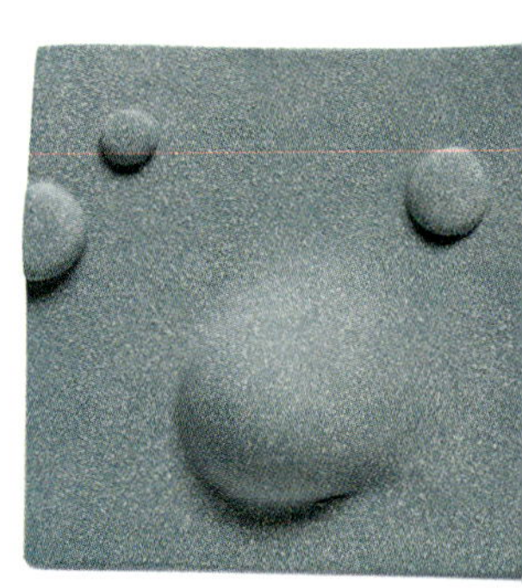

Blue maquettes for *Bubbles* by Mari-Ruth Oda, 2008. Scarva's Earthstone Handbuilding clay with stains.

Photos by Mari-Ruth Oda.

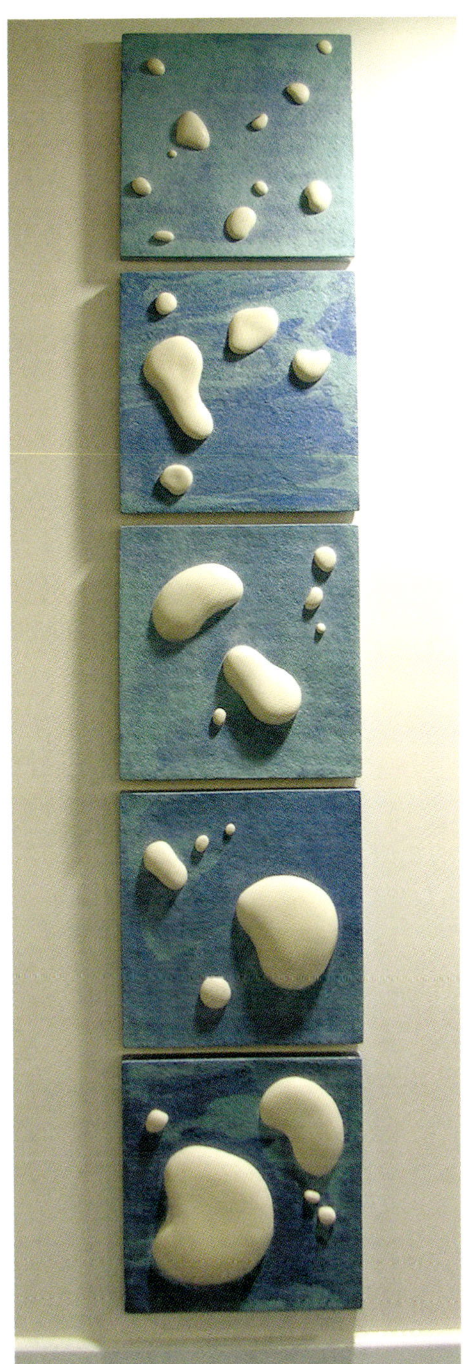
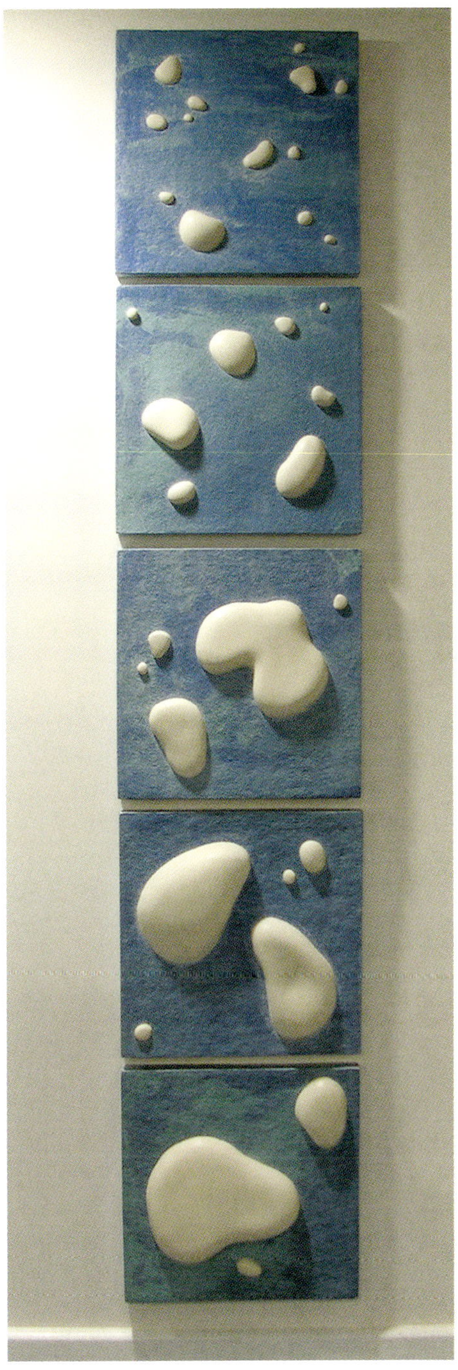

Bubbles, by Mari-Ruth Oda, 2008. Installed in the Main Hall at Brimble Hill School, Swindon. Size: 40 x 40 x 6 cm (16 x 16 x 2½ in.) each. Earthstone Handbuilding clay. *Photo by Mari-Ruth Oda.*

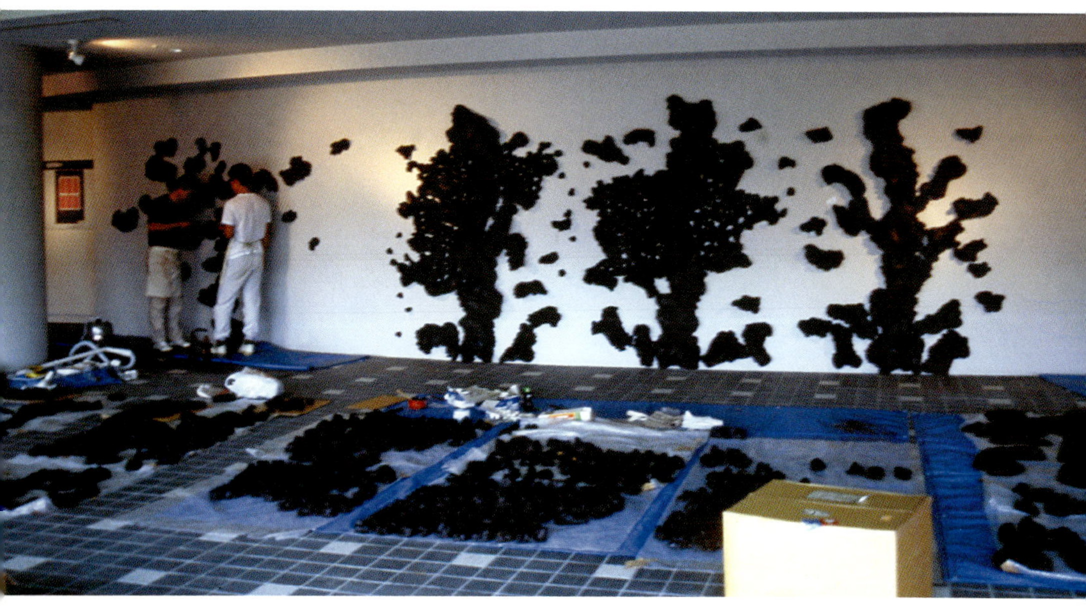

Birth of Bubbles, Ancient Woodland and Peat Deposits, by Satoru Hoshino, 1993. Ht: 27 m (8 ft 10 in.); W: 1.37 m (4½ ft); Dia: 3.5 m (11 ft 5 in). Earthenware smoke-fired. *Photo by Satoru Hoshino.*

be using and the fixings, so that there was no temptation to remove the pieces but still the chance to touch. (Some clients can be cautious about commissioning ceramics as they consider it to be fragile, so it might be wise to reassure them about its durable nature and tactile qualities too.)

Once you have found a location ensure you measure the space for your wall piece as this will have an influence on the design process and your budget.

It is always wise to find out what kind of wall you will be working on as this factor will take you back to the drawing board, most likely to alter elements of your design. Walls can be made from soft to hard brick, plasterboard partitions, wood or natural stone amongst other materials. Make sure the surface of the wall is checked, and if the wall is old, check for loose plaster as you will have trouble installing work securely if it is crumbly. It is helpful to check the thickness of the wall too. Just knocking on the wall with your knuckles can be a good start: a dull, heavy sound will usually indicate a solid wall, a light sound will indicate a thinner wall. Knock at intervals all across the surface. A very thin partition wall will not withstand heavy ceramics being hung on it, although it will probably be safe with a smaller, picture-sized work. Ask the owner, builder or architect what the wall is made from and its thickness before you plan your work (*see* p.41).

Restrictions and considerations for locations

Research on locations is essential. Sometimes the common perception of design can be about placing an idea on paper, but the design process goes far beyond a few drawings; it is also about being confident with the chosen materials, practicalities and space/location. You would not attempt to fire a new kiln without having read the manual, so why would you embark on a 65 ft (20 m) wall piece without research?

Once you have looked at the location from a design and concept point of view, consider and research the restrictions of the space you are creating for. If you are creating work for contemporary interior living spaces, it will be useful to have an idea of the sort of space available in the average front room – possibly not a great deal!

Consideration of space when hanging

When you come to hang your pieces it is essential to consider the height and location where the piece will be hung. It might need to be hung above a piece of furniture, or over a fireplace, so it will need a certain clearance above the ground. For one of my client commissions they required a piece for their dining room, so it was key that firstly the piece was designed with the exact scale in mind, and secondly that once completed it was hung at a height to be able to view when sitting in the room at the table. Check the heights and see if the location is sound. If the ceramic work is very delicate it might be wise to place it in an encased frame to ensure the surface and form is preserved successfully. Avoid hanging work above radiators as the heat can damage the work, cause wood to warp, and create problems with glues.

The following is a list of other key factors to consider:

Weight

The weight of the work is an important factor wherever your piece is to be hung. Interior walls can often be very thin so it is wise not to make very heavy pieces which a plasterboard partition may not be able to support (often these walls are hollow inside and will not withstand hefty weights, screws or brackets). A brick wall can normally withstand a fair amount of weight, while a stud wall (plasterboard over timber frame) will not. It is important either way to use several fixings and to distribute the weight out across the surface. If your work is going to be very large, and installed in a public or even private space, it is important to ensure that the owner or yourself check out the weight-bearing limits of the wall. Structural engineers or builders may be able to help advise with this. If the work is in a public space, you will need to ask the health & safety advisor to check it and then give written permission to install your piece. This might be in the form of a risk assessment, or it may already be written into the contract. Most large companies will have their own health and safety officer or/and site manager. If not, you can get further information from your local authority, and the Health and Safety Executive. Many local authorities have planning and construction officers who should be able to advise on the safety and suitability of the location.

The Health and Safety Executive main office is based in Caerphilly and there are regional offices all across the UK (*see* p.126). They provide guidance to help work in a safe way that follows the government regulations for health and safety. For example, if the project requires installation at a height, there is a clear set of guidelines that should be followed to prevent risk. Please note that employers, the self-employed and any person who might contract others are responsible for a safe working place and must ensure they are up to date with the current regulations. If not, and an incident occurs, they could be liable. It may be worth taking out public liability insurance, or checking it is covered by the contract.

There are guidelines on the Health & Safety Executive website on creating a risk assessment. A Risk Assessment is a document that should assess all possible risk while carrying out the installation of the wall piece. This assessment should be carried out before the project begins, and must be available when working in a public environment. It is essential to weigh your final work, including any backing or mounting materials, so that an accurate assessment can be made.

It is worth bearing in mind that if the wall piece is going to be placed on the exterior of a listed building you will have to apply for planning permission, which can take a minimum of eight weeks. Each local authority has a conservation department, which holds a list of all listed buildings within their area, so it is worth checking with them first.

Surface

The surface of the wall will also have an impact on the work. You need to consider the colour of the background in relation to your work. You also need to consider the suitability of the surface – does it need painting, repairing or just covering? This may be an aesthetic decision, as any blemishes can become very noticeable once the work is hung. Perhaps covering the wall in sheets of ply means that the work can easily be screwed in and has a good clean surface behind it. Or perhaps the point of the work is to cover up a bad wall – in which case, will the work serve its purpose? Does it need to be mounted onto something to help with this? A rough or uneven surface, such as a natural stone wall, or very old plaster, may need repair or covering before anything can be attached to it, and will obviously alter the way the final piece interacts with the surroundings. What looks great in the studio may not look so good against an old, grey, flaking wall. In the worst case scenario, if the wall is or has been very damp, it might be impossible to drill into the plaster without it breaking up, and the location might need to be changed.

Also check to see what is behind the wall (i.e. pipes or wiring). A simple tool called a 'stud and metal finder' can help to locate electrical wiring, pipes or nails. This is important, as drilling into an electrical cable or water pipe is very dangerous. As a simple rule, do not drill directly above or below electrical sockets, as there will always be wiring at these points.

Access

It is important to consider how you will install the work. What is the access like? Will you need scaffolding, ladders or other equipment? If the work is heavy, will you need transport to bring it right up to the wall – and will this be possible? If it is very fragile, how will you access the space if it is inside a busy building or area? Many makers lay their work out on the floor or a table before attaching it to the wall in its final position – will this be possible?

Satoru Hoshino is a good example of a maker who lays his work out on the surface (*see* p. 40) before it is assembled and arranged on the wall. The pieces are placed on large sheets of plastic so that he and his assistants can ensure the correct position is given to each piece.

Kathryn Clifforde also uses this method for her work. Before she begins to hang, each individual piece's position is selected and the wall is marked with a pencil dot. *Black and Blue* (opposite) uses casts in earthenware taken from speakers as the source of her pieces. The large-scale wall piece is designed to span across the surface, creating an amazing wash of intense, rich, blue and black tones.

Weather

The weather may affect your design if the work is outside. Anything that is free

Black and Blue, by Kathryn Clifforde, 2008. 170 x 170 cm (67 x 67 in.). Slipcast earthenware ceramics with underglazes. Initial preparation prior to installation entails Kathryn laying out the ceramics on a flat surface in order. *Photo courtesy of Kathryn Clifforde.*

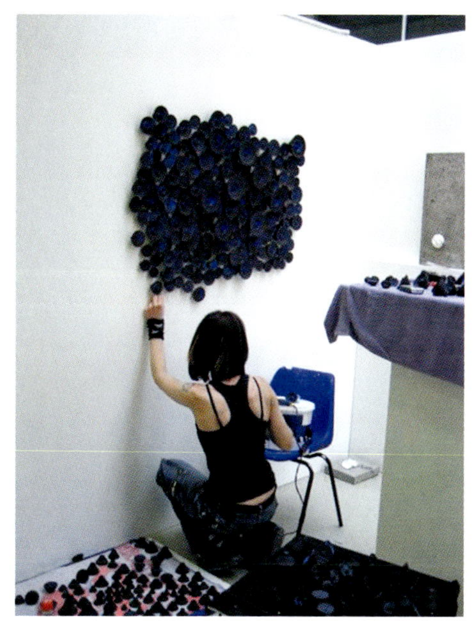

BELOW *Black and Blue*, by Kathryn Clifforde, 2008. 170 x 170 cm (67 x 67 in.). Slipcast earthenware ceramics with underglaze. *Photo courtesy of Kathryn Clifforde.*

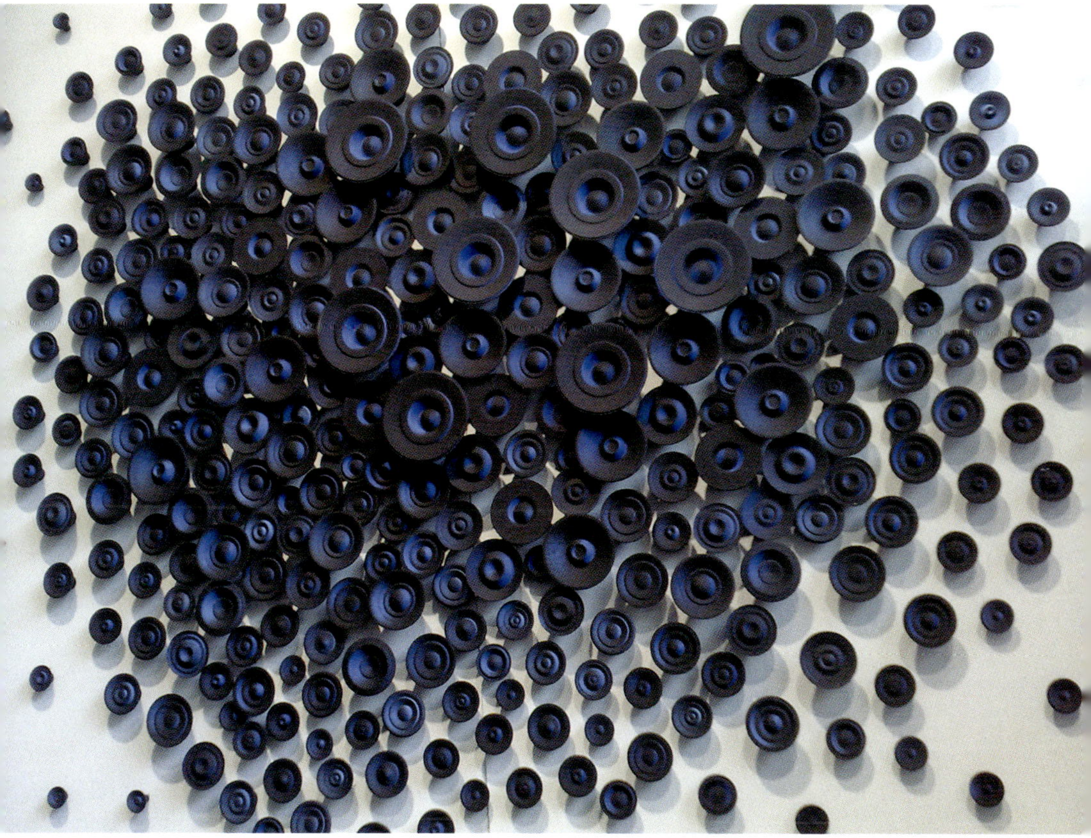

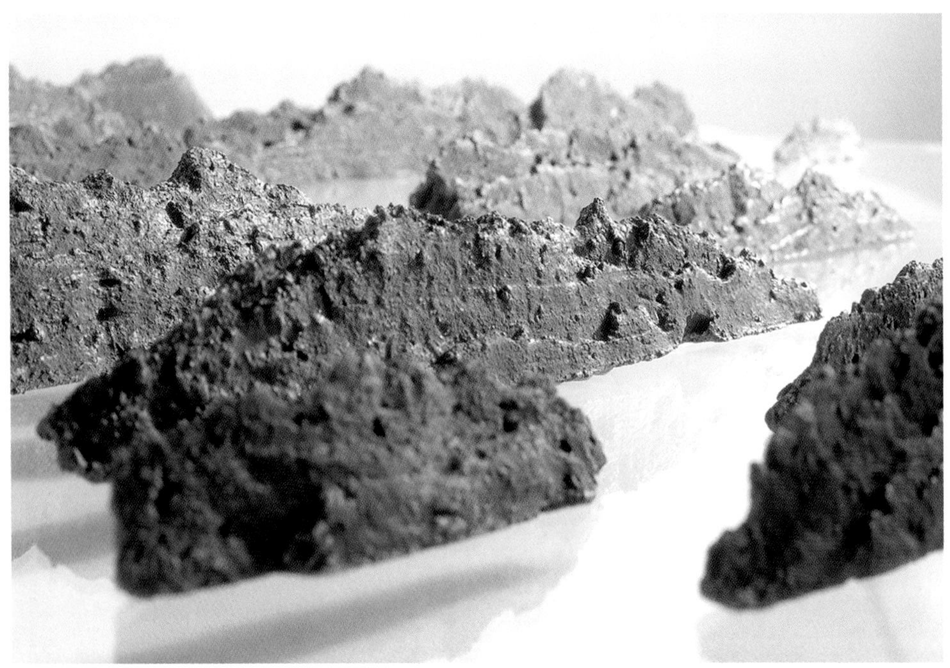

Rock 5, by Dominique Bivar Segurado, 2005. Detail of ceramic wall piece, 75 cm (29.5 in.) x 1 m (3.3 ft). Stoneware ceramics with glaze washes fired to 1240°C–1260°C (2264–2300°F).
Photo by Dougal Waters.

to blow around may easily get broken, and then be a danger to others. How will it be securely fixed? Will rain affect it, making it slippery, or making wooden frames prone to swelling? Will hard frost damage the surface or cause cracking? This may affect your choice of clay. You should also consider the weather while you install the piece. It may take several days to put up, and rain, wind or cold could hamper the work. You may be able to rig up some protection, or else keep an eye on weather reports and plan around a good break in the weather to carry out the installation.

Equipment

The equipment needed to produce the wall piece will have to be considered as this could affect the design process. The kiln size and/or the kiln shelves might limit the scale or size of the final design. Will the piece fit in the kiln, for example, or will it need to be made in sections? If so, can you make a feature of this? A number of makers do work in sections as this can help to simplify matters with scale, kiln firing, transport and installation if you are restricted by space.

With my own work *Natural Fragments* (*see* p.46) you will note that some of the fragments are arranged in one long progressive line and vary in size. This is for three reasons: first, the design helps the eye to move around the composition; secondly, it is not possible to fire one section longer than 60 cm (24 in.) in my kiln; and thirdly, it helps to spread the weight across the surface of the glass.

Marie Bornet's piece, *A Swiss Ceramicist's Rêverie* (*see also* pp.95–96), was inspired by mountain landscapes.

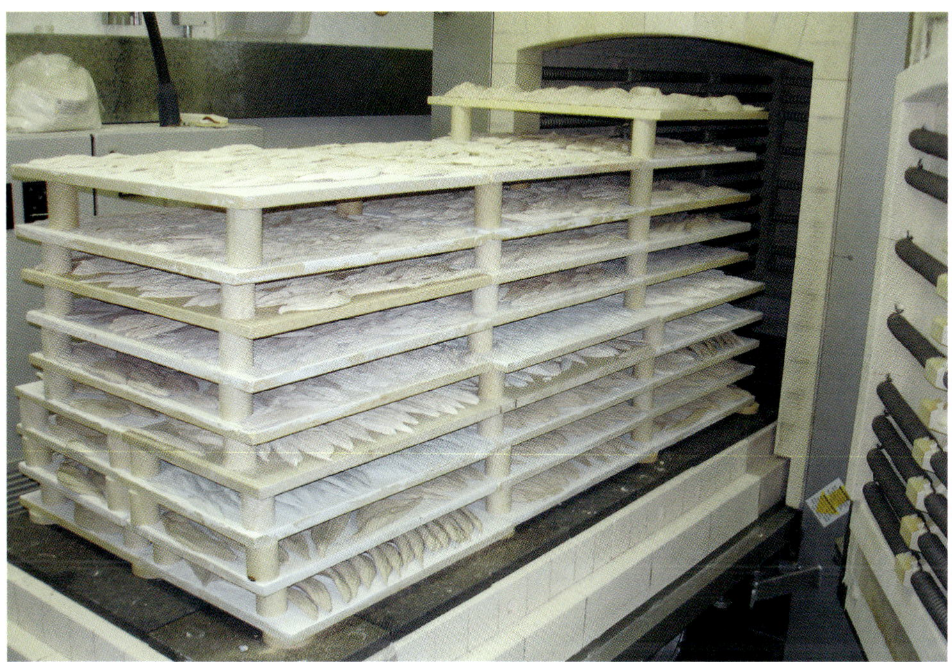

Rêverie by Marie Bornet, 2008. Size: 7.40 m (24 ft) x 3 m (9.8 ft). Porcelain. Raw firing in a trolley kiln between 1240–1260°C (2264–2300°F).

RIGHT The location for *Rêverie*, by Marie Bornet.

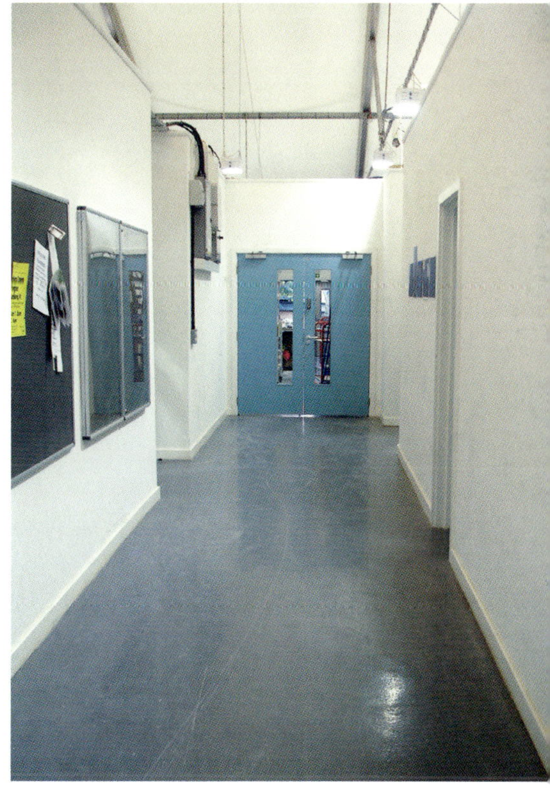

It required a clear approach to the design and planning, from the drawing to the final kiln firing, as the piece was composed of 1000 ceramic pieces. As the piece was to be sited in a corridor it was essential for Marie to consider at what height it should be displayed, and how to use the length of the space to ensure she remained true to her original idea of structure and fragility: 'I was looking in my piece to have geometrical but very delicate and fresh lines.'

Her research into the design for the piece had to consider all elements, from the number of coats of paint on the wall (three in total) to the raw firing between 1240–1260°C (2264–2300°F), as the porcelain was delicate. The use of the trolley kiln ensured that the 1000 pieces

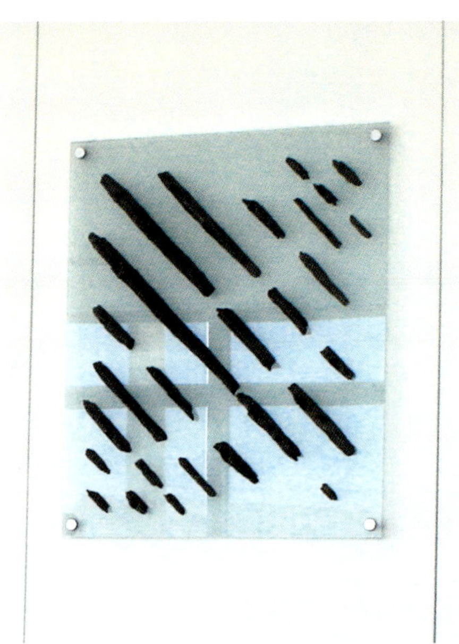

Natural Fragments, by Dominique Bivar Segurado, 2007. Private client commission. Size: 70 cm (27 in.) x 80 cm (31 in.) . Stoneware ceramics with glaze washes, mounted on toughened glass. *Photo by D. Bivar Segurado.*

to create the *Rêverie* were able to go through a shorter amount of firings.

Marie also describes how it was essential to draw on the wall as part of her design process, to transfer the design from page to location. This gave an opportunity to check the measurements and resolve any errors. As this piece relied on being placed directly onto the wall the planning was critical. This was also an opportunity to check that the correct amount of ceramics had been catered for. For this piece Marie was able to place the ceramics directly onto the wall with an adhesive. This did require a good deal of research, as it was important that the glue used did not damage the wall, but equally that it could support the ceramics in this temporary location.

Key questions to consider

As a guide, these are some crucial questions to ask when planning to hang a piece of ceramics on the wall, which will have a direct influence on the design and making process:

1. Where is the piece going to be placed?
2. What scale is the piece going to be and what scale is required?
3. What is the wall texture – for example does the backing need to disguise the surface? Does the entire surface need covering?
4. Can the wall take the weight of the ceramics and backing material?
5. What fixings are preferred or suitable to support the ceramics and/or the backing material?
6. How best can the design and style of the piece work in the location? (It is crucial, if possible, to conduct a site visit.)
7. Does the clay need any holes or changes made in the making process to help it hang or be placed on a backing material (i.e. holes for screws, ledges for brackets)?
8. What is the total weight of the ceramics, including any backing or mounting?
9. What is the thickness of the wall and structure? You should be extremely wary of thin partitions, and equally cautious if mounting something onto a solid but uneven surface such as stone.

These are general questions and give a basic checklist. With each new piece created, more questions and design issues will arise. (For more detailed information on hanging and mounting see chapter 3.)

It some cases the actual installation might need to be handled by a specialist company. Their experience and knowledge can ease the stress, and result in a successfully hung piece of work. There are a number of specialist companies who work with fragile artworks, for example Art Move and 01 Art Services. Art Move, who have installed some of my glass wall pieces, are based in London. They specialise in fine art installations, and the shipping and delivery of works of fine art. So it is useful to know they can collect work from all over the world, deliver, and hang the work if required.

There are a few details the installation company will need to know to ensure the piece is hung correctly: the size and weight of the piece, as it might need more than two people to install, the location, the type of wall and the height the piece is to be hung, as it might need scaffolding.

Making your piece

Preparation

One of the first starting points is to consider what you will be creating and why. For example, will this piece be an extension of your current work or is it a separate idea that has been burning away for a number of years? Is it suitable for the location and purpose of the space? Once these questions have been answered the next step is to begin the formal design process of the actual piece. One suggestion would be to ensure the idea becomes reality through a sketch first, this can of course vary in scale and material. My preferred choice is a pencil, pen and a ruler, as these materials in particular relate closely to the lines and structural qualities in the fragments created, but obviously any medium is good.

If you have been commissioned to create a wall piece and this is new territory for you, it is even more important that you begin by drawing out your ideas, as you will probably need to show these to the client. Once you have captured the broad idea, take the time to make a scale drawing; this could begin simply with A4 or A3 (standard copy) paper. By this point ensure that you are happy with the scale, the materials you will be using,

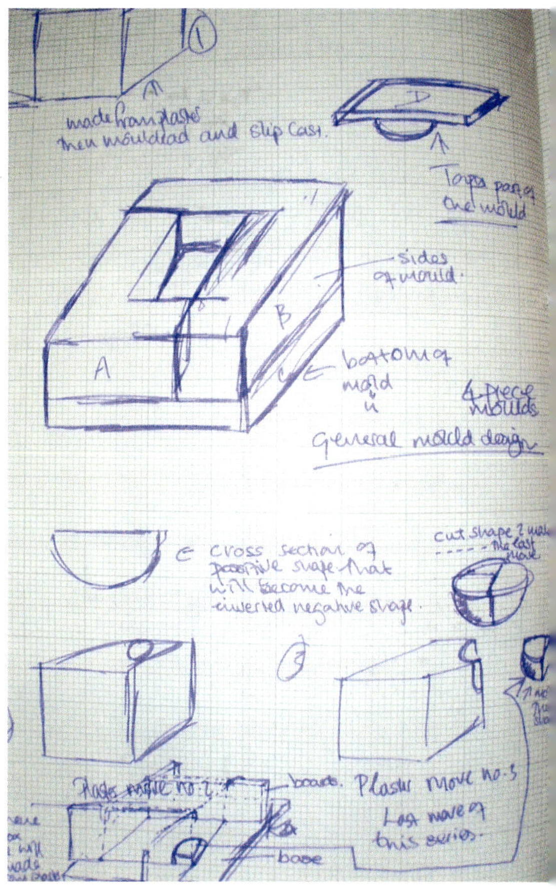

Louise Goddard: the making process, stage one. Design and working out. 'At the design stage I create a cube with an inverted semi-sphere, but if looked at with a bird's eye view you could then identify the square (male) and the circle (female)'.

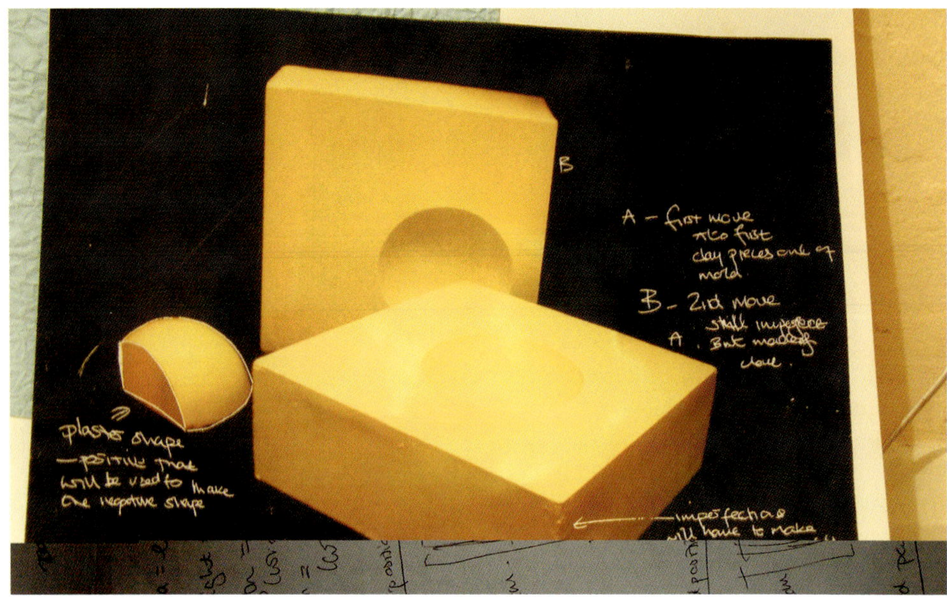

Louise Goddard: the making process, stage four. Plaster of paris forms created for the design of mould making and casting. Two practice pieces plus the plaster positive. *Photo courtesy of artist.*

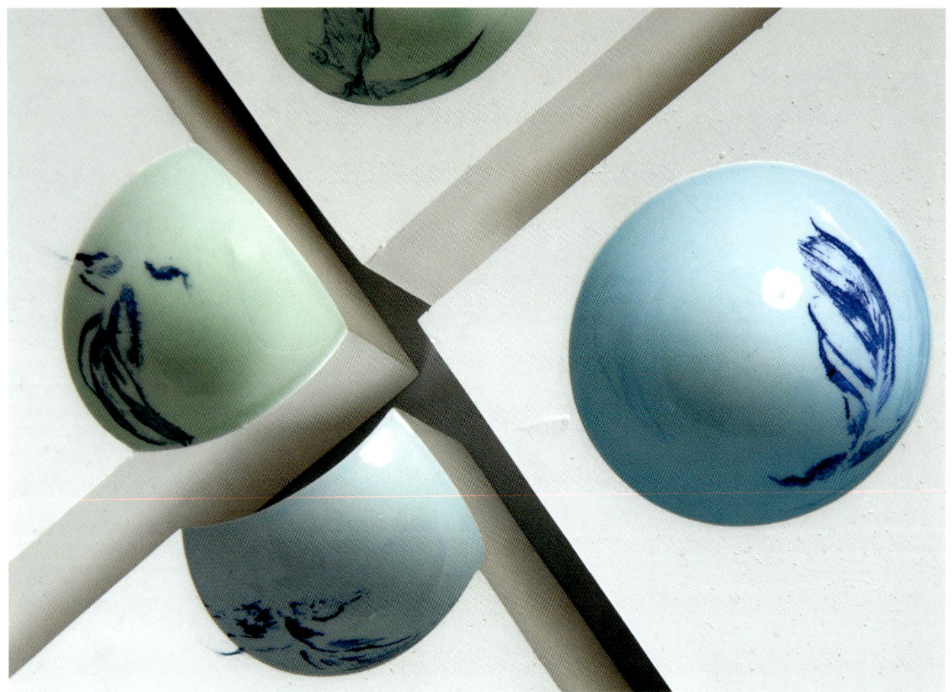

Detail of *Blue and green cubes with cobalt carbonate feathers*, by Louise Goddard: 2007. Each cube: 23 cm x 23 cm (9 x 9 in.), ht: 10 cm (4 in.). *Photo by Martin Avery.*

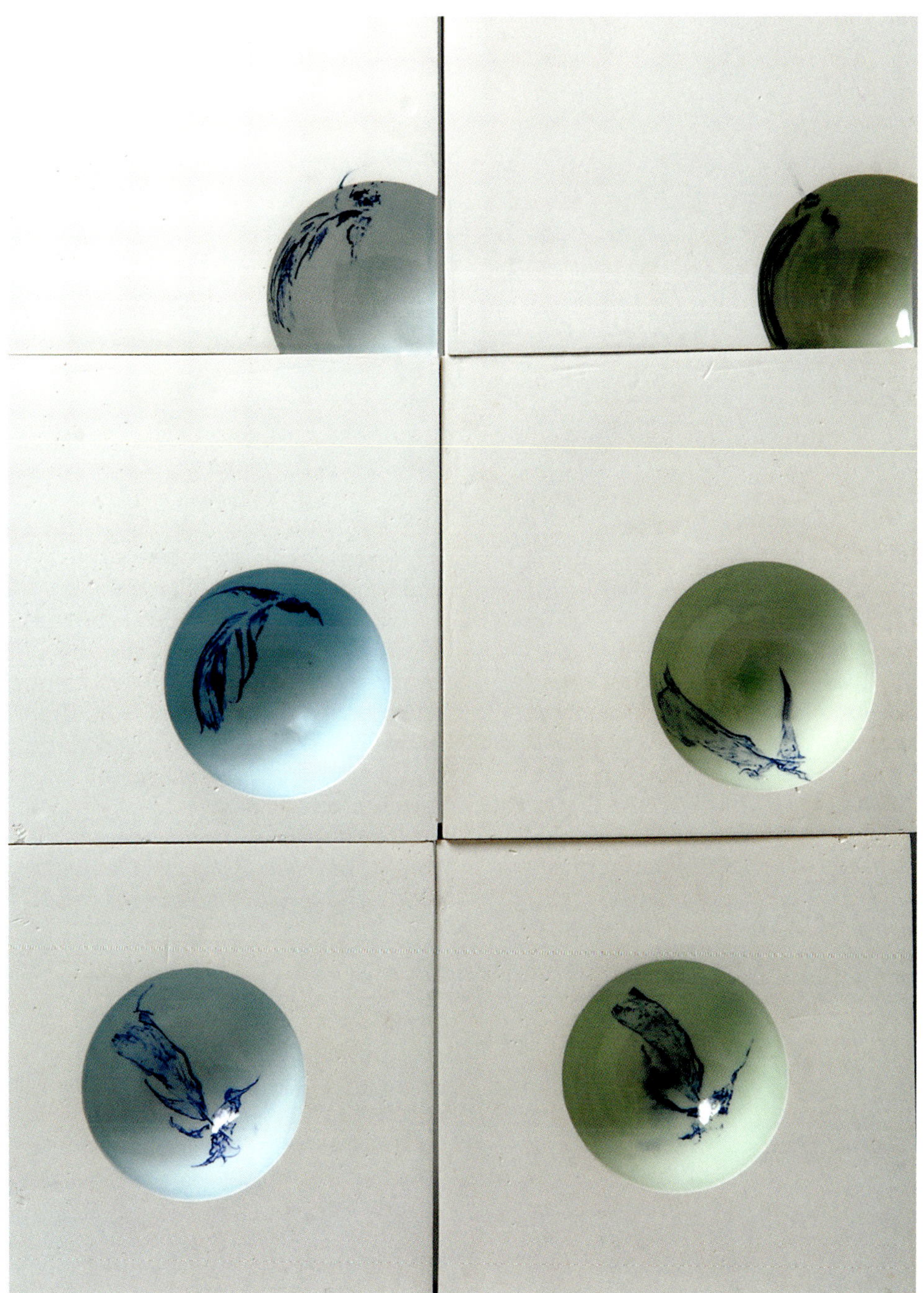

Blue and green cubes with cobalt carbonate feathers, by Louise Goddard, 2007. Each cube: 23 x 23 cm (9 x 9 in.), Ht: 10 cm (4 in.). White earthenware casting slip, fired to 1100°C (2012°F) and then a final firing of 750–850°C (1382–1562°F) to incorporate the delicate feather in response to male and female form. *Photo by Martin Avery.*

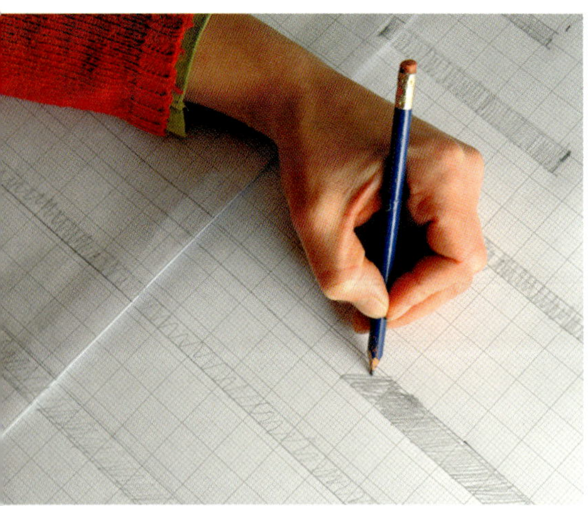

Dominique Bivar Segurado: Design planning for a *Natural Fragments* wall piece. Drawing with a pencil on a large sheet of graph paper. *Photo by Mark Harvey.*

the method of making, the fixings you have in mind and where this piece will be hung. (See chapter 3 for more discussion of fixings.)

Many makers use graph paper for their scale drawings. Louise Goddard makes earthenware wall pieces and ensures that all her slip-cast mounts, designs and ideas are noted on graph paper, all of which are key to the final wall piece, as each slip-cast block forms the final composition of six blocks. The design pattern is noted on graph paper too.

The process of creating an A4 (8.5 x 11 in.) or larger-scale drawing can also help when presenting ideas to a supplier, client and/or contractor. It also allows scope for playing with ideas and composition. This is then developed finally by re-drawing the design to the exact scale (if possible) using A1 (24 x 36 in.) graph paper (and obviously scaling down if not). The paper may need to be joined with other pieces to achieve the scale need. It is important to measure and check both your space and planned work well so as to avoid any problems with fitting the work later on.

Before you make your work, you need to consider not only the concept and feel your work will have, but also the type of clay, and practical installation factors as previously discussed. Will your work be made up of one large block? Many tiny pieces? Will it be possible to clean the work, and is this relevant or necessary? Consider the type of clay you will use and if it needs to be very high fired for durability and/or frost protection. If the work needs to fit or allow for screw holes, brackets, mounting or frames, it is important to consider shrinkage of the clay and allow for it in the design. Once all of these are thought through, you can begin to make the piece(s).

When the sculptor Walter Ritchie made his *Creation* piece for the Bristol Eye Hospital (*see* opposite and pp.52–53) he constructed a temporary work area to build and carve his wall panels. To deliver the work a lorry with a hoist was needed and several members of his team, to ensure the panels could be installed successfully due to the weight. These are all important factors to consider when creating large wall pieces.

Budgets

Before sitting down in the studio to begin making with clay it can be very useful to ensure you have considered your budget for creating the wall piece. Otherwise it might be a surprise how quickly money can disappear on a project, whether it is a commission or not!

Working out a budget can help you to focus on every aspect of the project; it is also wise to consider the time you expect this project to take. Working on a project for two months can be very different from working on a project that might take three years. Make sure your budget allows for

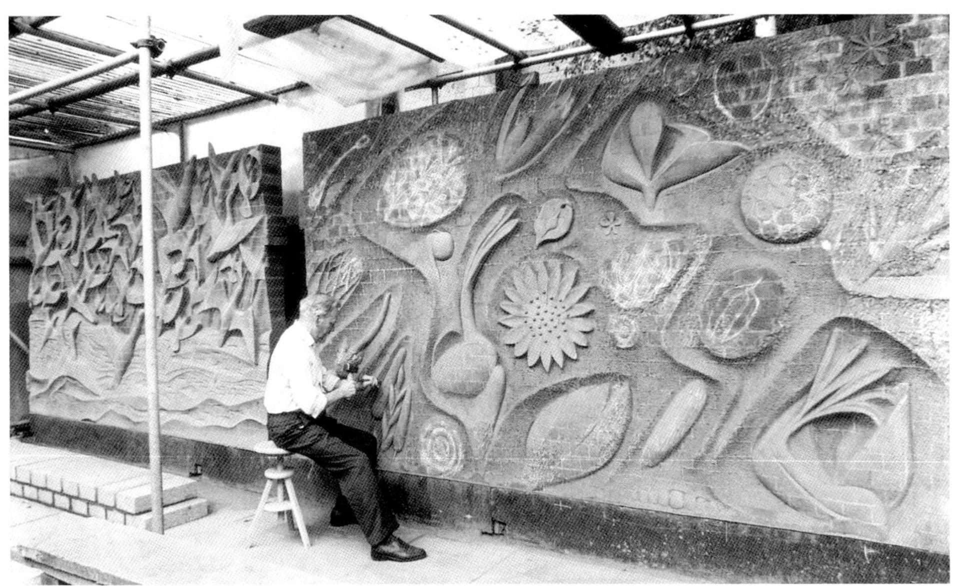

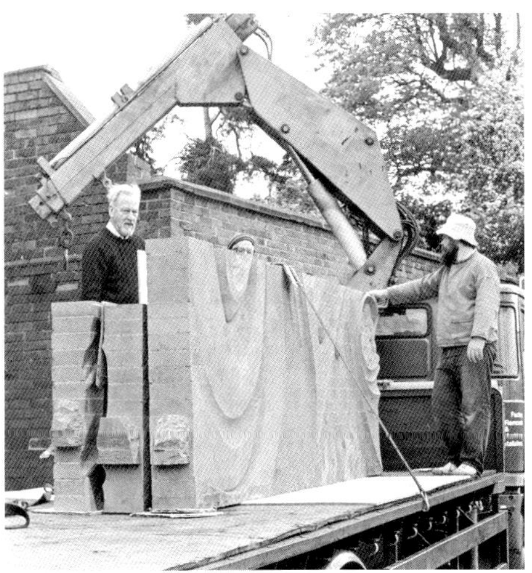

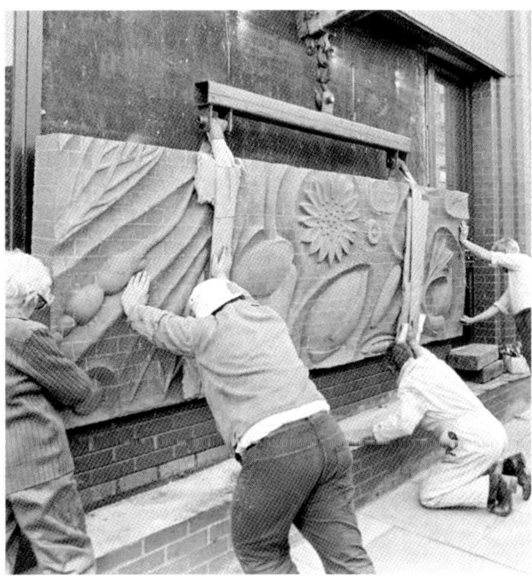

Creation by Walter Ritchie, 1981–1986. TOP Walter Ritchie working at home, under a temporary shelter of scaffolding, plastic sheeting and timber. Concrete beams form a base for the panels. Tools in hand – hammer and chisel – used throughout.

ABOVE LEFT The panels being slung on to a lorry from Walter Ritchie's home. Note lugs at the end of the panels, to help with fixing, which are cut off once the panels are in position. Note also use of soft board to protect panel.

ABOVE RIGHT Fixing at Bristol Eye Hospital: the panels are secured into position using rawl bolts.

Photos courtesy of Sally Taylor, Trustee of Walter Ritchie Foundation.

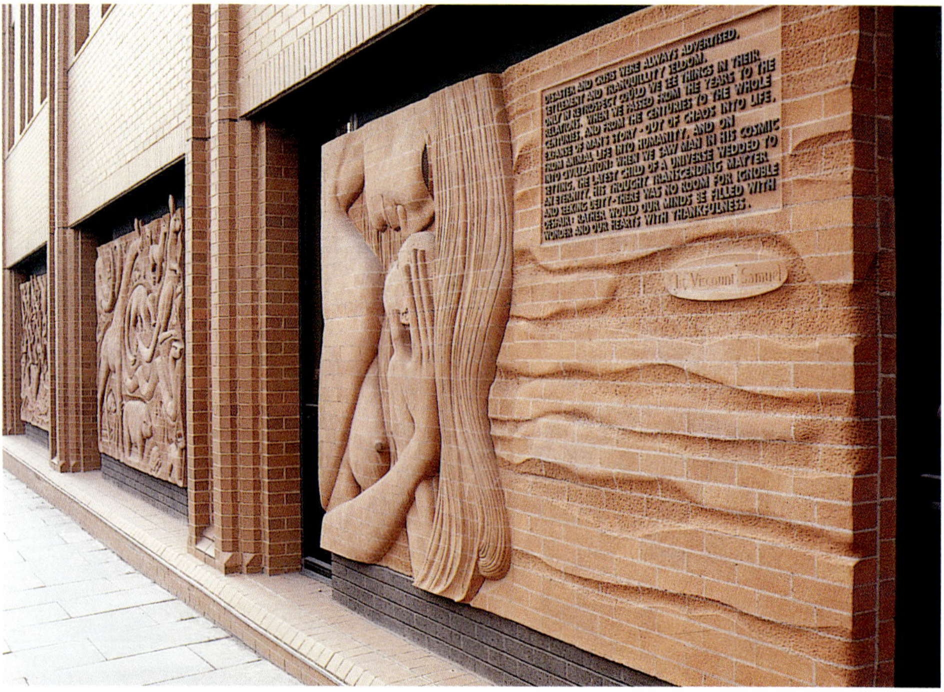

Creation by Walter Ritchie, 1981–1986. Five panels, each 3.58 m (11 ft 9 in.).

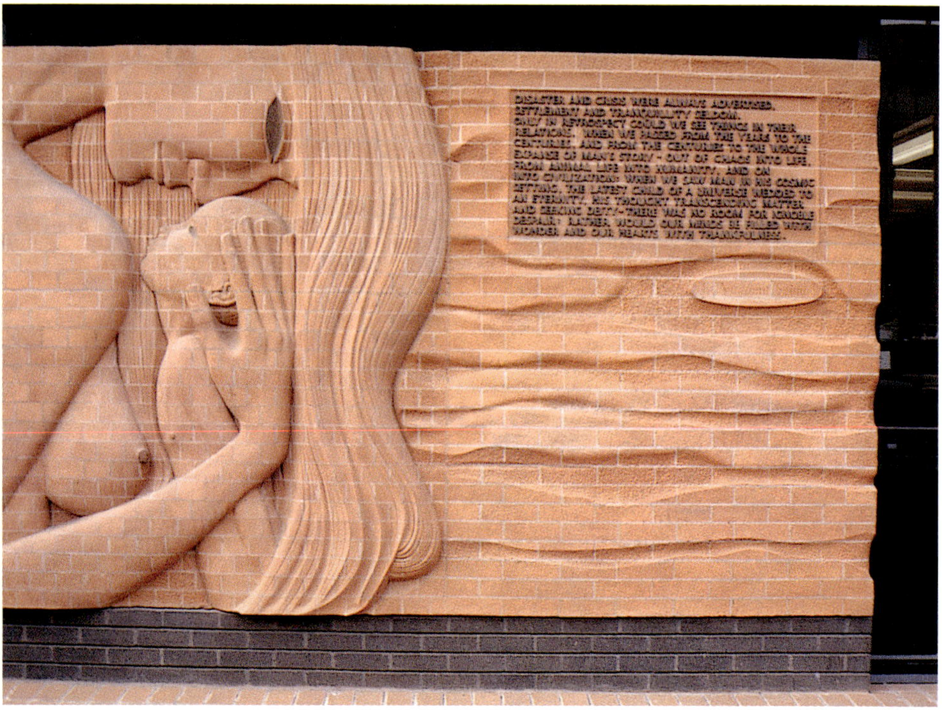

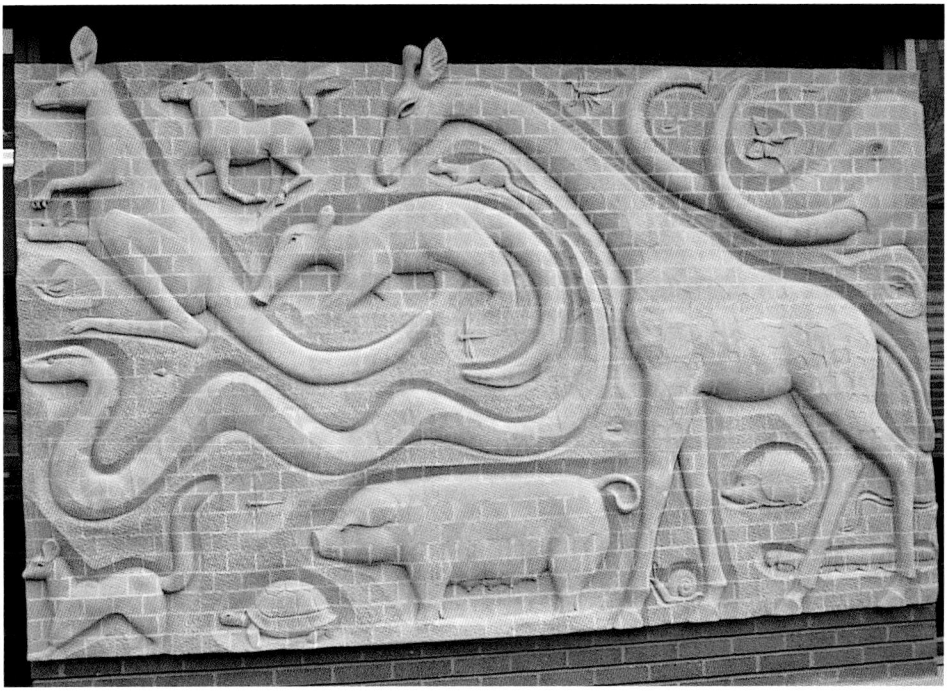

Commissioned for Bristol Eye Hospital, UK. Red rustic brick (Ibstock Brick Ltd), rmc mortar.

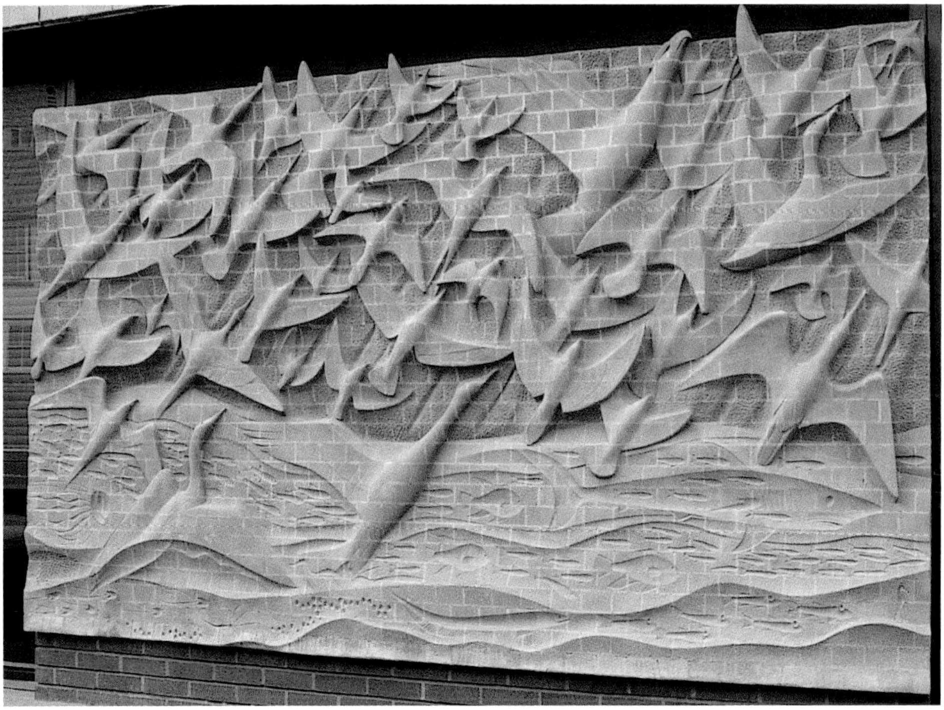

this too. A time plan with deadlines can be useful to run alongside the budget.

If you are submitting a proposal a budget might be required as part of the submission, along with the designs. It is a useful practice to be familiar with all the costs of creating a new project before getting started in the studio.

Try to include the following in your budget:

- Time to create the piece (i.e. your time, your rate per hour or per day).
- The material costs for the actual ceramic work, including everything purchased for the project from the glazes and clays to new tools and pencils for designing.
- Fixings (they can be expensive so ensure you do your homework on the costs and suitability).
- Mounting materials and backings for the work if needed, including any materials needed to render or improve the wall.
- Any help or contractors needed, for example builders or assistants in the making process and/or when installing (ensure you get quotes before you commit yourself).
- Transport costs. Will you need to hire transport? If not, remember to keep a note of your mileage, parking and fuel.
- Equipment – will you need to purchase any new equipment before beginning to make the work?
- Time and costs to create a model or maquette first, if required.
- Any extra space requirements to make the work – possibly hiring an extra studio or larger kiln if the project is very big.

NB: If you are working with a client don't be shy to ask for a deposit – for example enough to cover the materials, or 10–20% of the whole project cost. If the project is large and/or costly it is wise to discuss and draw up a contract.

Commissions and set project briefs

If you are commissioned to create a wall piece in a specific location, you will normally be given a brief, or a number of set objectives for the project, by the client. If you are commissioned by an established organization, it is worth finding out whether a budget has been set. You may need to supply your own budget breakdown, or at least see if theirs is realistic before taking the project on. Once accepted, the commission is confirmed normally through a contract.

Thereafter it is essential to ensure that a constructive and successful dialogue occurs between you and the client – it might be up to you to set a meeting date and visit the client. Do a little homework on the company beforehand, and then ask for feedback on past makers who have worked with this organisation. A number of the makers featured here, such as Mari-Ruth Oda, Alice Mara, Chris Wight, Jim Robison, Margaret O'Rorke and myself have been commissioned by organisations familiar and comfortable with commissioning arts, such as Art for Offices, Artpoint Trust, Free Form and Project Art, as well as local county councils and regional councils.

Artpoint Trust specialises in managing projects for the built environment and public space, and all their projects involve a creative response to space. They follow a clear structure when selecting and working with artists. Although each commission is unique, there are similar guidelines they tend to be set by their clients: they require the artist to produce and work to a high standard, have experience in handling similar projects in the environment (although this is not always essential) and be able to engage with the clients involved in the project – this might also involve the wider community.

Once the applications have been short-listed there is normally an interview to meet the artist and discuss possible ideas for the project. This is an ideal opportunity for the client and Artpoint Trust to consider what individual approach each artist will bring to their commission. Following a successful interview a number of meetings occur normally with the client, possibly the wider community and Artpoint Trust. This can also enable the artist to witness the use of the space by individuals and to assess its function. The meetings would involve viewing the space, meeting with the client/commissioning body, hearing their needs and aims, and discussing the practical issues for the project and any further matters. On occasions, if the project is connected with the local community, often leading members or spokespeople from the local community are invited to engage in these meetings to help build a stronger understanding of the requirements for the project. This all helps the artist to develop a clearer understanding of the concept and purpose of the piece of work that will be created, and ensures the community will feel engaged with the project. On occasions, in order to develop further the relationship of the community with the project and to build an understanding of the artist's role in the commission, artists are asked to run a number of practical workshops (often connected to the local school or community group). These activities do provide a really interesting chance for both parties (artist and community) to build a good relationship, and can often inspire and motivate people.

In contrast, companies who have never done this before may decide to commission works, in which case it will be up to you to set the guidelines for what is possible and practical. Communication, and forming a relationship with your client, is then even more important to avoid any misunderstandings, as this can cause problems later on when you have already invested time and money in a project. So from the start it is essential to maintain regular contact with your client, to keep them updated with progress, changes, or possible delays to the commission. A helpful approach can be to send clients photos of the work in progress through email – this might even be a requirement. Documenting a project from start to finish can also be helpful for future reference.

It may be that the commissioned project you are working on will involve architects, in which case your designs and planning will need to be viewed by them. Be open-minded, as there could be a need for technical changes to your designs. Use the experience and knowledge on offer as a welcome addition to your creative practice. Make sure you contact the relevant people and get them involved from the start, to avoid having to redesign and change your plans halfway through, otherwise you may suddenly be told about restrictions, rules or requirements you had not been aware of.

Obviously commissions will vary depending on each commissioning body, but this is a broad outline of what to expect.

Chapter 3

Hanging and mounting

With all the key elements discussed in the previous chapter, we can now move on to the next stage – hanging and mounting a wall piece. This chapter focuses on the practical aspects: the fixings, fittings and materials to consider when making and installing a wall piece. There are a number of approaches and a variety of materials available, some more obvious and easier to obtain than others, but it is important to find both a method and materials suitable for the final design. Be open-minded, as sometimes the simplest method can be the most suitable. Plan ahead before buying a selection of materials that will never be used. The ideal result is to find materials and methods which will not only enhance and support the ceramic, but which will work well aesthetically with the wall too.

This chapter looks at several makers' methods of hanging and their approach to installation. It is exciting to see how each maker's approach is a unique and successful integration of their concepts and the use of clay.

Materials such as glass, ceramics, wood and metal have all been used as a valuable addition to the ceramics, some acting as an additional feature or embellishment to the work, as well as a backing material, while others operate as the key support when placing ceramics on the wall. Some makers will use a material in a purely functional way to help hang the ceramic, while for others it becomes an inherent part of the work itself.

One innovative work is a collaboration between two Japanese makers, Kaz Kondor and Ikuko Iwamoto, entitled *Insect Collection* (opposite), which uses the spines of old leather-bound books. The spines act as a backing material for the small, hand-carved and press-moulded porcelain insects which are joined to the backing by small pieces of Velcro. It resonates with a traditional feel, reminiscent of the Victorian enthusiasm for collecting butterflies and insects in specimen cases. This small, delicate piece takes a traditional concept and gives it a contemporary feel, combining old and new in an interesting way. These makers spend many hours looking around antique and second-hand shops for their source materials. The piece demonstrates the point that found or second-hand backings, frames or fixings can be an alternative idea, if other materials do not suit the overall concept of your work.

The use of Velcro in *Insect Collection* is an unusual idea because it allows for the possibility of change. If a client wanted a certain kind of insect, they could easily be swapped over. For a changeable or temporary installation, Velcro might be a useful idea as a fixing material to use on a wall, the only downsides being that it will only hold lightweight work, and will most likely damage the wall, as the glue from the Velcro will probably take the paint off when you try to remove it.

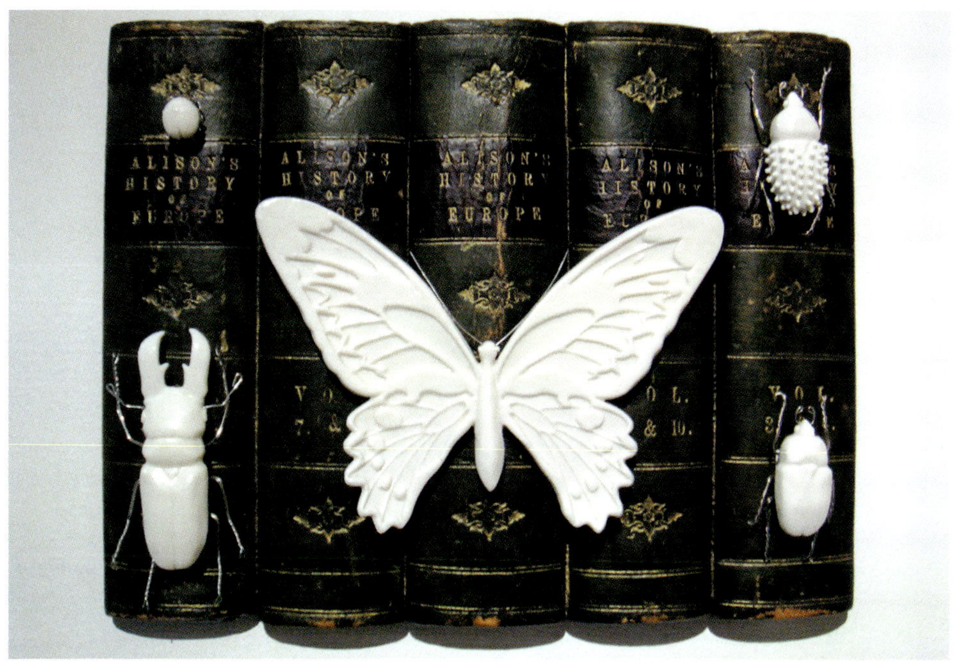

Insect Collection, by Kaz Kondor and Ikuko Iwamoto, 2008. Size: 18 × 23.5 × 3 cm (7 × 9 × ¼ in.). Porcelain, stainless steel wire, book spines and wood. *Photo by Ikuko Iwamoto.*

Materials used to hang ceramics

Many makers have their preferred materials, designed and chosen to suit the piece they are creating. Every material, wood, clay, Perspex, metal or glass, has its own attraction and if used successfully will not only support the ceramics but enhance the final outcome. You don't need to be a specialist in using these materials, but it does help if you understand how your chosen medium will support the work.

A builders' merchant, timber yard or trade shop can be a good starting point, as they should be able to give some basic advice on the materials they have for sale. Don't be afraid to ask questions, and explain clearly what you want to use the material for, as they might be able to advise and point you in the right direction.

Conducting your own tests on a small-scale sample can be a wise investment of time and money. Before you spend a fortune on materials ask the suppliers if they have any off-cuts. For example, as I often use glass with my work, I have in my studio a selection of glass off-cuts which vary in thickness and sandblasted surface texture. This also applies to fixings and fittings as it might be hard to envisage them against the work. Try asking for a test sample, or one fitting, before committing to a large order. This will also give you an idea of scale, and how the fitting is to be attached to the ceramics and the wall.

The following are some examples and suggestions of materials that can be used to hang ceramics.

Ceramics itself – using loops and holes

Ceramics itself can be used in many forms to support wall pieces. One of the easiest is to create a simple loop on the back of the piece. It is essential to note that the loop(s) must be of a reasonable size and thickness to support the weight as ceramics, though strong under compression, does not respond well to distortion and pressure. The larger the work, the more loops or holes are needed to spread the weight. Equally, if you are boring a hole in your work to thread wire through, it must not be too near an edge, as otherwise the weight of the work may break off the corner or edge where the hole has been made. The hole needs to be well within the piece, but without being visible.

John Butler, who creates wood-fired ceramics, uses a simple approach – string and ceramic loops on the back of his large platters. The large dishes are created in a mould which is an old satellite dish.

Originally, Butler used picture wire to hang his ceramics, but discovered that because of the weight, the hard ceramic surface was rubbing away the coating on the wiring, which in the long term would lead to the wire rusting, and eventually snapping. He now uses nylon picture-hanging string that can take a weight of 30kg (66lb); the string is doubled to ensure it can support a heavier weight. John chose to mount the platters on the wall after having a discussion about their fantastic surfaces (achieved through wood firing and by placing salt on them beforehand). As many people lack space in their home for large platters, Butler thought the idea of being able to hang them on the wall would be of great interest. So he began experimenting, until he arrived at this solution.

I also use loops in my ceramic work sometimes. When I fired my shards and wall blocks I discovered that the loops needed support during the firing. The porcelain and stoneware blocks are fired on a deep bed of grog, and the back of

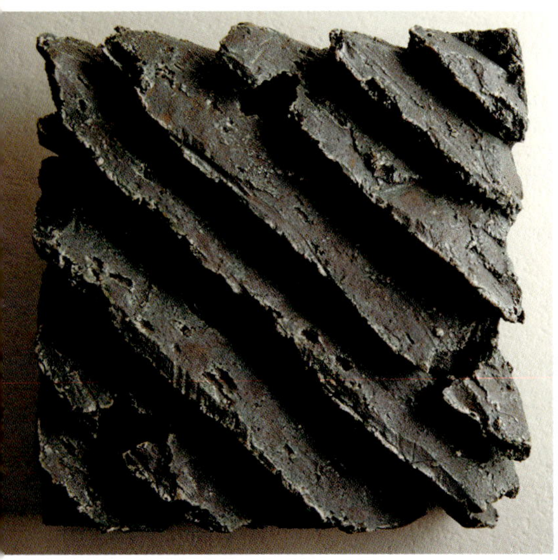

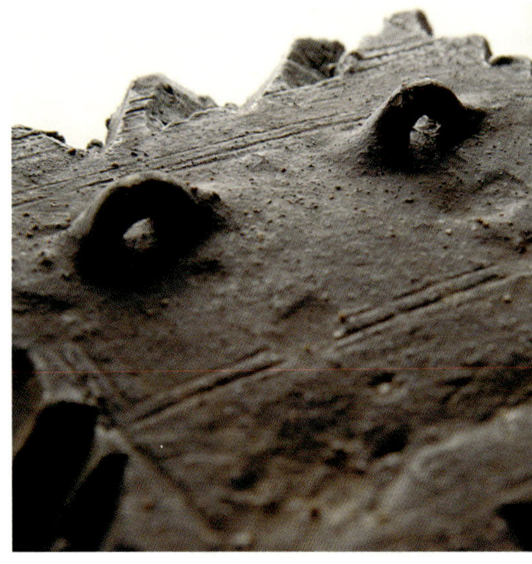

Stoneware wall block, by Dominique Bivar Segurado, 2008. Size: 30 × 30 cm (12 × 12 in.). Detail (*right*) of ceramic loops on the back of the ceramics block. Scarva's Earthstone Handbuilding clay, with glaze washes, fired between1240–1250°C (2264–2282°F). *Photos by Mark Harvey.*

The back of *Satellite Dish*, by John Butler (see below). Wood-fired stoneware clay. Threading nylon string through the lug on reverse of dish. *Photo by John Butler.*

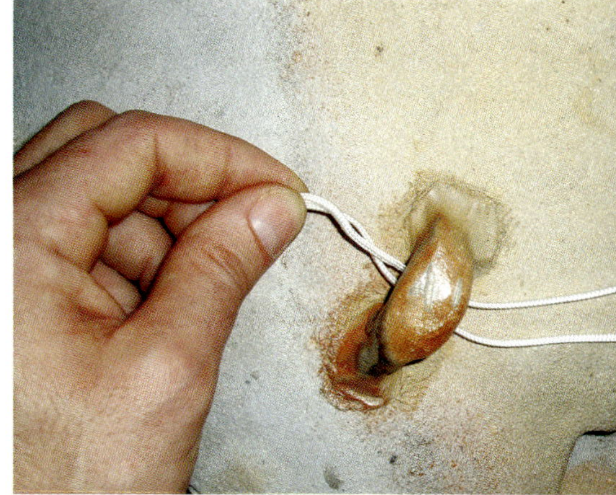

BELOW *Satellite Dish* by John Butler, 2008. Dia: 55 cm (22 in.). Wood-fired stoneware clay. *Photo by John Butler.*

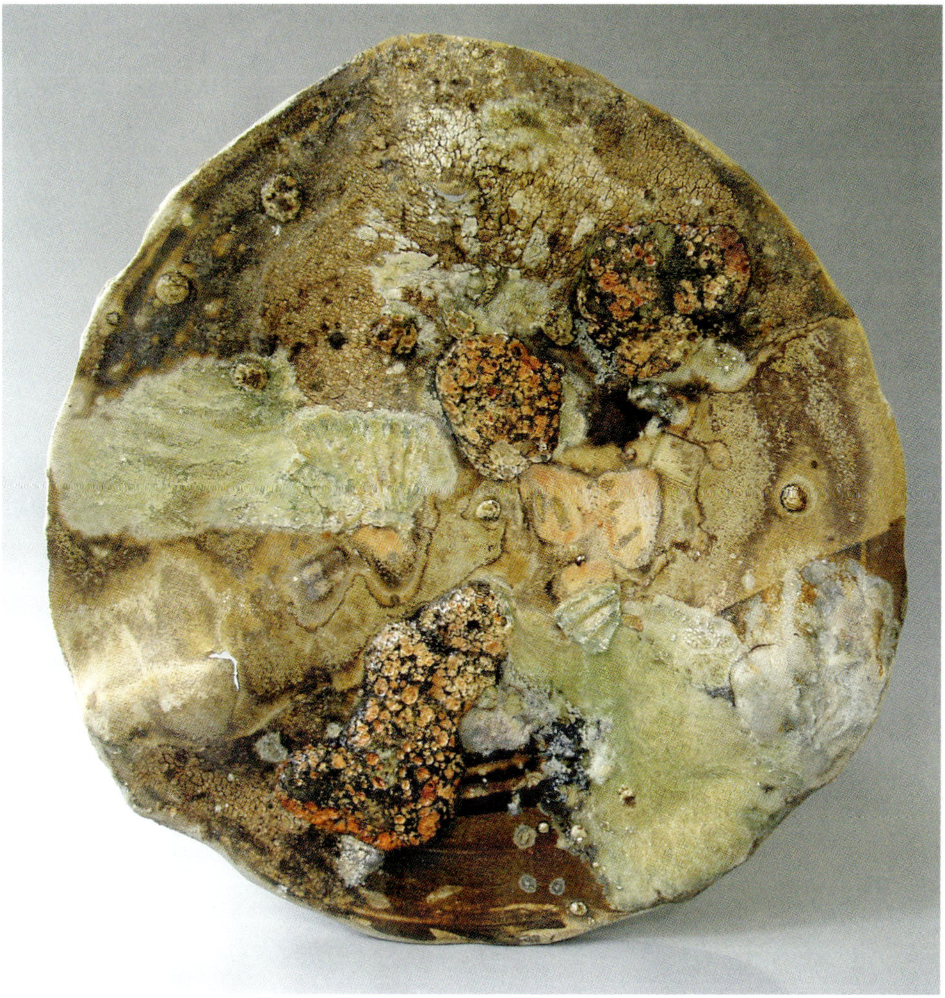

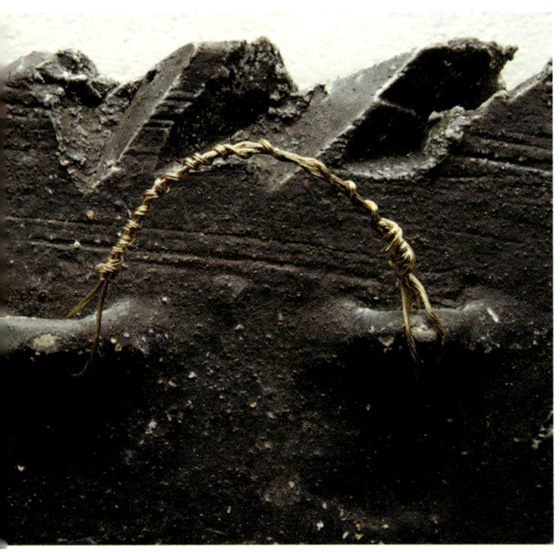

Stoneware wall block, by Dominique Bivar Segurado, 2008. 30 x 30 cm (12 x 12 in.). Scarva's earthstone handbuilding material, with glaze washes, fired between 1240–1250°C (2264–2282°F). Detail of ceramic loops with picture wire thread on the back of the ceramics wall block, ready for hanging. *Photo by Mark Harvey.*

the piece with the loop on is placed on the bed of grog to prevent cracking. These blocks cannot be fired face down, as it will warp the decoration.

Using loops is a method used by many other makers. For example, Claudi Casanova uses large, thick loops of clay on the back of his large plates which are hung on the wall. Strong wire is threaded through the loops, giving a good support to the plates which can be anything from 60–150 cm (23–59 in.) in diameter.

Wire and string

If the wall piece is to be hung like a canvas or a picture in a frame, wire can be one of the simplest and most suitable materials to use. There are varying thicknesses of wire that can be used: picture wire is good for lightweight pieces, thicker, galvanized wires are recommended for heavier pieces, and when hanging ensure the weight is distributed. Most wires can be found in hardware shops, often by the yard or metre, and the shop should be able to recommend a wire providing you know the weight of the work.

Type of Wire	Advantages	Disadvantages
IRON WIRE / BLACK ANNEALED STEEL WIRE	It is versatile because it can be both spot-welded and soldered when using the appropriate solders and fluxes.	Will rust in its natural state and therefore isn't appropriate for outside use. However, you can buy a galvanized version that is able to withstand the elements.
STAINLESS STEEL WIRE	Can be spot- or laser-welded.	Very tough to manipulate. It tends to spring back on you, and is difficult to control!
COPPER WIRE	Can be used outdoors as it doesn't rust.	It is very soft and may change shape and distort after manipulation, especially after soldering.
BRASS WIRE	Can be used outdoors as it doesn't rust.	It's quite a hard metal and therefore not the easiest to manipulate.
ALUMINIUM	Can be used outside and doesn't really discolour, unlike brass and copper.	Has a very low melting point therefore can't be soldered. You can only bind or twist with it.

For cutting or joining wires it is wise to invest in a pair of pliers. It may be possible to weld the wire together, but a simpler option is to join the wire by overlapping the pieces and twisting them tightly together (*see* left). As mentioned earlier, wire can rub against the ceramic, in which case another material, such as nylon, may be better.

Fishing wire can also be a good, strong wire to use. Similar to metal wire, it comes in varying thicknesses, to support different weights, so check on purchase. Be aware when hanging that it can have a tendency to stretch.

String and thick cords act in much the same way as wire, but bear in mind that if they are outdoors they may rot eventually. Bulky knots can sometimes distort and push the ceramic piece away from the wall, creating an unwanted gap between the wall and the piece.

Wood

Wood is an excellent resource as it comes in many forms, colours, textures and hardness. It is also widely available, and has the advantage that it can be glued onto, screwed into, nailed, drilled and painted. The use of wood can vary from being a backing material to acting as a frame for the piece – or both. Many makers do use wood as a backing material as it is durable and easily obtained. A wooden surface is something to consider seriously if the wall you will be working on is uneven, cracked or unsuitable in some way, or might not be a permanent location. If the wall is very large, it might be worth considering employing a contractor.

Before the installation of the collaboration piece *Flock* (*see* p.34) it was essential to line the wall with sheets of marine ply. This is wood sheeting that is water-resistant and comes in varying thicknesses. This makes it is an ideal material for outdoors, though preferably still protected from the weather. In the case of *Flock* the site was under a covered walkway. By attaching the wood to the wall, the wood acted as a smooth, even backing surface. Covering the wall with marine ply, and the joining and painting, was handled by the university contractors. This also involved the site engineer, who checked the total weight of the wood and ceramics to ensure that the wall was able to withstand the weight. This is something to check if the weight of your work will ultimately be very heavy – you must get permission and a safety check that the wall can bear the weight (*see* p.41).

The sheets of ply were drilled, screwed and placed on wooden battens which were directly attached to the wall using screws and rawlplugs. The wood was then painted to match the surrounding walls, using several coats of paint. This gave a neutral backdrop for the ceramics, and a strong, durable surface to support the piece. Each piece of ceramics was screwed into position with security screws, which need a special screwdriver bit. These fixings ensured that the ceramics could not be unscrewed or taken off the wall easily – the makers were concerned that people might want to take the small, attractive pieces off the wall.

The installation of the work at the Regent Street Campus was quite a lengthy undertaking. A record of the event was written by Kyra Cane, from the University of Westminster, the ceramics course leader at the Harrow campus, who initiated the project: 'The colossal task of installation became increasingly apparent as boxes of parts were sorted and organised. In early January of 2003,

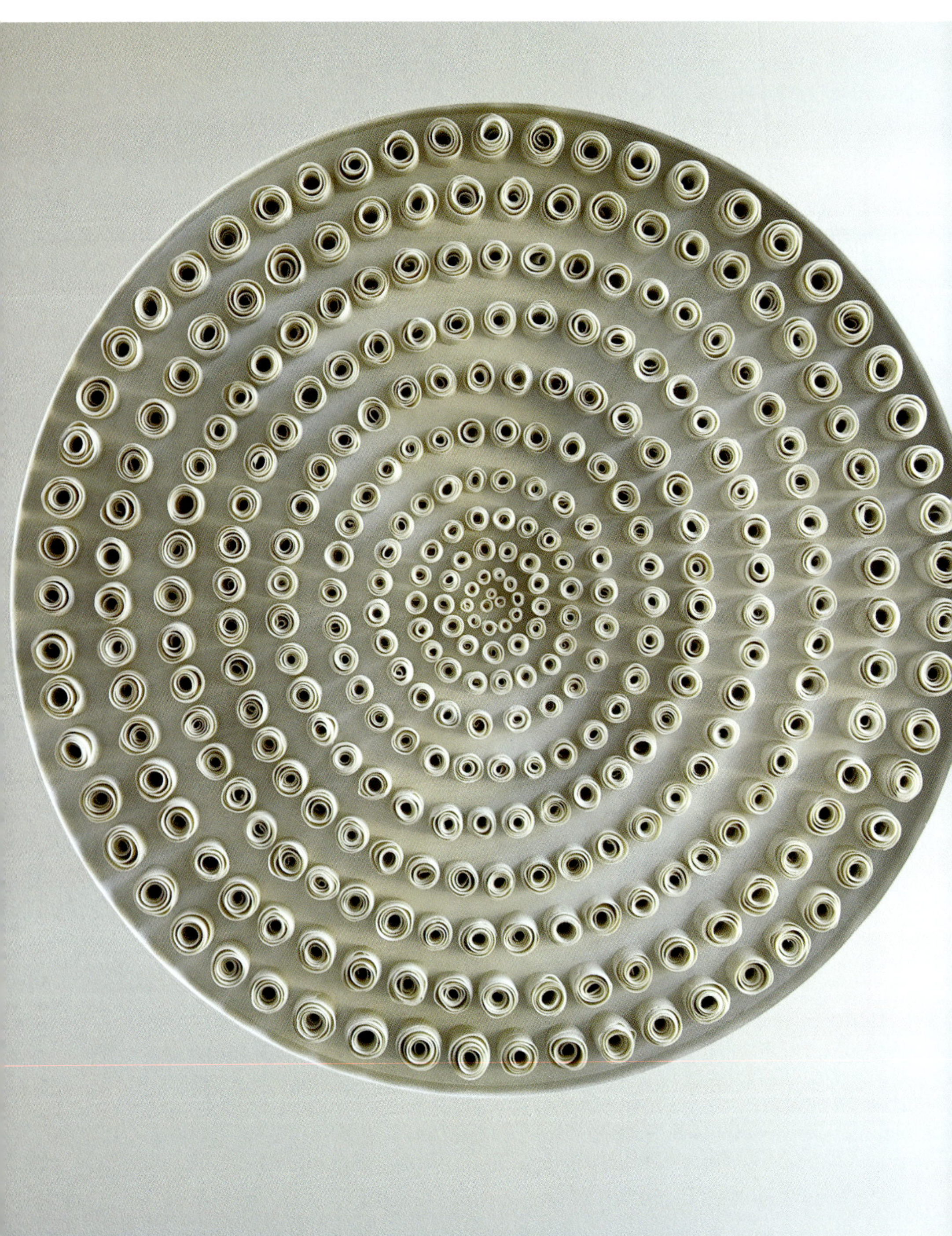

Roses by Valéria Nascimento, 2006. Size: 100 x 100 cm (39½ x 39½ in.). Royal porcelain fired to 1260°C (2300°F). Mounted on wooden backing with recess. *Photo by Christopher Pillitz.*

with snow on the ground, vehicles were packed, scaffolding towers erected and the final stage began. The wall was gridded out to match that of the floor of the adjoining room where for the first time the whole piece was being laid out. As the curls were screwed into the boarding the beautiful blues and greens created an impression of colour that broke down as you got closer to the piece and the desired pixelation effect really did become an effective metaphor for those crowds which break down into individuals as you draw nearer.'

Flock used a wood backing on a large scale, but of course it is possible to use wood on a smaller scale, and wood sheets can be cut to size in most hardware shops. Although marine ply is a popular choice for larger panels indoors and outdoors, another engineered wood substitute is MDF, although not so water-resistant. Choose your thickness depending on the weight of the piece, as the heavier the ceramics the more likely the MDF is to warp: a timber yard will be able to advise you on the weight it can bear. Remember to consider the overall weight in relation to the wall – once you have found the weight your wall can take. If you are cutting MDF yourself it is important to wear a mask as the compacted particles of wood, fibre and resins are not good for the lungs.

Wood has the advantage of allowing nails and fittings to be drilled in at odd angles as required. When I began to create my ceramic fragments series the backing material used was MDF with a thickness of 8–10 mm (3/8– 1/2 in.). The

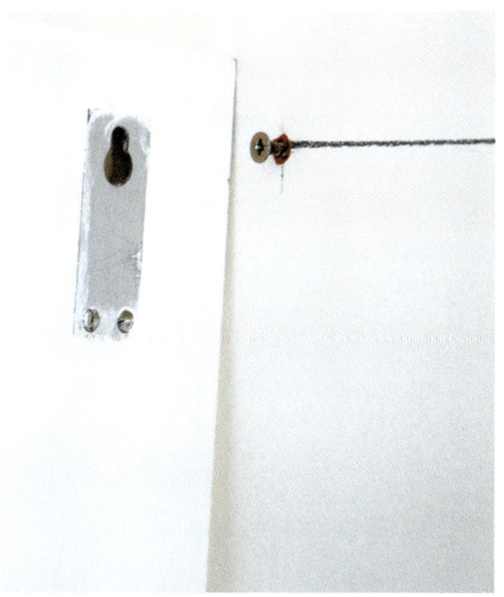

Ceramic Fragments, by D. B. Segurado, 2000. Detail of keyhole fitting, rawlplug and screw head before hanging piece on the wall. *Photo by D. Bivar Segurado.*

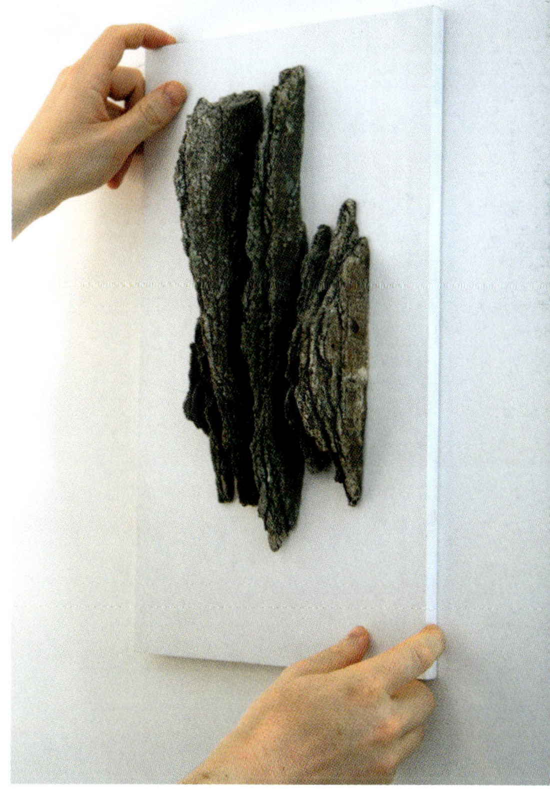

RIGHT *Ceramic Fragments*, by D. B. Segurado, 2000. Positioning and hanging the piece on the wall. *Photo by D. Bivar Segurado.*

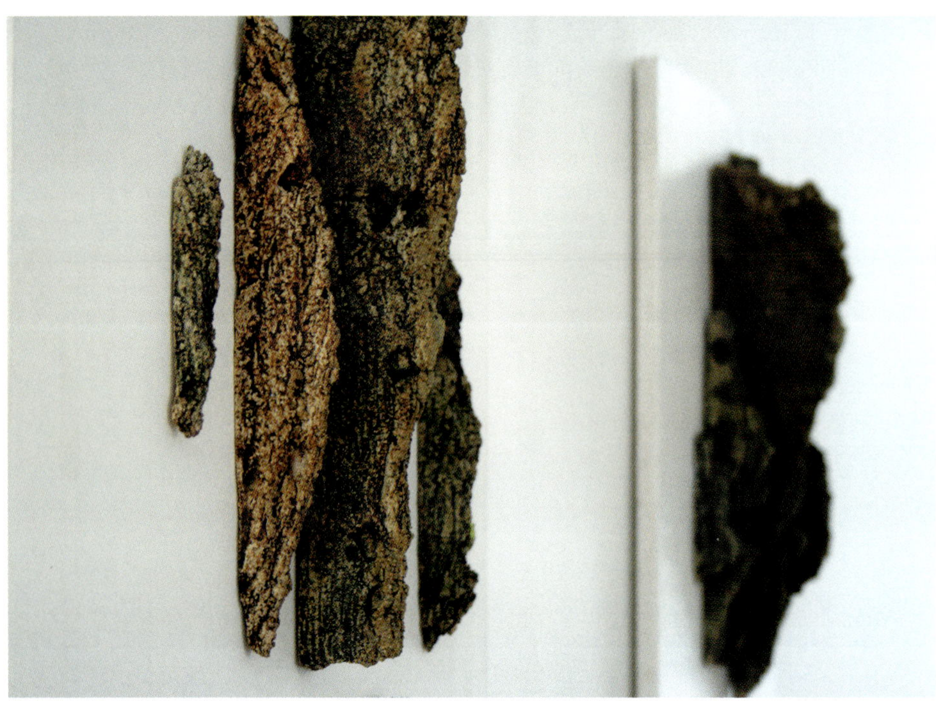

Ceramic Fragments by D. B. Segurado, 2000. 25 x 40 cm (10 x 16 in.). Stoneware ceramics with glaze washes, mounted on MDF wooden backing. Final hanging on wall. *Photo by D. Bivar Segurado.*

MDF was cut to size at the hardware shop and then painted with several coats of white emulsion. Each coat was gently sanded with wet and dry to remove the brush marks, helping to create a perfect, even surface. Two holes at a slight upwards angle were created in the back of each ceramic shard during the making process, so that once fired and glazed they could be placed on the backing. Once the position of the shard was confirmed, a very small pencil mark was made to position the two galvanized pin nails to hold the shard in place; this was in the same position as the holes. Each nail was then was hammered in at the same angle as the ceramic hole. On the end of each nail a small amount of strong durable glue (araldite) was placed as an extra support. As the holes in the ceramics were deep, the nail and glue were well disguised.

If the backing material can be cut or dug into, like wood, a key fitting (*see* p. 63) can be used. A small recess is created with a chisel and the key fitting is placed in the recess and fixed with two small wood screws. The recess creates a space for the screw head to fit in, to support the piece when hung on the wall.

Hanging a wall piece

The illustrations on p.63 show an easy way to hang a small wooden-backed wall piece. First it is important to check for any wiring or pipes. The space is measured between the two fittings and the correct distance is allowed. A straight line is drawn on the wall and the first drill hole is made for the rawlplug. Once the rawlplug is in

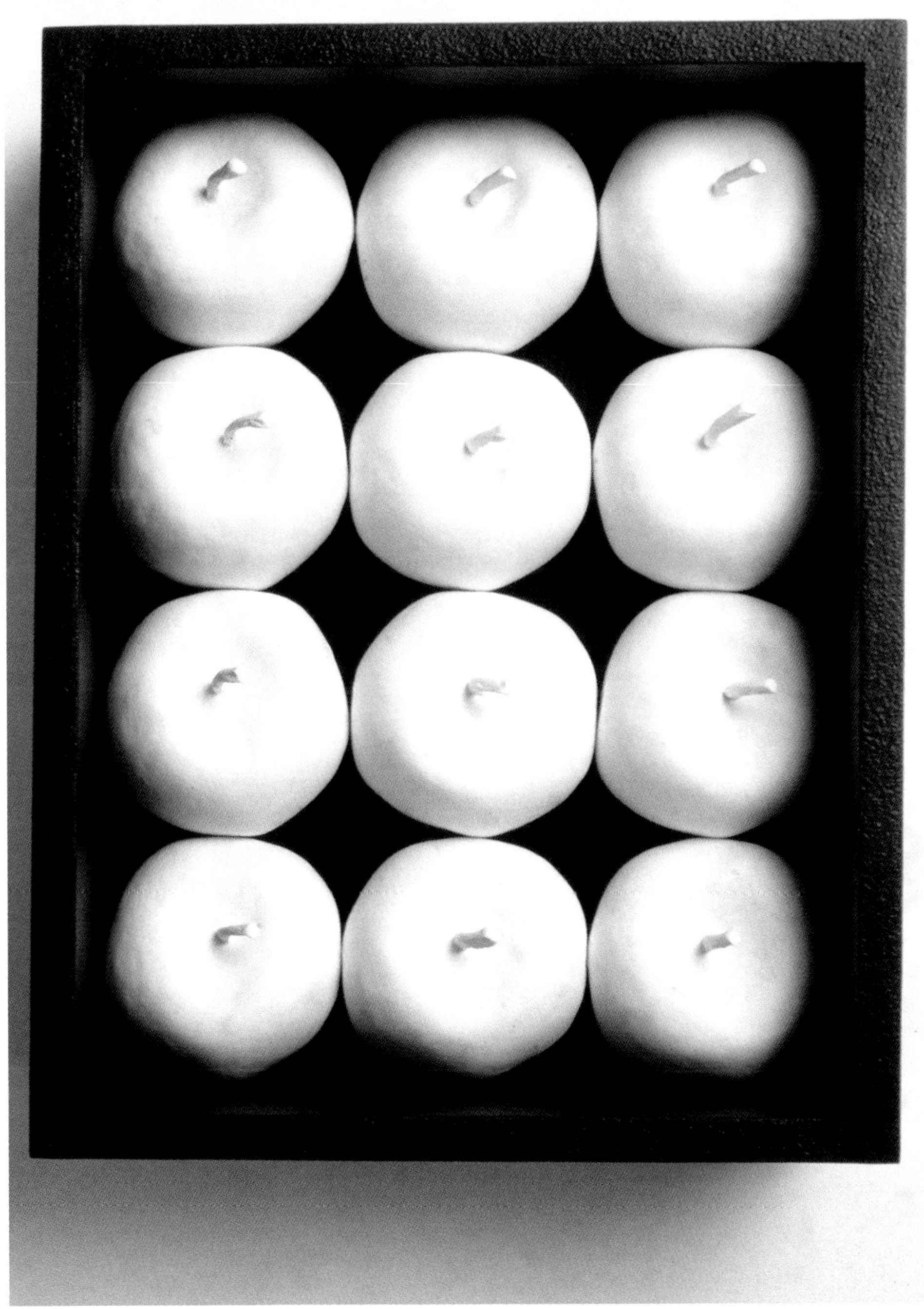

Apple by Andrea Hylands, 2000. 22 x 29 x 12.5 cm (8½ x 11½ x 5 in.). Bone china slipcast and handbuilt, secured in a wooden box. *Photo by Andrew Barcham.*

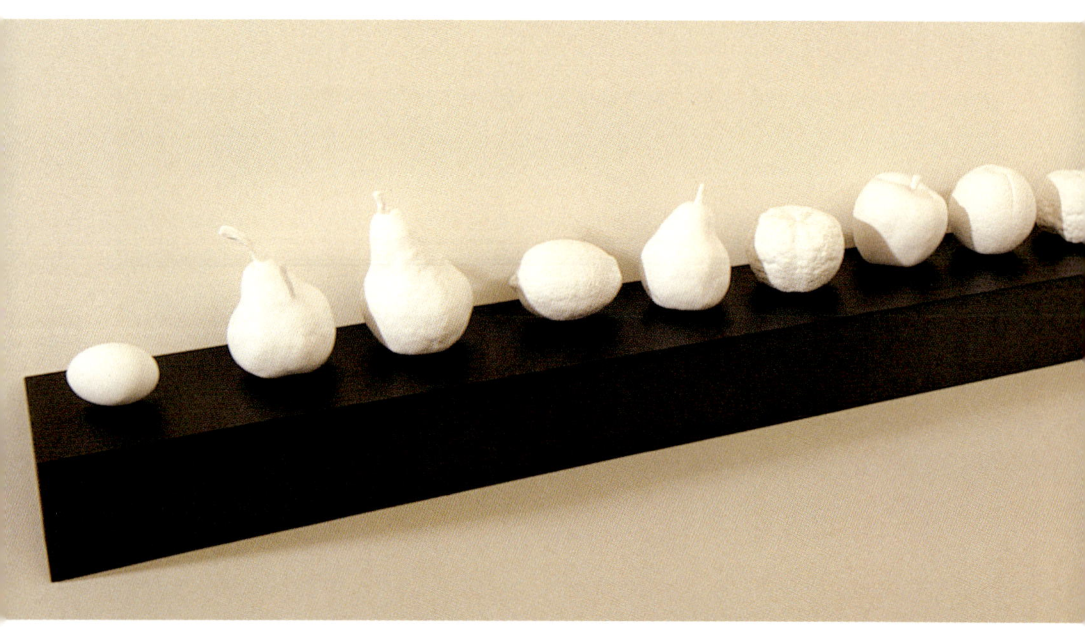

position and the screw put in, the level is checked with a spirit level; the next hole is drilled and screwed, and the level is checked again. The fittings on the back of the piece are designed to be supported by the head of the screws. The piece is then hung and the level checked once more.

Wood can also be used as a frame, to enhance and unify the piece. Placing ceramics in a frame can also provide a secure and practical approach to hanging the work. *Apple* (*see* p.65) created by Andrea Hylands (Australia) is a beautiful example of using stained wood to create an attractive box in which to house her white slipcast fruits. Curious to explore the patterns and physical concepts of nature, Hylands encases these fruits in the frame. As the ceramics is unglazed, the frame adds depth to the overall finish of the piece once hung on the wall. The frames are made by Hylands and have screw hook fittings to hang them on the wall. Each fruit is glued in place with a high impact adhesive to ensure no movement.

This maker has also gone further than simple wooden frames to her work. In *Still Life* (above), a composition of unglazed bone china fruits and egg is placed on a dark wooden shelf. The shelf is secured to the wall with rawlplugs and screws, though the fixings are hidden. Shelves with hidden fixings and fittings are now widely available from DIY shops, but often will not take a great weightload, so check on purchase. You might prefer to approach a specialist carpenter, as you will be able to get exactly what you want to support your work.

Emma Johnstone is a maker whose use of backing and display material has developed from using wood to Perspex, and she now creates pieces specifically for the wall. As Emma's work is non-functional, there was scope for variety in the way the work was displayed. Originally, the wooden display boxes Emma made were for individual bowls, but this changed when a client was impressed by an arrangement of four

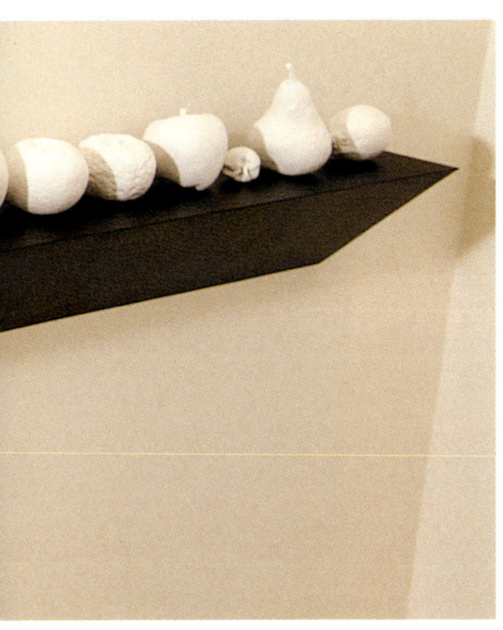

Still Life by Andrea Hylands, 2001. W: 1.5 m (3.2 ft). Bone china fruit and egg, slipcast and handbuilt, on painted wooden shelf attached to a wall. *Photo by Andrew Barcham.*

RIGHT *New Warriors 008* by Andrea Hylands. 59 x 22 x 9 cm (23 x 8½ x 3½ in.). Bone china, slipcast, with found wood backing. *Photo by Andrew Barcham.*

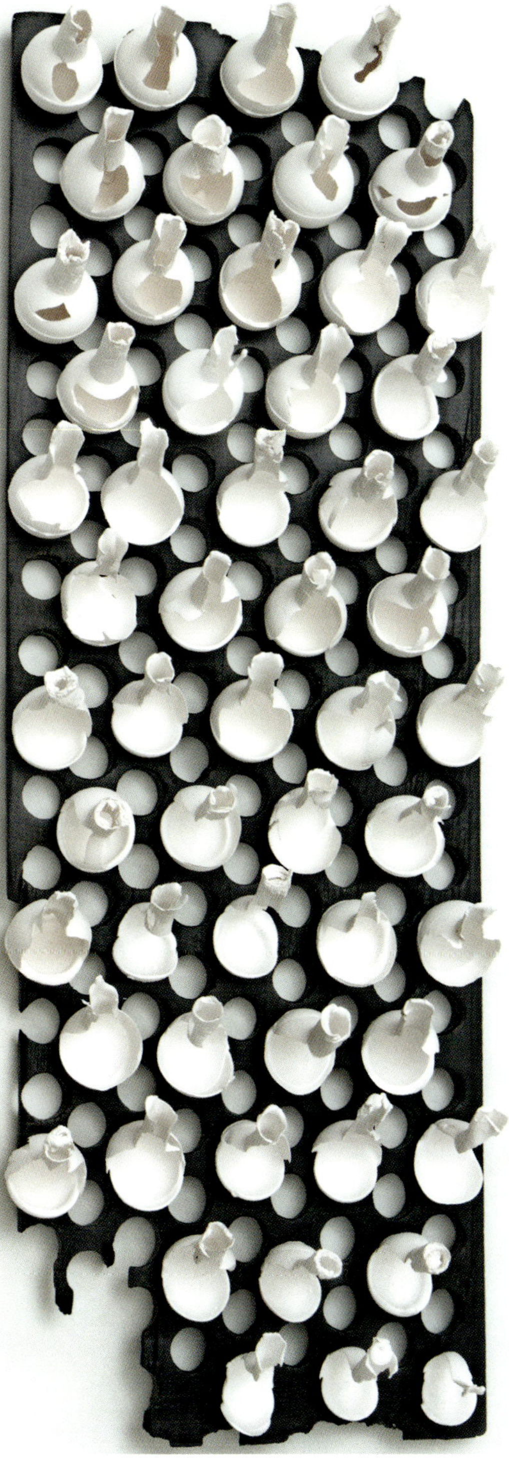

specific bowls. The appealing surfaces of her pieces have a real contrast between the dark edges and cracks of the raku and the rich gilded interiors of gold, silver and bronze leaf, and they look fantastic when seen directly from above. They also catch the light and have a lovely sheen on the interior, so it made sense to mount them as precious objects on the wall. The wooden display boxes use cut sections of wood, and each one houses four bowls. Each box with three shelves is attached to the wall by several screws: there are holes located in the top and third row of the box. Each bowl weights about 1 lb (470 g), so the overall weight is not too

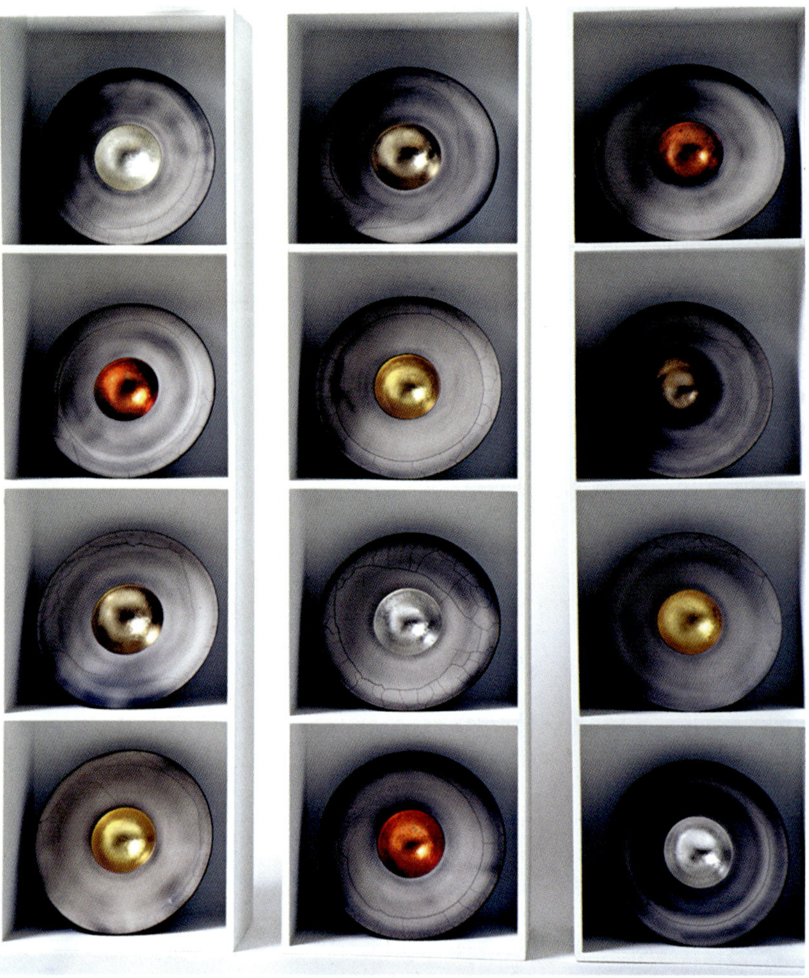

Bowls in wooden display cases, by Emma Johnstone, 2000. 20 x 80 cm (8 x 31 in.); Dia: 15 cm (6 in.). Scarva's Ashraf Hanna clay, raku-fired. *Photo by Dan Smith.*

heavy for the wall. The bowls are kept in position by special clear rubber adhesive pads known as 'bump-ons', which can be found in hardware shops or specialist suppliers (*see* p.125).

Another use of a wooden frame also incorporates a metal finish, creating a successful marriage between media and enhancing the ceramics of Vanessa Cox Pendray (*see* p.69). She uses wires to join her sections of paper clay to one another as well as to the wood frame. Around the edge of the wood frame there are metal eyelets so the wires can be threaded to support the delicate ceramics.

Wood can also be recycled and reused. If you live near a beach or woodland you might find driftwood or fallen twigs or branches that can be incorporated into the work. Andrea Hylands' *New Warriors 008* (*see* p.67) is a good example of a piece using a found wood backing to support and display the bone china.

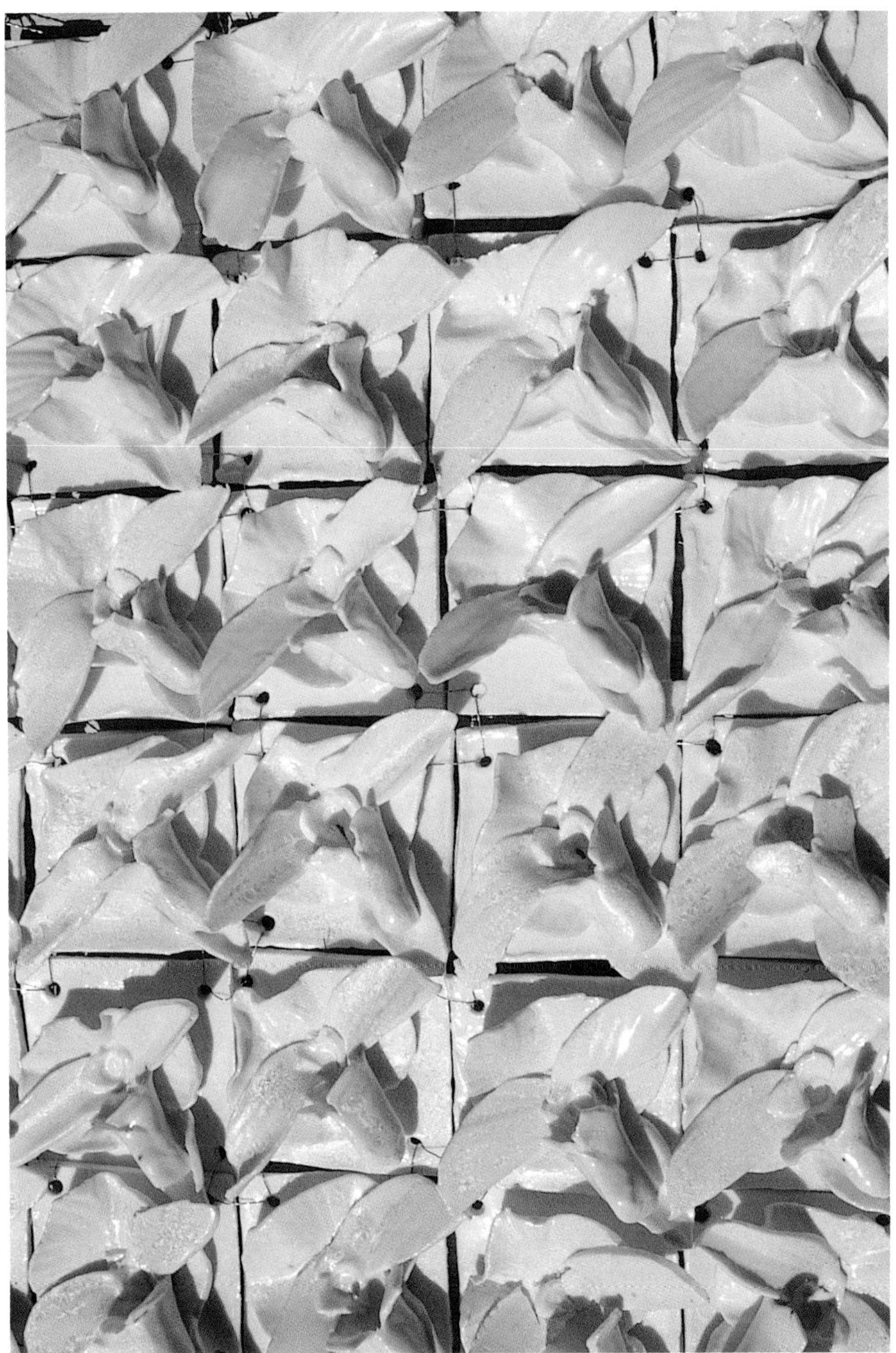

Wild Orchids, by Vanessa L. Cox Pendray. 40 x 40 cm (16 x 16 in.). Porcelain clay orchids fired between 1200°C–1220°C (2192–2228°F) with crystalline glaze, joined together with wire and mounted in a frame. *Photo by V. L Cox Pendray.*

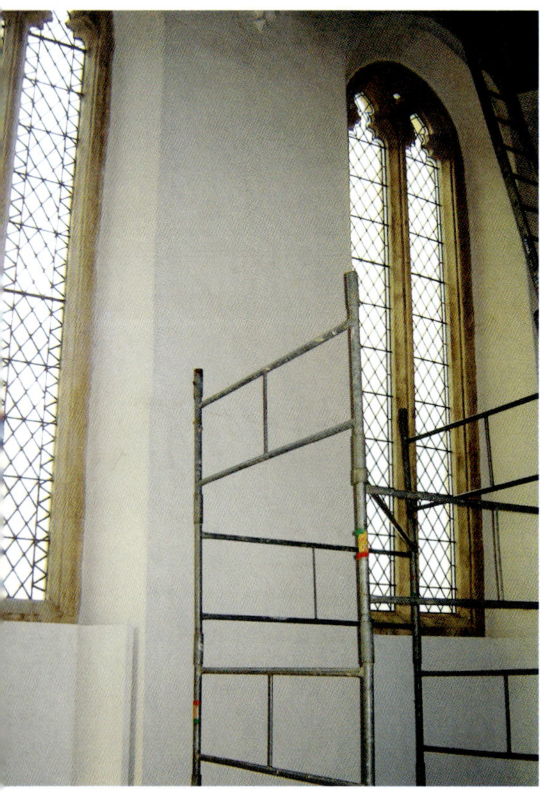

LEFT TO RIGHT *North Sea* by Viv Allen, 2006. Scaffolding tower being assembled to enable the work to be installed.

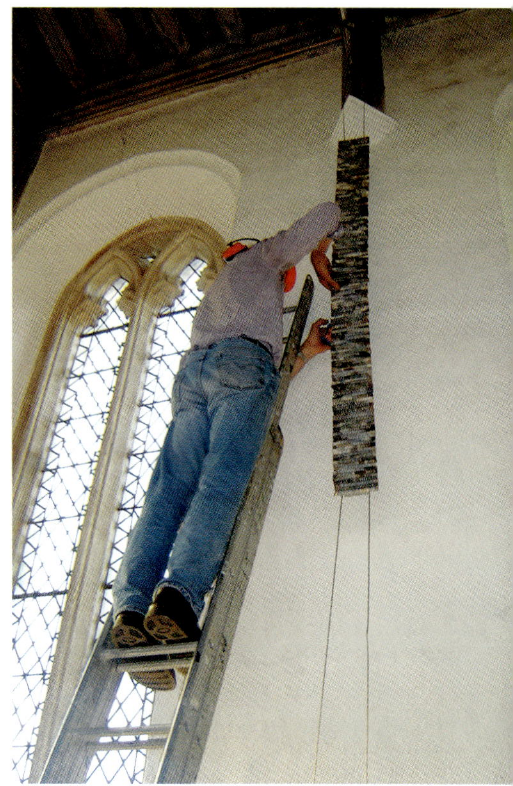

The first stages of the installation of *North Sea*. Two sections being secured to the length of cable using small metal clamps. The cable was looped through one of the wooden roof trusses.

Perspex/acrylic

Perspex, also known as acrylic, acrylic glass or plexiglass, is a successful material to use as a backing: it is durable, weather-resistant, soundproof, lightweight and easy to drill into and join ceramics to. Another advantage is that it can be obtained in many forms – clear, opaque, coloured – and also in varying thicknesses, so there is vast scope to interact with the wall surface or disguise it if needed. As a material Perspex also has a very modern feel, if that is what you need.

The Salthouse Exhibition, held every year on the picturesque North Norfolk coast, is known for encouraging its artists to interact with the surrounding area and Salthouse Church where the exhibition is held. A show exploring the theme of 'Cross the Boundaries Between Art and Craft,' was inspiration to the maker Viv Allen, prompting her to create her piece *North Sea*. She wanted to respond directly to the vast, pure white space of the church interior, but also to reflect the natural, rural qualities of the surrounding environment. She selected a wall space that was a narrow wall, 5 m (16½ ft) high and 1 m (3¼ ft) wide.

Allen created over 4000 hollow tubes using Earthstone Original clay, which she decorated with green and

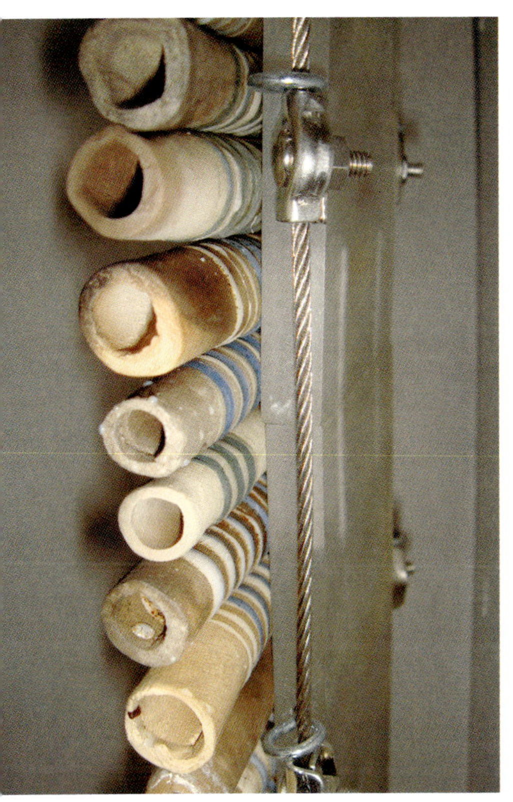

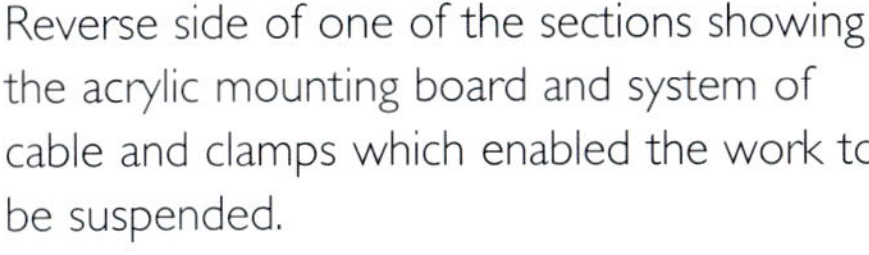

Reverse side of one of the sections showing the acrylic mounting board and system of cable and clamps which enabled the work to be suspended.

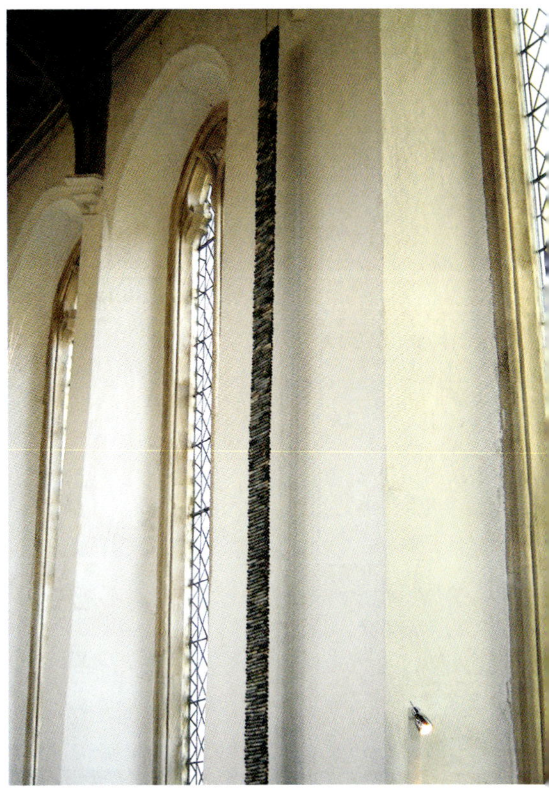

Scarva's Earthstone Original clay with slips and glaze. The smoke-fired tubular ceramic pieces (over 450 tubes), were mounted on 5 x 1 m (16 ft 4 in. x 3 ft 3 in.) acrylic boards. Each board registered with the one above using metal dowels and was then clamped onto the length of cable with small metal clamps. Installed in Salthouse Church North Norfolk, as part of the Salthouse 06 Annual Exhibition.

Photos by Viv Allen.

blue bands of slip, glazed after the bisque firing and finally smoke-fired to give an organic quality to the work. To achieve the scale needed, the ceramic was mounted on an acrylic surface. The final piece was made up of 1 m (3$^{1}/_{4}$ ft) sections. Each sheet of acrylic was sanded gently to create a non-reflective surface, and to help provide a suitable surface for the adhesive. Viv describes how this process of working with the acrylic was achieved: 'small metal eyelets were fixed into the sides of the acrylic, and dowelling was drilled into the top and bottom edge of each section. I glued each clay tube to the acrylic so that they touched each other and remained square to the acrylic backing board throughout its length. Once the ceramics were attached and the dowelling pegs in place to align the boards, fine steel cable was threaded through the eyelets and the sections held in place with small metal clamps.'

Scaffolding and a ladder were needed

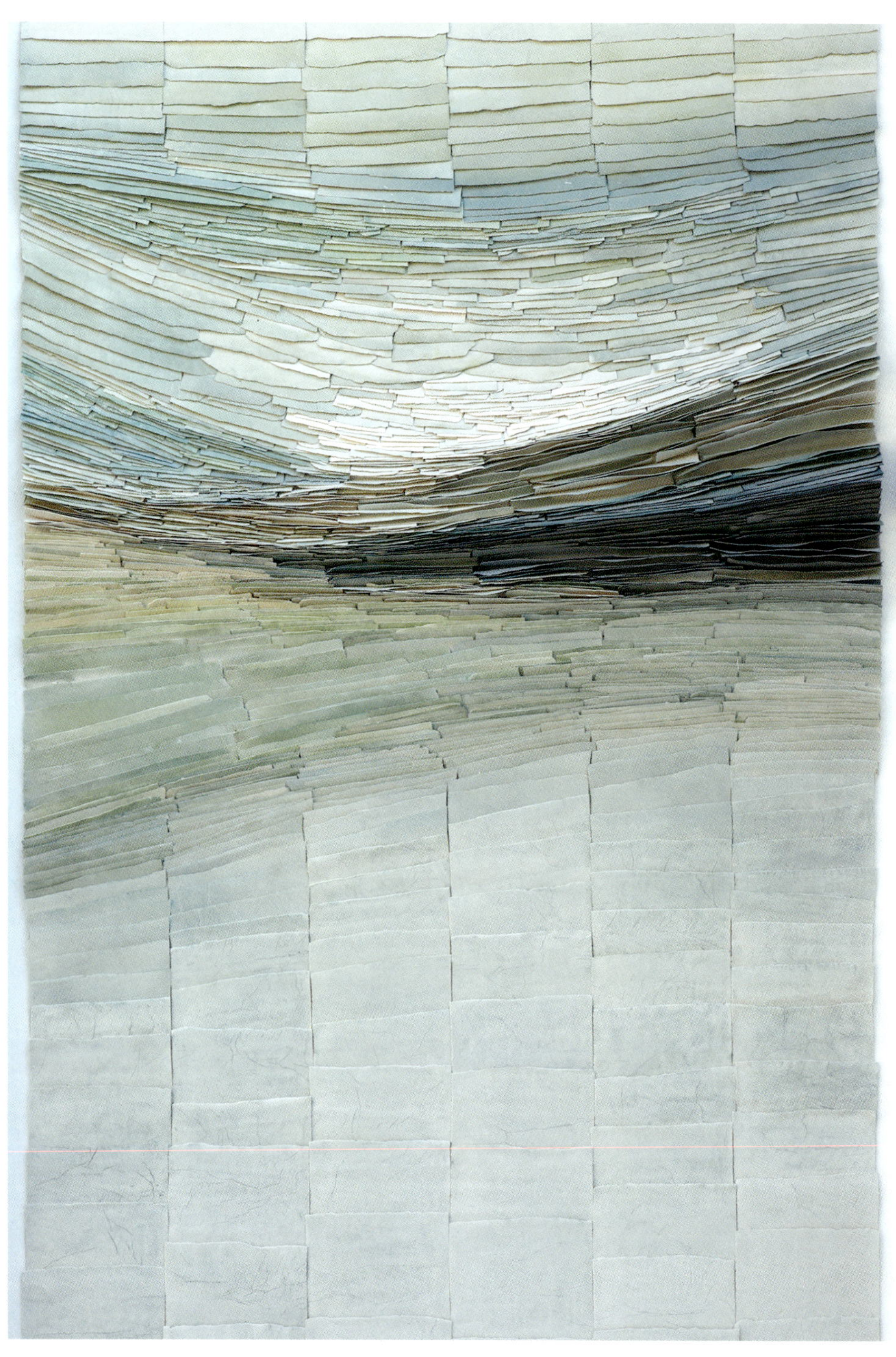

Green by Jeanne Opgenhaffen, 2007. 1.2 m x 2 m (3 ft 9 in. x 6 ft 6 in.). Coloured porcelain, fired in an electric kiln at 1260°C (2300°F). *Photo by S. Van Hul.*

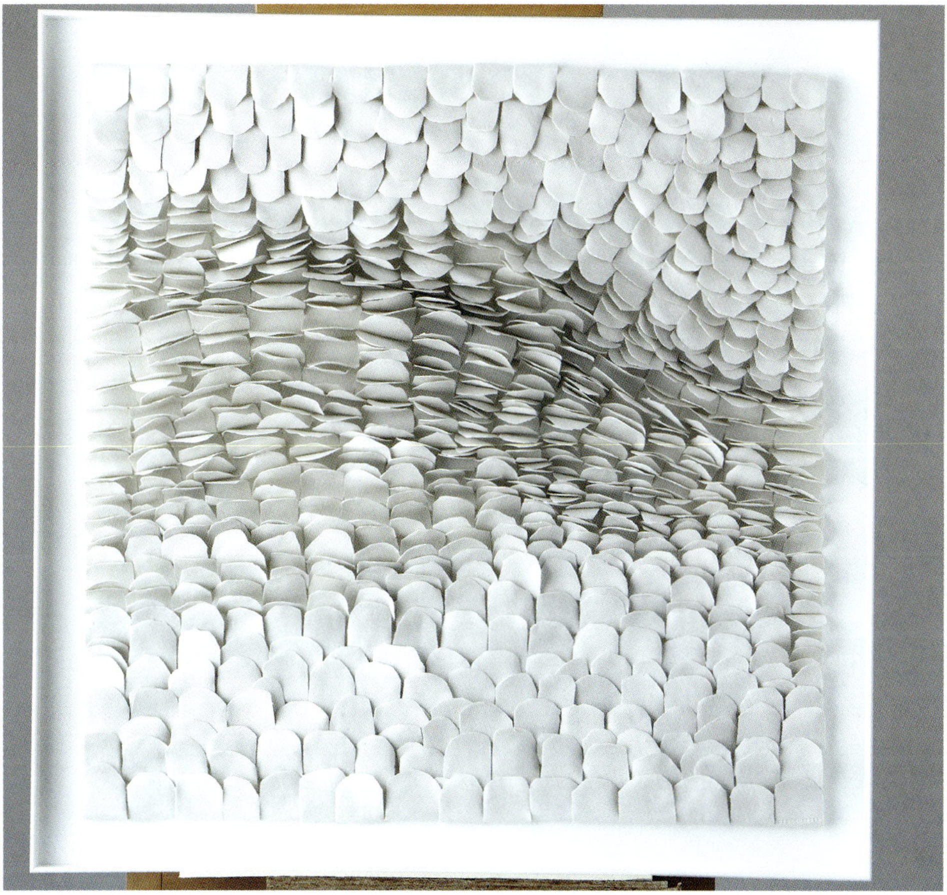

How the Wind Blows by Jeanne Opgenhaffen, 2008. Size: 85 cm x 85 cm (33½ x 33½ in.). White Limoges porcelain. Fired in an electric kiln to 1260°C (2300°F). Mounted on white Perspex. *Photo by S. Van Hul.*

RIGHT *How the Wind Blows* by Jeanne Opgenhaffen, 2008. The fixing and hanging system. *Photo by S. Van Hul.*

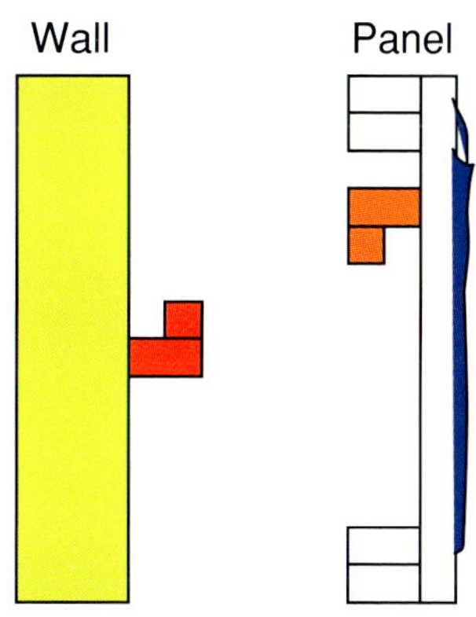

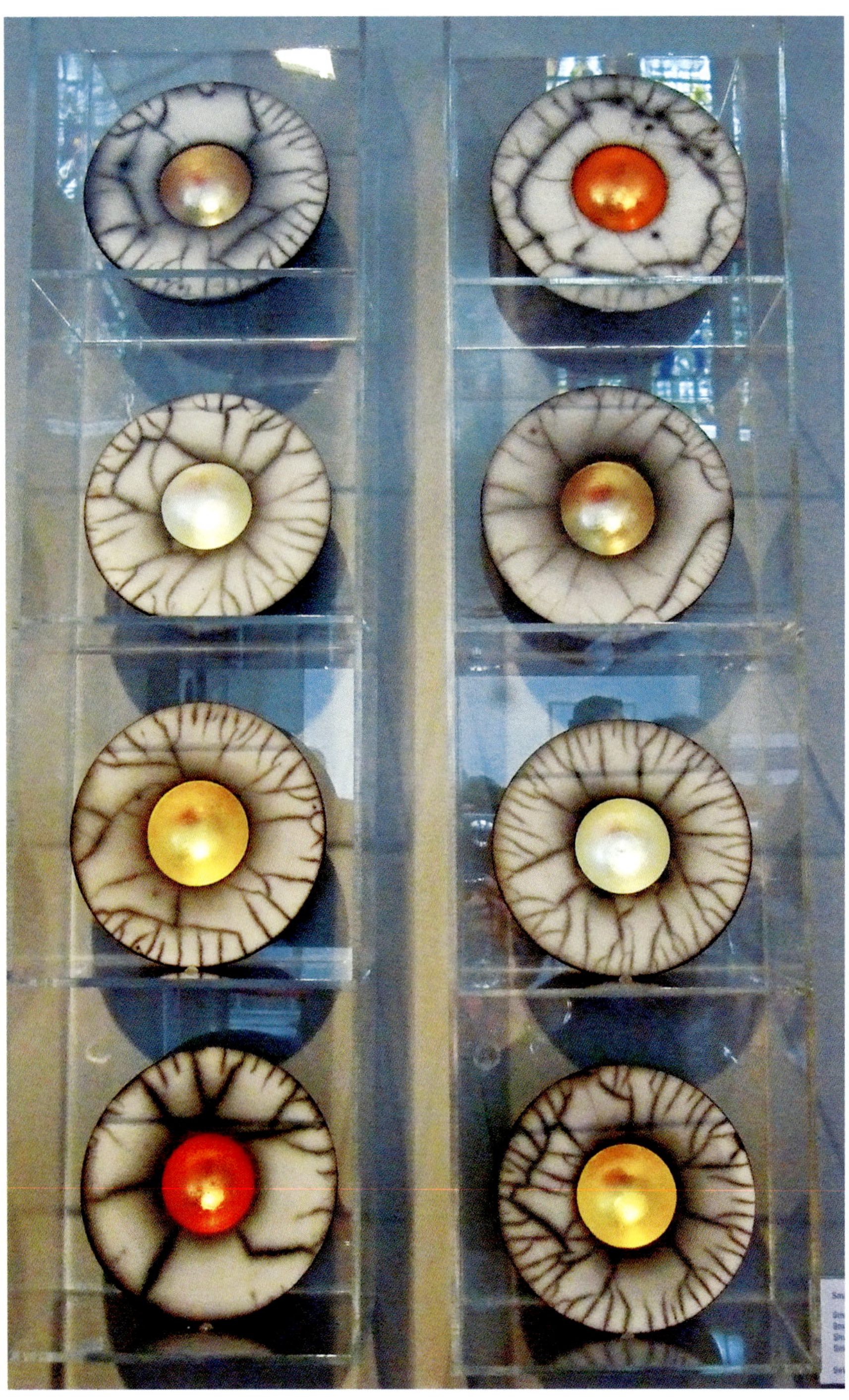

Small bowls in Perspex case by Emma Johnstone, 2008. Bowls 20 × 80 cm (8 × 31½ in.), Dia: approx 15 cm (6 in.). Scarva's Ashraf Hanna clay, raku-fired. *Photo by E. Johnstone.*

to ensure the piece was safety installed. The installation of the sections was carried out on location, the scaffolding providing a safe platform to join, position, thread and secure each of the sections to the long steel cable with the metal clamps. The process began at the highest point and gradually worked its way down. The weight of the piece does ensure lack of movement, though a small weight was secured to the base to limit any movement, since it was in a public exhibition.

Perspex can also be used as a frame or box to support and display ceramics successfully, and it can provide a clean and also coloured backing if required.

The Belgian artist Jeanne Opgenhaffen, who works with coloured and printed porcelain, conveys elements of rock strata and the natural landscape through her ceramics. In *Green* (*see* p.72) she has captured the element of movement throughout with the subtle use of porcelain. Worked in small, thin sections and tiles, the pieces give a sense of life to the visual experience. Perspex makes an ideal clear white lightweight backing to support her pieces in *How the Wind Blows*, where each individual piece is positioned on the surface (*see* p.73). The Perspex is then attached to the wall by a wall bracket fixing. It could be described as a ledge with a lip (on the wall) and then the Perspex slots on to this ledge.

Emma Johnstone, as mentioned earlier, has also used Perspex cases to display her work (*see* opposite). The Perspex means the viewer can see all aspects of the form. At the back of the case on the two middle levels there are two counter sunk holes so the case can be placed on the wall using screws and rawlplugs. These are then hidden by the bowls in their display positions.

Metal

Metal is a material that can add an interesting surface and backing for ceramics. It is able to support weight and comes in many forms, thicknesses and colours. It can be drilled, welded, bent, painted and corroded. There are 86 different varieties of metal, though some may not be suitable for decorative and functional use. However, metals in an accessible format such as sheet metal, which can be bought in a flat length or coiled strip, are widely available. Aluminium, brass, copper, steel, tin, nickel and titanium can all be bought as sheets, and all vary in pricing. The more expensive precious metals such as gold, silver and platinum will most likely not be suitable for backing purposes due to the expense (although they might be used in smaller quantities for decoration).

The thickness of a metal sheet is called a gauge; the lower the gauge the thicker the sheet. If the metal sheet is to be cut, bent and given an individual approach it might be wise to visit a specialist metalwork company (*see* suppliers list, p.125) who can help and advise you. Metalworks may also be able to drill specific holes for you if needed. Although this may well cost extra, it will save a great deal of hard work and cost in obtaining drills and bits.

Steel

Steel is a strong, durable metal that can be welded, shaped, formed and drilled (if the thickness is not too great). It is also relatively affordable and widely available. It comes in a range of thicknesses and there are a number of surface treatments that can prolong its life. A thickness of 3mm (1/8in.) would provide strength and limited weight, but with anything thinner there would be movement, which would possibly not make for a successful backing material.

Bare steel without any coating is not suitable as it will rust. The steel needs to be cleaned and painted, and the best paints to use are normally epoxy paint or polythene paint, which tend to be used as industrial paints. These paints can come in a wide variety of colours and tones.

Before the steel is painted it is essential to 'blast' the metal to ensure it is clean, and free of oxides and dirt, or it will continue to rust. This process can normally be carried out by an industrial specialist, or the local metalworks. Alternatively, if the metal is on a smaller scale, you can clean and paint it yourself. First clean the surface with wire wool; you can buy a special attachment for a drill to ensure a thorough job. When spraying a colour it is recommend to use an airless spray as this will provide an even coating. A car paint could be used successfully, or a paint such as Hammerite, which protects metal. It is possible to use a paintbrush, but only if the metal surface is not to be seen, as the brush marks will be visible.

Galvanized steel

Galvanising is a process that thinly coats the steel with zinc. This ensures the metal does not rust, as long as the galvanized surface is not scratched. Galvanized metal has a life of about 20 years in a non-industrial environment, but if the surface is in contact with sea spray the life span is reduced dramatically.

It is highly recommended to galvanize all pieces of steel that are intended for outdoor use. For this you need a specialist company. Most metalwork companies can offer this service (but they may even outsource to a large-scale galvanising company). You can approach them directly but you will need to be prepared to deliver or collect the item. Galvanized steel has a matt, industrial-looking surface which might not be suitable for the wall piece, but this can be painted with hammerite or by an industrial specialist. Before you galvanize steel it is essential all cutting, welding, drilling and joining is done first, as any of these processes can remove the surface and once again expose the steel to rust.

Stainless steel

Stainless steel comes in a selection of types and grades: the recommended ones are 304 and 316. You can weld stainless steel and as a metal it is durable, flexible and will not rust, even at the coast. It is not very expensive, although it can be a little difficult to buy in small quantities (contact a local metal supplier to enquire). Once again, if the metal needs to be cut, drilled, welded or bent, and you don't want to do it yourself, you can source and use a local supplier.

Aluminium

Aluminium is a relatively lightweight metal, suitable for outdoors, that can be bent, drilled or welded. However, it does have a few limitations: welding aluminium requires specialist equipment; and although the surface is shiny, as soon as it is exposed to the air it forms an oxidized surface which becomes dull, and can detract from the quality of the piece.

Copper

Copper does not rust, but outdoors it will turn green over a period of time. The green surface could be described as a mould or oxidized layer. Indoors it will tarnish, and might need polishing with a specialist cleaner, but should keep its original colour. It is not particularly strong and therefore would only support a light weight if used as a backing

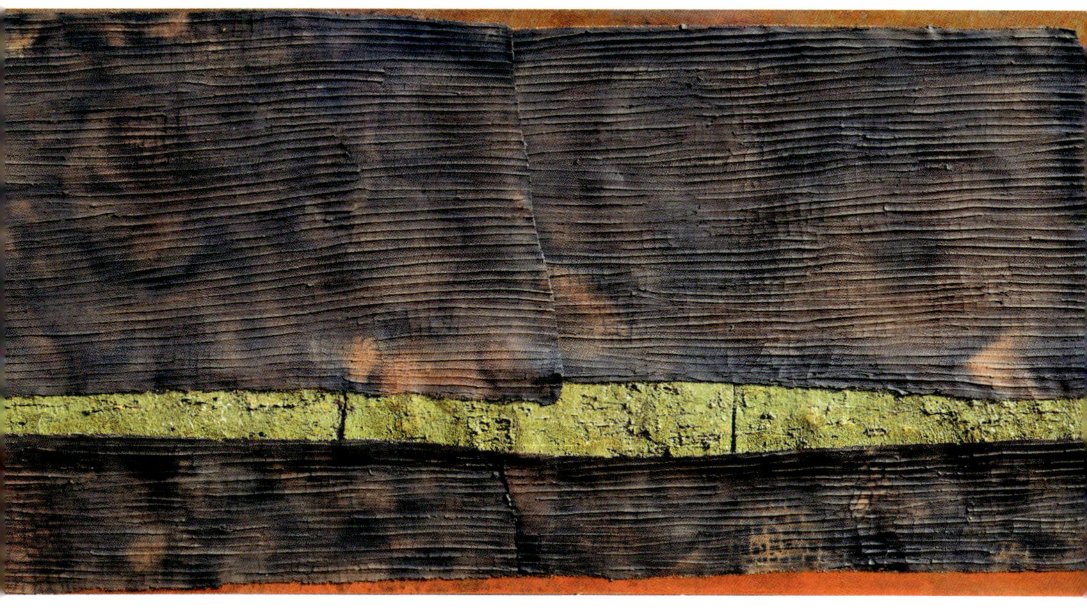

Toile d'argile by Olivia Chagué, 2008. 2 m x 97 cm (6 ft 6 in. x 38½ in.). Earthenware fired onto mesh between 600–700°C ((1112–1292°F), with a raku-fired mixture of refractory clay, faience and green ground bottle glass, which is glued on afterwards. *Photo by Francis Bourgueur.*

(i.e. maximum of 1 kg /2.2 lb). It can be easily bent and manipulated into shape.

Olivia Chagué (France) works with steel metal sheeting as a backing for her pit-fired ceramics, which can reach temperatures of 700°C (1292°F) or higher. Her work shows a fascinating, unique approach to the use of the metal as a material in combination with clay. Chagué is inspired by the colours and textured surfaces created by the pit firing. If the surface does not have the desired result she will re-fire the work, even when it has successfully reached its correct temperature. It is the memory of the process left on the ceramic that captivates her, and an interest in the colours generated: the rich yellow ochres, the reds and the blackened surface. She works with a steel mesh encased in the clay, which can vary from terracotta and stoneware to local clays, the metal mesh creating the cracked surface texture which the pit-firing highlights. The metal mesh also gives a certain flexibility to the ceramics.

The combination of ceramics and metal mesh gives Chagué the chance to cut selected parts from the fired work and rejoin them to other pieces, to create compositions. The ceramic mesh forms are glued with an epoxy resin glue to the coated, rusted steel metal backing. Normally the backing is cut by a company and then the metal fixing on the back of the piece is added, which allows it to be hung easily on the wall. Chagué will then leave the metal outside for several months to advance the ageing process which can increase a rusted surface. It is then coated and preserved with epoxy paint to ensure the rust is fixed.

It is important for Chagué to consider the weight of the ceramics and the metal together: usually between 3 kg (6½ lb) for the small work and up to 6 kg (13 lb) for the larger pieces. Each piece is relatively

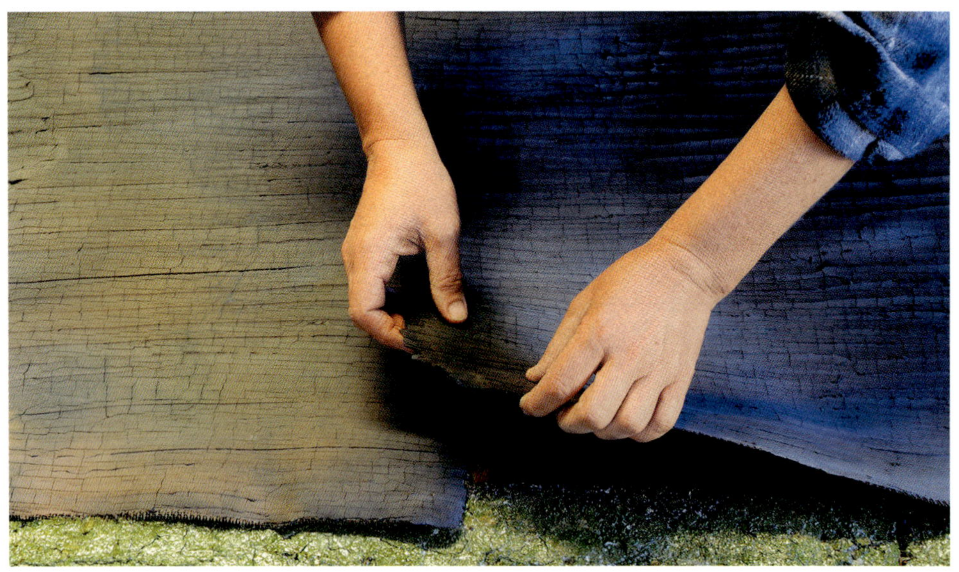

Toile d'argile by Olivia Chagué, 2008. 2 m x 97 cm (6 ft 6 in. x 38½ in.). Construction, laying and fixing the brown earthenware fired between 600–700°C (1112–1292°F), mix refractory ground and sandstone 1080°C (1976°F) on to the metal backing. *Photo by Francis Bourgueur.*

light to place on a wall: the use of the ceramic with the mesh enables Chagué to create a piece with a light, flexible quality. They are hung on the wall with a simple hook on the back of the metal sheeting, similar to a painting.

Considering the colour and quality of the metal surface is also essential for Jeanne Opgenhaffen, who has successfully worked with metal to complement the porcelain in her piece, *Power of Running Water*. The dark grey zinc-coated steel backing heightens the contrast with the light porcelain.

Glass

Glass is a contemporary, clean material, currently used very successfully in new buildings, wall pieces and as a feature in bars and contemporary spaces. Glass comes in a variety of thicknesses, colours and surfaces, and has the advantage that it can offer a transparent backing for the work. Unlike many other materials it cannot be drilled easily (only by specialists) or take a large amount of uneven weight or pressure due to the fact that it might crack. Glass has many seductive and attractive qualities, but it carries more complications and risk than many other materials, as it is both breakable and heavy. When choosing glass as a backing material it is recommended to use toughened glass, which breaks into small square pieces that are not sharp, unlike normal glass which will shatter and can be dangerous to handle.

The correct thickness of glass to support the ceramics is also an important factor; if the glass is too thin it might bend and break, if too thick it might be too heavy for the wall. This will vary with each maker and the size of the ceramics. Chris Wight (*see* pp.110–12) works with layers of toughened glass to sandwich his ceramic disks in place. The top and bottom of the sandwich are each composed of over three

Ceramic Fragments by Dominique Bivar Segurado.

FROM TOP Grinding a ceramic shard on a spare sheet of toughened glass using coarse silicon carbide, in preparation for mounting on to the glass backing.

Fitting used for glass wall pieces. Note the black rubber washers which the glass sheet sits between to ensure the metal and glass have limited contact.

Detail of glass fitting supporting toughened glass wall piece on the wall.

Photos by Mark Harvey.

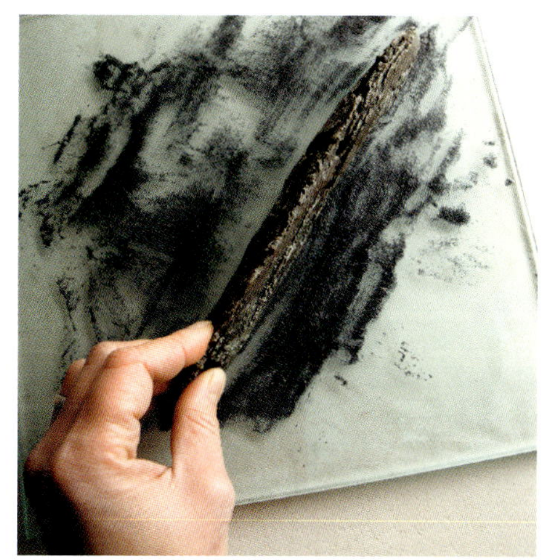

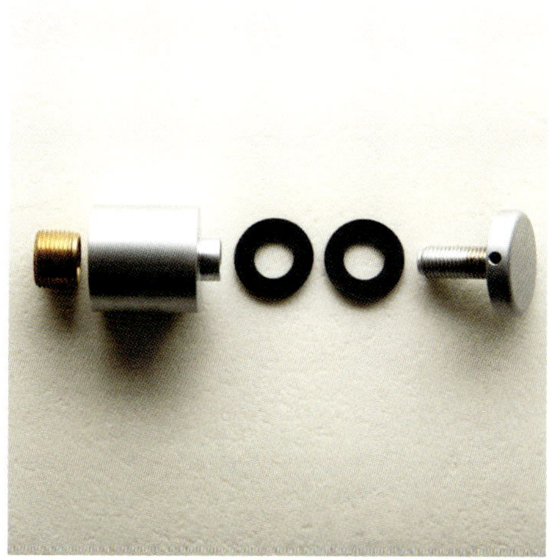

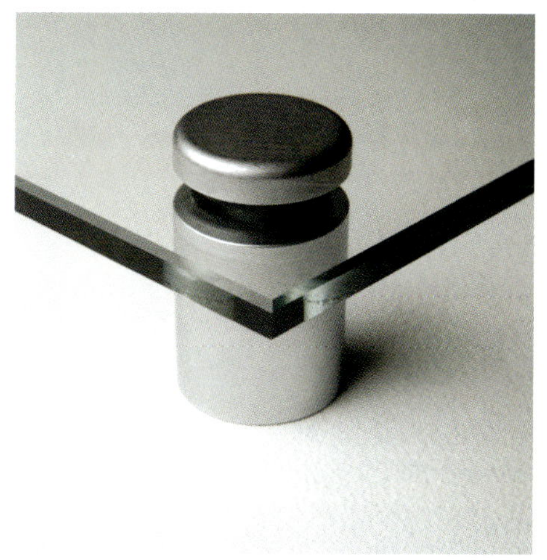

layers of glass; the work is positioned and stuck between these two layers.

Currently, in my own work, I use a toughened glass with a thickness of 6–8 mm (1/4–3/8 in.), depending on the scale and weight of the ceramics. On some occasions the glass backing has been sandblasted, so that the texture of the wall is not a distraction.

It is important to remember that ceramics has a tendency to scratch when placed on a glass surface. For my wall pieces it is essential that the ceramic fragments sit flush with the glass so that the silicon adhesive will not be seen. I have developed two methods for this.

First, the ceramics is prepared with a groove in the centre to ensure the adhesive can be applied successfully (*see* p.97). The fragments have a tendency to warp, i.e. the base might not be completely flat, and so they are ground down on a sheet of glass using silicon carbide granules with a little water. This helps to flatten and soften the base, and ensures that each shard is flush with the glass.

The design for the piece is placed underneath the glass sheet as this helps

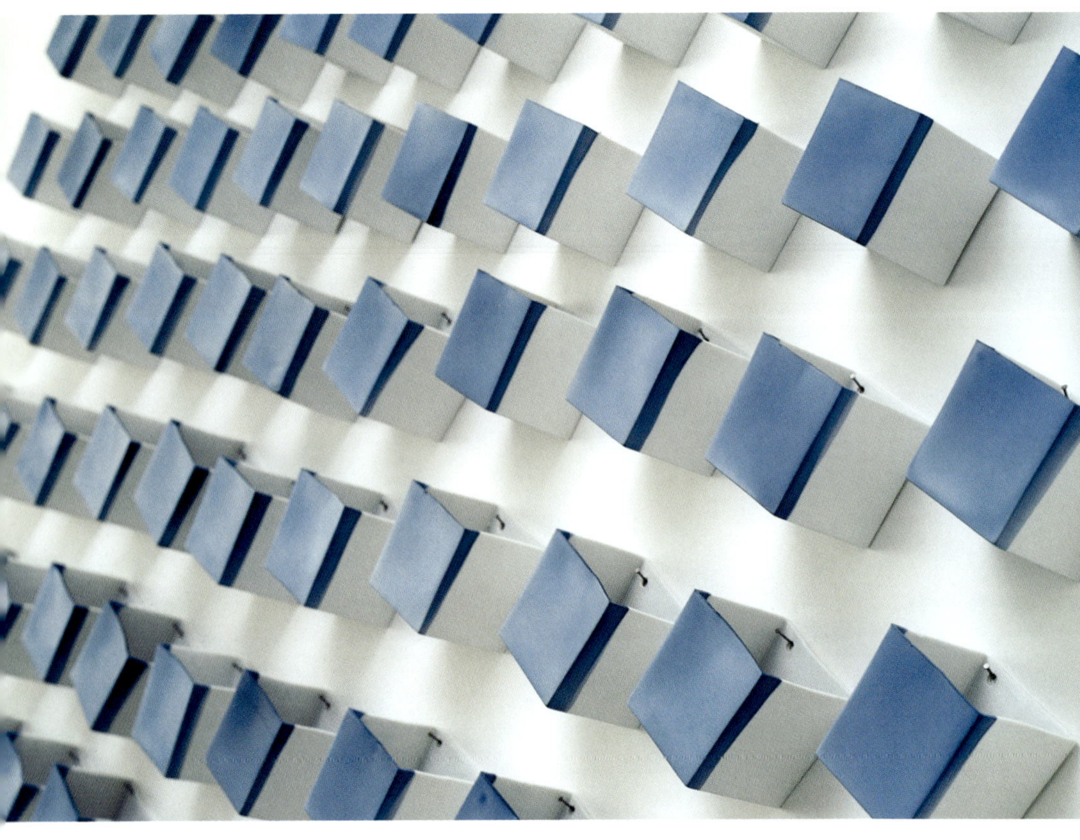

Untitled, by Piet Stockmans, 2001. Slipcast boxes with glaze held up simply by a nail. Installed in the Gardiner Museum, Toronto. *Photo courtesy of Pieter Stockmans Studio.*

to ensure the ceramics is positioned correctly (*see* p.97 for images). Once each shard is in the correct position, the gluing begins, starting with the furthest piece. As the adhesive has a long curing time it is essential to first ensure that the ceramic piece is in the correct place, and second, that it does not get knocked. The glass cannot be moved for about a day. Each shard is checked before the glass is cleaned with specialist glass cleaner, handling it with gloves to limit the finger marks.

The toughened glass backing is supported by fixings supplied by a local company called Fairfield Lighting and Displays. The fixing sizes and colour do vary. However the glass does require a drill hole of 12 mm ($^1/_2$ in.) for the fittings in each of the four corners which the supplier (Unit Glass Art, Norwich) ensures is provided. All toughened glass suppliers should be able to provide this service. It is important to consider if polished edges or rounded corners are required, as the glass will come with sharp edges unless specified. A clear drawing with sizes, or a job list, should be provided to ensure the job is completed successfully.

The drill holes are positioned from the edge of the glass with an equal clearance of 25 mm (1 in.) on both corners. This helps to support the glass, distribute the weight of the ceramics and glass on the wall, and ensure against cracking. The fittings are metal, and it is essential that the glass and metal should not come into contact with each other, so two rubber washers are used on either side, between both the glass and the metal fittings. These washers can be found in trade suppliers or large DIY stores.

Attaching to the wall

Nails, screws, rawlplugs and hooks

If the piece is light, putting a nail in the wall can be quick and efficient as long as the wall is able to support the nails. A hole can be made in the ceramics which the nail will be able to hook through. In Piet Stockmans' piece at the Gardiner Museum (*see* opposite) the simple use of a nail is perfect to display the lightweight slipcast box.

However, when the piece does have some weight, screws and rawlplugs should be used. Depending on the size of the piece it might require more than one point of support. Consider how the weight will be effectively distributed on the wall: the heavier the piece, the more points of weight distribution are needed.

All screws and rawlplugs come in different sizes. The rawlplug in many ways is a vital fixing as it acts as a key support to the wall piece; it is designed to fit the hole and support the screw, which in turn will support the wall piece. They are designed to suit a variety of walls, for example if you are drilling into a plasterboard wall you will need a special rawlplug that will anchor itself effectively into the wall to ensure it can support weight, and the same for a masonry wall. When selecting a rawlplug it is essential to choose a size smaller than the screw. Once the correct size of hole is drilled into the wall for the rawlplug (check the rawlplug size against the drill bit and make sure they are the same) gently tap it into position with a hammer, and then the screw should successfully be screwed into place. When drilling the hole for the rawlplug make sure it is not at an angle; always drill straight!

Rawlplugs are normally made from plastic, and expand once a screw is screwed into them. However, if you need an extra strong fixing, a durable metal plug exists, known as an 'anchor bolt'. This galvanized bolt fitting with a nut and thread top has a metal end section

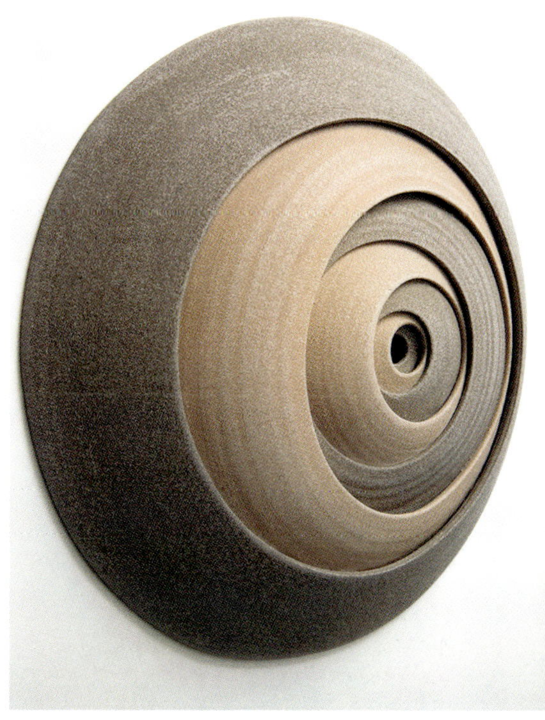

Crescent by Matthew Chambers. Ht: 30 cm (12 in.); W: 30 cm (12 in.); Dia: 8 cm (3¼ in.). Thrown sections joined together. Stoneware clay with coloured oxides and stains fired between 1160°C–1170°C (2120–2138°F). *Photo by Steve Thearle.*

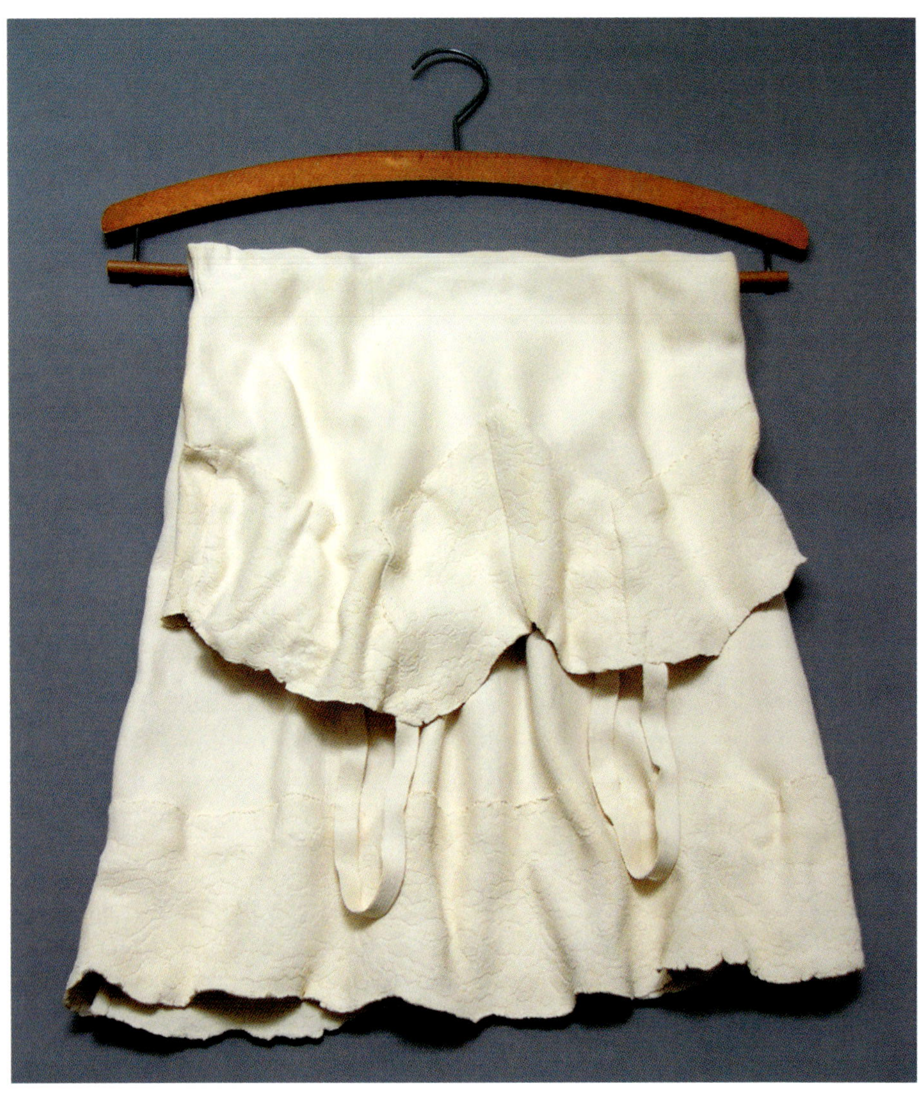

Camisole Dress by Kaori Tatebayashi. 42 x 46 x 3 cm (16½ x 18 x 1¼ in.). Hand-built Scarva's Earthstone Handbuilding Material (clay) fired between 1240–1250°C (2264–2282°F) and mounted on a wooden hanger. *Photo by K. Tatebayashi.*

which acts as an anchor into the wall, enabling the fitting and bolt to be tightened accordingly. This type of fitting is suitable for heavy or more permanent pieces of work and is mainly used by the building industry.

Matthew Chambers (UK) creates a lip in his work to sit on the screw head. The wall pieces then hang on the wall by this simple lip created during the making process on the back of the ceramics. Chambers is inspired to create forms that explore and push the boundaries of abstract form by working with the traditional process of throwing, and is fascinated by geometric art forms. Each piece is made with thrown sections, using stoneware clay which has coloured oxides added. The wall pieces can consist of up to eight sections which have been sanded and polished.

Kaori Tatebayashi (UK & Japan) works with handbuilding techniques to create pieces that remind us of the presence of the everyday and are also a reminder of our own past. Her work captures the soft qualities of the fabrics the person might have worn: shirt, blouse or vest. She captures in the stoneware clay a sense of absence (*see* opposite).

She uses metal picture hooks attached to the back of the ceramic forms with glue. This method simply requires a screw or nail to be placed in the wall to support the piece. Some of her pieces involve wooden hangers, but these do not act as a support for hanging the piece on the wall.

Fixings and fittings

Hanging wall pieces with a supportive fixing or fitting on the wall can give an opportunity to ensure the piece is flexible for easily installation, with the possibility of moving positions and locations. We have discussed the possibility of hooks, screws and nails, but the backing material used might also require a special fitting, particularly when the weight of the piece starts to increase. A very useful guide to this subject is *Installing Exhibitions* by Pete Smithson (*see* bibliography).

A fitting that can be hung quickly and works effectively is an important consideration if you are short of time. There are several fixings and fittings that can be used for glass and Perspex. Some that can be used are wall and signage fixings, and come in several finishes from chrome, black, polished brass to warm chrome, (if in doubt check with the supplier).

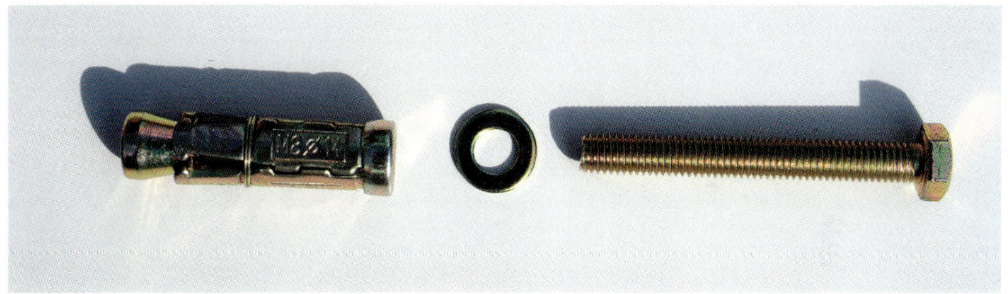

Anchor bolt fixing, size: M8, 6.5 cm (2½ in.) long. Used for solid walls such as solid brickwork, masonry or concrete. Please follow manufacturers guidelines for installation.

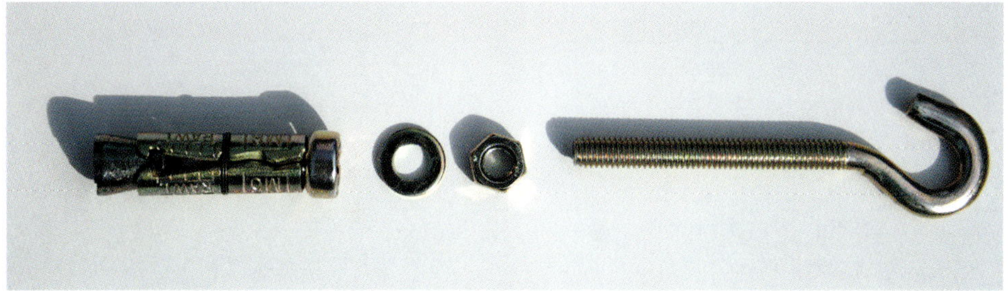

Hookbolt brickwork fixing, size: M6, 8 cm (3 in.) long. Used for fixing into masonry, solid brickwork and concrete. Please follow manufacturers guidelines for installation.

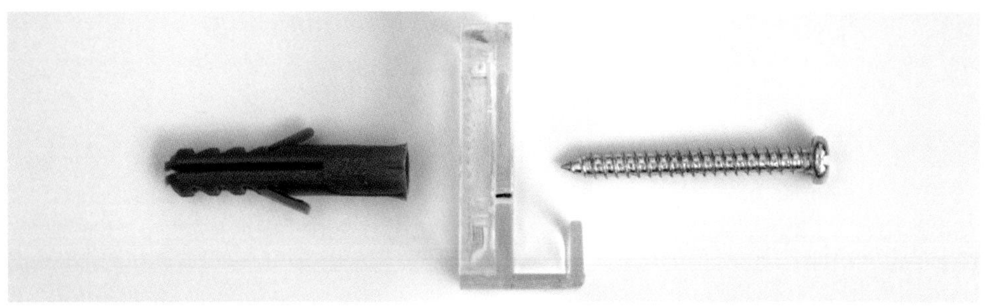

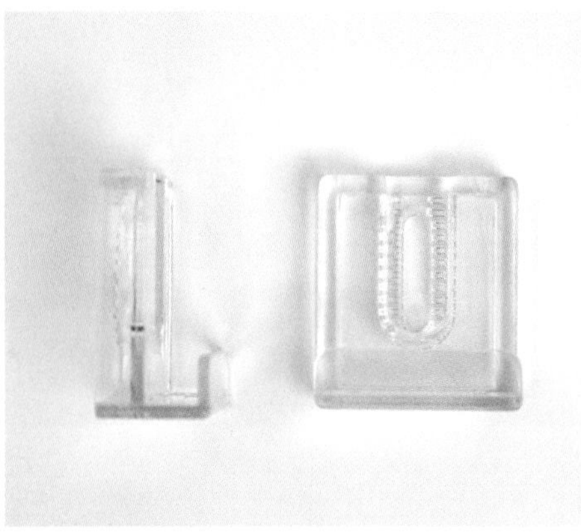

ABOVE Rawl plug and screw with plastic mirror fitting. 1. Measure the location for the screw and ensure the wall is suitable for drilling. 2. The screw is screwed into the rawlplug through the plastic fitting, keeping it in place to support the work. (Please consult the manufacturers guidelines for further details.)

LEFT The two parts of the plastic mirror fitting, 2.5 x 2.5 x 0.7 cm (1 x 1 x 1/4 in.). Four fittings are used to support a lightweight piece with these, two at the bottom and two at the top.

A company that I have used for this are Fairfield Lighting and Displays. These fittings can sometimes require more that one person to install, particularly when the piece is heavy. They are designed for a more permanent location, so consider this and ask for advice.

If you need a fitting to be made to support your piece on the wall, a specialist engineering company or foundry could be helpful. Write down the weight and scale of the piece, as this will give a clear idea of the number of fittings and the design that is required. If you show the original design when discussing fixings with a supplier it will ensure they are clear about the needs of the project. If you know the weight the supplier should be able to advise you.

There is the option of creating the fitting yourself. Stine Jespersen uses a bent metal strip stuck with glue to support her work on the wall (*see* opposite). Each piece is given two metal strips (the metal strip is placed with a small gap between itself and the ceramics to ensure the piece can be attached to the wall). On the wall three screws with reasonable screw heads are drilled into place: two on the same line to support under the metal strips and one near the bottom of the piece to ensure the piece has an equal gap from the wall to create shadows between the wall and the piece. However on the small pieces Stine Jespersen threads picture string through the metal strips and they hang on one nail.

Adhesives and glue

It is not generally advised to try and stick your work directly to the wall. However, a range of adhesives and glue have been mentioned throughout this chapter and it is clear that many makers do use glues within their pieces, or to attach the work

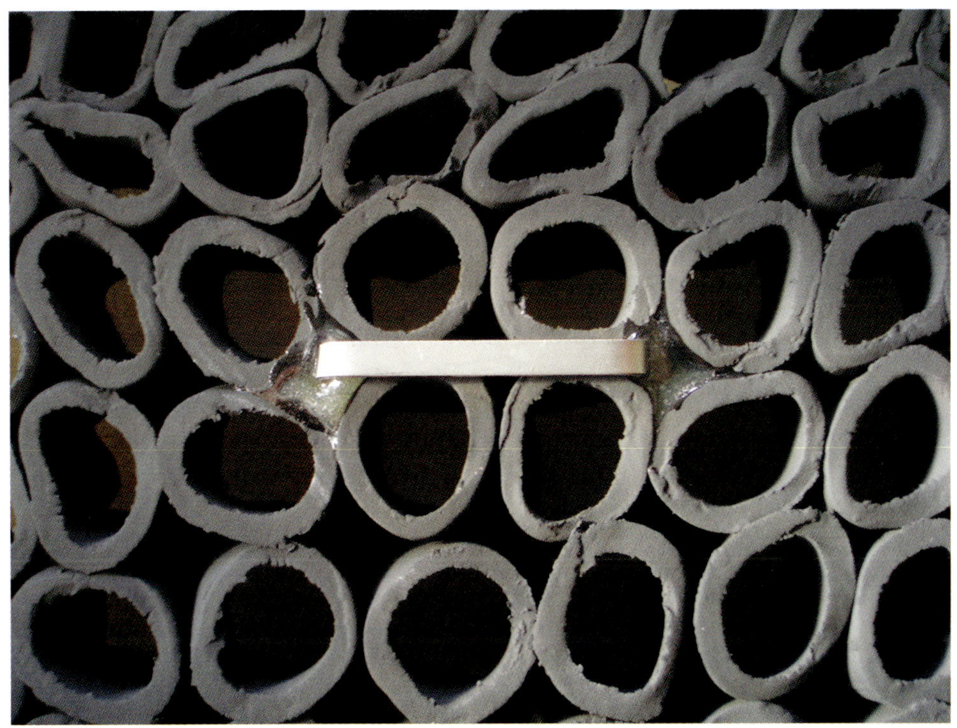

Wall piece by Stine Jespersen. Earthenware fired to 1080°C (1976°F). Detail of back of wall piece with metal fitting glued into position. *Photo by S. Jespersen.*

to a backing and even the wall. Finding the right adhesive is essential as many are not suitable to hold, stick and work with ceramics. It might not be just the ceramics you want to stick: bear in mind the other materials you are fixing too.

Some of the common glues used by makers are: araldite (a glue with two parts, which sets when mixed); chemical metal (an industrial glue with two parts which also acts as a filler); silicon adhesive (normally used with glass, also gives a flexibility to ceramics for transport and comes in different colours); high impact glue (a quick-setting glue that can withstand shock); grab adhesive (fast-acting glue, suitable for ceramics); a glue gun (it heats up and has glue sticks which melt). Adhesive pads can also be a useful tool to ensure the ceramics remain in position, such as the previously mentioned 'bump ons' – these are clear rubber adhesive pads.

It is also possible to use a clear gel to keep objects in place. Known as 'museum gel' this can be purchased from specialist suppliers (*see* p.125). The gel is used to support pieces, and does not damage the surface of ceramics. It is used by exhibitors, galleries and many museums, especially when pieces are on display in a public space or liable to be knocked, or even in areas prone to earthquakes.

If the location is outdoors and requires drilling into a brick wall and the use of metal fixings, the fixing can be secured with an adhesive/mortar for extra support called injection mortar. Again, this can be purchased from specialist suppliers, but you may want to hire a contractor.

Special constructions

For very large work or special commissions it is possible to create purpose-built forms. For example, if working with builders you can ask them to build the wall with a ledge at the required height which panels of work can then sit on (see Walter Richie's panels being installed on p.51). Then, while also attached to the wall, their weight is at least supported in position. It is obviously a very unusual advantage to be able to do this. Alternatively, you could construct your work so that it actually stands on the floor, while being attached to the wall further up to prevent it falling forwards. Designing a structural armature that might require attaching to or cementing into the floor space, and then also being fixed into position on the wall can be a consideration for larger-scale work, but will obviously involve careful planning, research and permission.

If the location has exposed metal steel joists in the ceiling, near where the wall piece is to be hung, it may be possible to hang structures from the joist as long as they are load-bearing and the weight is not too great. The wall piece could then also be fixed at various points on the wall to secure it further. As each location will vary, it is important to conduct a site visit and consider the options carefully.

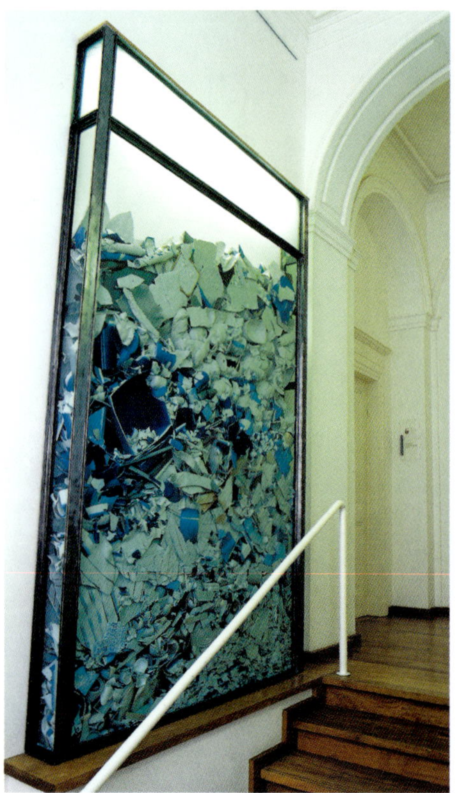

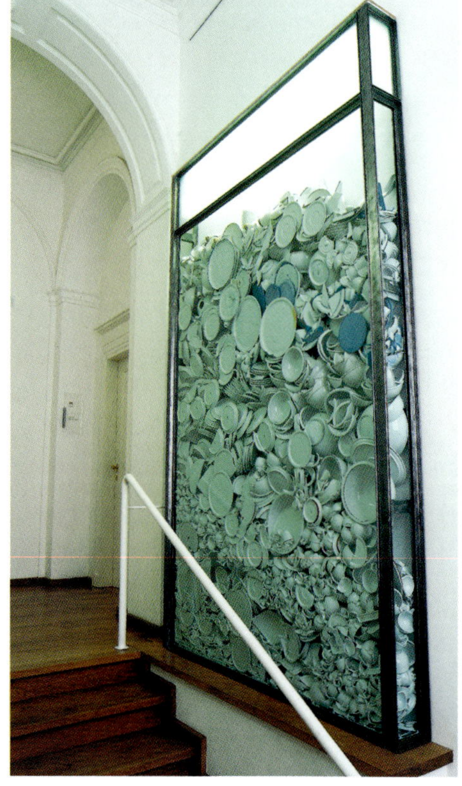

Everyone its History by Pieter Stockmans, 1995, at The Stadsmus museum, Hasselt, Belgium. These broken shards and pieces chronicles the artists work over time, showing the layers of development.

Chapter 4

Projects in action

These projects offer a valuable insight into the individual approach to space and process by several ceramicists. Understanding how other makers approach spaces can expand and develop our own practice, perhaps opening up new and exciting opportunities for us to communicate our creative ideas. The makers featured in this chapter offer a stimulating peek into some of their projects: a brief but broad overview of the project, including wherever possible, the beginning of the design process, the making and installation, up to the final outcome on the wall.

All the makers featured have designed and made innovative wall pieces that respond directly to a space and their personal vision to transform it. The projects discussed vary in their approach: some are temporary, some are permanent, and the locations vary from public space to private homes. However, all reflect a personal passion to demonstrate ideas on a wall and the use of clay in a contemporary manner. All the wall pieces were designed and made for specific locations. Some locations were selected by the makers, while some pieces are in response to a given location. Designing and making work for a specific location often pushes artists' boundaries to explore and develop new ideas.

One thing all these makers have in common is that their pieces are designed and made in sections. This has given them the chance to work with a variety of scales, and in some cases other materials. Working in sections can technically be a great help, from the start of a creation through to the final hanging. First, if there is limited studio space for drying and storage, lots of small pieces can be placed on shelves (as opposed to one enormous work). Secondly, firing in sections can reduce cracking, and of course there is the size of the kiln to consider too. Thirdly, transporting and storage of the work can be made easier if the work can be placed in boxes and assembled on site, and might reduce the cost of hiring a vehicle too. Boxes can also be stacked and carried relatively easily by one or two people. In chapter 2 the question of weight was discussed; creating pieces in sections can help in distributing the weight on the wall's surface. It can also simplify installation, as hanging individual pieces can often be easier than one large-scale work. Lastly, if installing the work high up, it might be wise to consider working in small sections as carrying work up and down a ladder can be difficult if supporting a heavy weight or a complicated form. (When installing, remember to arrange for assistance if the ceramics are a heavy weight, and also to consider if scaffolding is needed.)

In most cases the makers have had some form of help to install the pieces in location. Some of the makers have assistants, and others might hire a specialist company to assist with installation or ask a friend or colleague.

In most cases, when the date for installation is confirmed there is normally only one opportunity to install the final piece. This can mean all tests might have only taken place in the studio or at other locations. The final installation of the work could take anything from one day to one week (or longer). This of course depends on the scale and construction of the piece. Nevertheless, the forward planning each maker has applied, including the design and test runs, are all important for the final installation. Their preparation reflects a strong sense of professionalism and gives the opportunity for errors and mistakes to be corrected before the whole piece is made and before the final on-site installation.

Jim Robison (UK)

Jim Robison's ceramic work involves a personal curiosity with narrative and an engaging communication with the viewer. As a successful international ceramicist he has worked on a number of large-scale projects over the years. His ceramics take an individual approach to space, and in many pieces the organic colours and detailed mark-making depict a connection to or story of the location. Robison finds it essential to understand and be informed about the history or story of the project he is working on, in order for him to experience a true sense of personal connection while developing and creating a project.

Originally from the USA, Robison has been based in Holmfirth, West Yorkshire for the last 30 years. He is well known for his unique and bold use of slab building. In many respects, the larger the scale of the project, the more he rises to the challenge by pushing the clay and design. *My Liverpool Home* is an eye-catching piece which fills the space.

Throughout the process of designing and making, he remains focused on developing the work through its artistic story as well as its historical narrative and interaction with the viewer. Robison has always considered and planned within his creative approach; this also applies to considering the weight on the wall and how the clay/ceramics can be made to remain relatively light.

In order to keep his work relatively lightweight, Robison creates backless blocks, to which he then attaches 'T' sections of clay, followed by a clay sheet for the backing. This creates a strong form but means that it is not too heavy to hang. This method also helps with the drying of the clay and firing. The hollow pieces mean that screw shaped holes can be placed in the back of the work, so that they can be hung on the wall easily.

Robison decorates his slabs with coloured slips, then the pieces are raw glazed and fired to stoneware temperatures. During the making process each panel has three (keyhole-shaped) holes cut into the back to ensure that once fired they can successfully hang on the wall on screws. The panels are also given a number, which corresponds with the hardboard design. During the installation the hardboard acts as a template and indicator of the correct positioning of the screws and drill holes in the wall.

Working in sections gives Robison the freedom to expand the desired scale of the piece and to mount each piece on the wall easily. Numbering each piece is also helpful for the people who are installing the work.

Robison uses a ceramics frame around the piece, which acts as a border to the central story. It is

My Liverpool Home by Jim Robison. Size: 2 m^2 (21½ sq. ft).

FROM TOP

Stoneware clay with slips and glaze, fired to cone 8, 1260°C (2300°F). Mural surface under construction.

A pencil or crayon rubbing is taken from the back of each tile when fired, and transferred onto hardboard. This locates the position of support screws and facilitates accurate drilling of the wall. Note the inverted keyhole opening in the tile.

Holes are drilled through the hardboard and into the wall for mounting screws.

Photos by J. Robison.

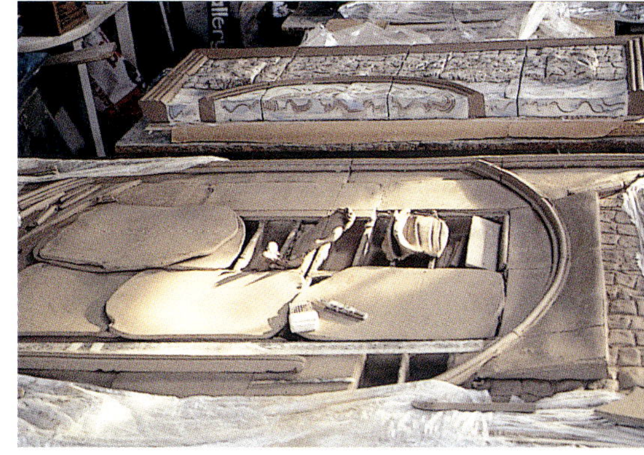

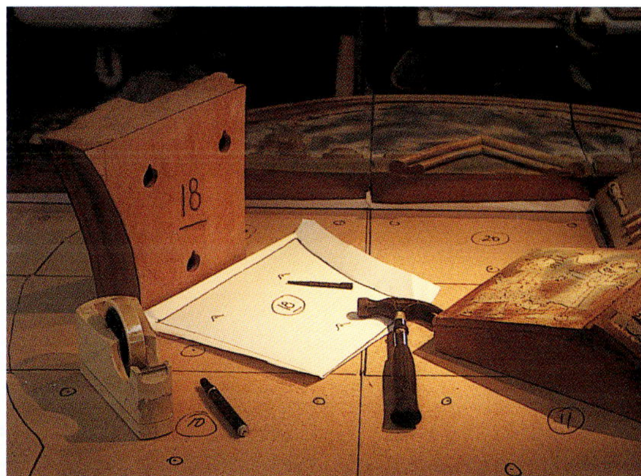

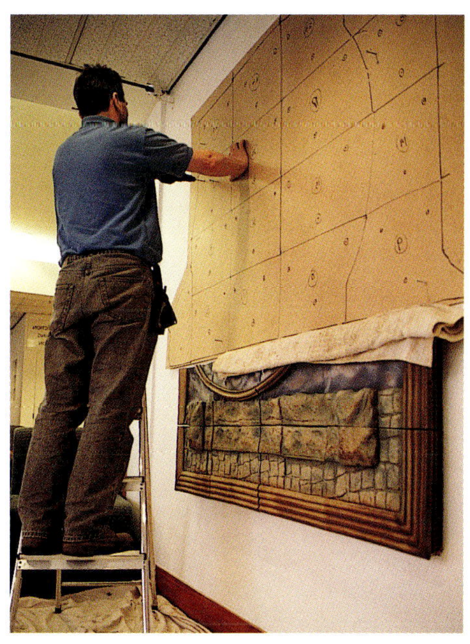

interesting with this piece to see how he has chosen to move the forms out of a standard-shaped square frame; the use of the circle and triangle give an element of shape that the viewer can relate to instantly, and at the same time the gaze is drawn across the form with the position of the shapes, adding an exciting, eye-catching dimension to the piece.

The pure white wall on which the piece is hung gives it a clean, neutral surface. The lighting has also been considered, and the piece is enhanced by the spot lighting positioned to highlight the detailed surface. Lighting can make a real difference to a wall piece. This should be something considered at the design stage, and you should always consult and use a qualified electrician when installing lighting.

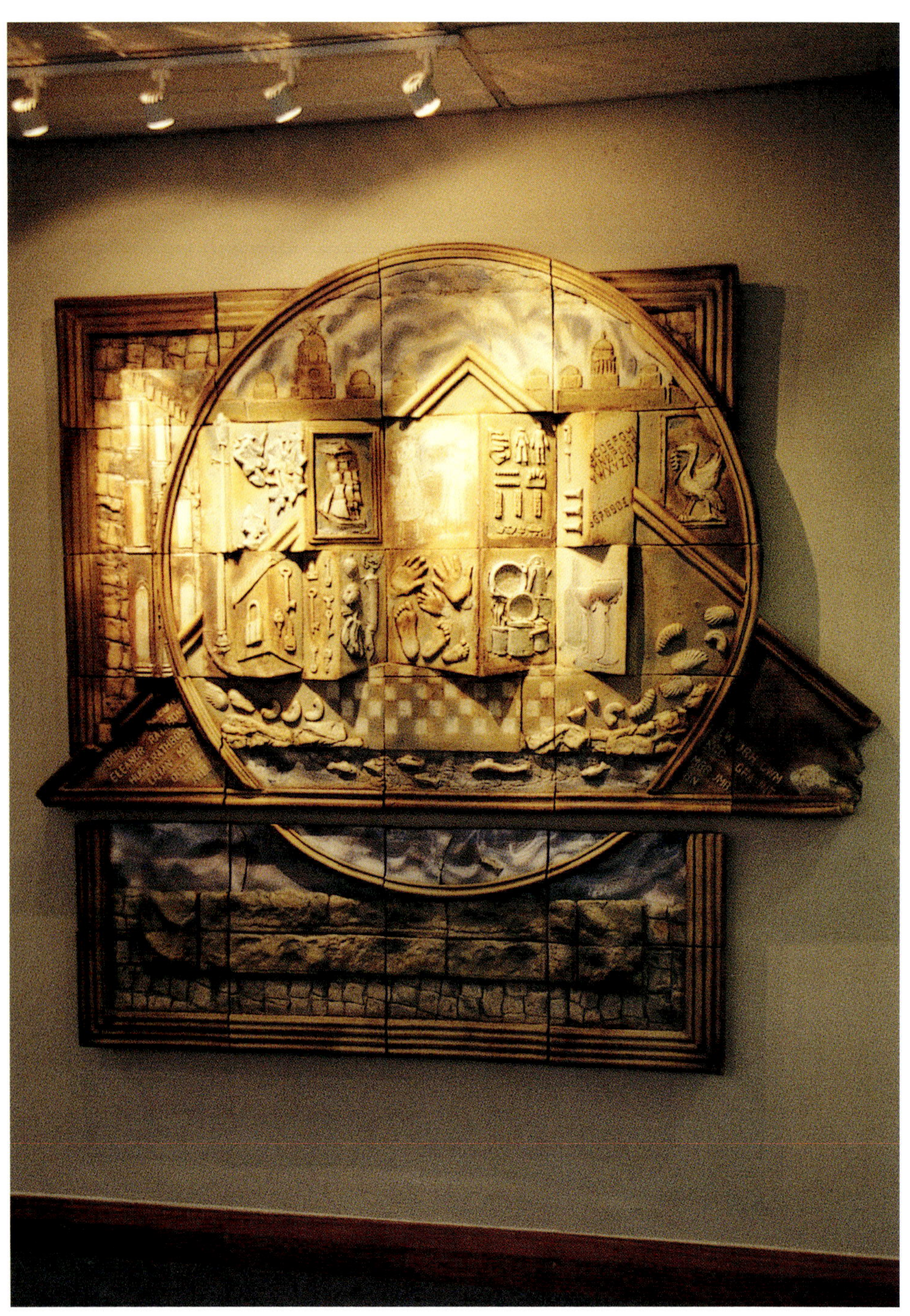

My Liverpool Home by Jim Robison, 2000. Size: 2 m^2 (21½ sq. ft). Material: Stoneware clay with slips and glaze, fired to cone 8, 1260°C (2300°F). Commissioned for the Riverside Housing Association. *Photo by J. Robison.*

Satoru Hoshino (Japan)

Satoru Hoshino's impact on this space is an expression of the tactile qualities he applies to the clay forms. His wall pieces reflect an organic and inviting presence on the space they occupy. His expanded shapes request the viewer to consider the impact the material has on our interior spaces, from the way the forms grow and transform across a surface.

Birth of Bubbles, Ancient Woodland and Peat Deposits is a prime example of how this maker has considered the design and the visual impact required for the location of the Mitsuke Cultural City Hall, Arcadia, Japan. The wall is located in the main auditorium, giving an opportunity for a large number of people to interact with the space.

The blackened clay, originally bisque-fired between 700–900°C (1292–1652°F), is then taken through the process to 'dye' the ceramics, this technique is the same used on the blackened roof tiles in Japan. First, the clay is polished or burnished with a stone or iron spatula to create a glossy surface and then given a layer of terra sigillata slip on the clay surface. The pieces are then smoke-fired with pine needles, sawdust and

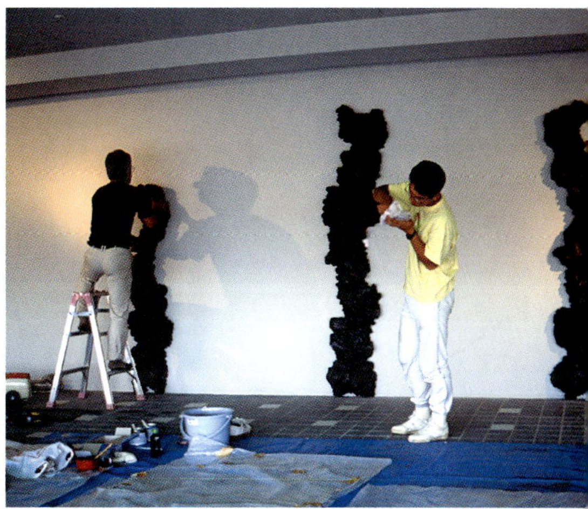

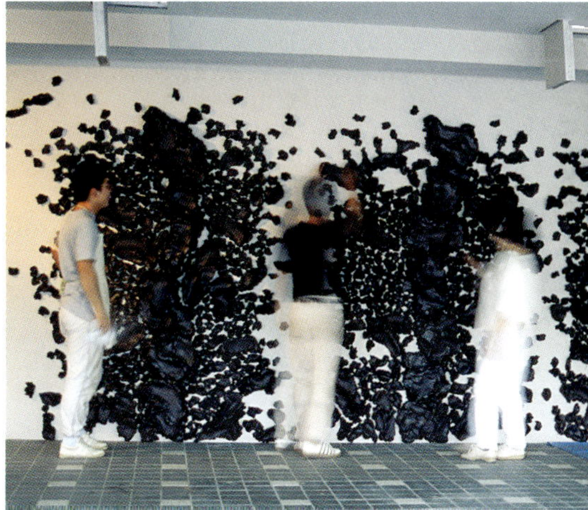

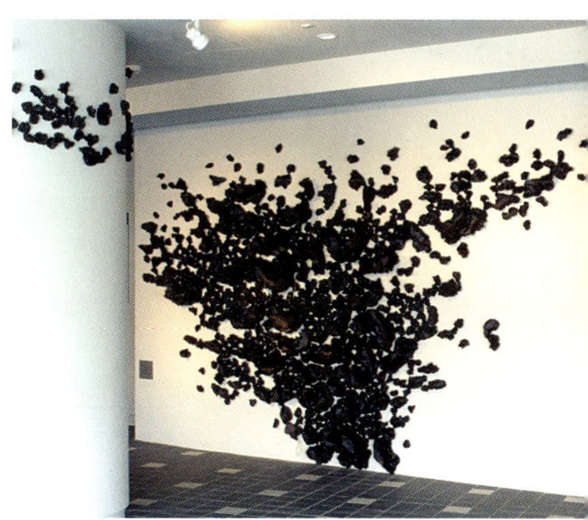

Birth of Bubbles, Ancient Woodland and Peat Deposits, by Satoru Hoshino, 1993. Ht: 2.7 m (8 ft 10 in.), W: 13.7 m (45 ft). Smoke-fired earthenware. Installation of wall piece in Mitsuke Cultural City Hall. Arcadia, Japan.

FROM TOP

The larger core pieces are glued to the wall, working from the base upwards.

Artist Satoru Hoshino oversees the process, checking the final positions of the pieces.

The completed work.
Photos by S. Hoshino.

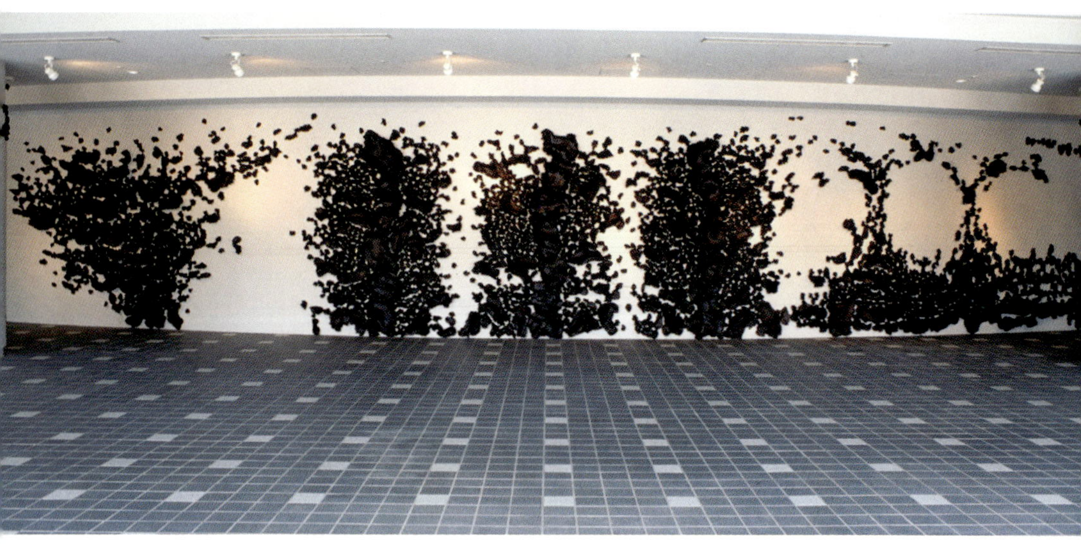

Birth of Bubbles, Ancient Woodland and Peat Deposits, by Satoru Hoshino, 1993. Ht: 2.7 m (8 ft 10 in.), W: 13.7 m (45 ft). Smoke-fired earthenware. Installation of wall piece in Mitsuke Cultural City Hall, Arcadia, Japan. *Photo by S. Hoshino.*

occasionally old tyres and waste oil to develop the deep black colour.

The pure white wall on which *Birth of Bubbles, Ancient Woodland and Peat Deposits* is displayed defines the rich black piece and allows it to make a strong, animated statement. It is also interesting to see how Satoru Hoshino has used small eye-catching forms at the top of each pillar to draw the gaze across the forms and towards the centre.

Before it was placed on the wall each piece was laid out on the floor on plastic in its correct grouping, to confirm its position and location on the wall (*see* p.40). The ceramic pieces were then placed on the wall with an adhesive following the designs for their location. Satoru Hoshino has several assistants who help with large installation projects, and they were on hand for this project due to the vast scale of the piece, giving Satoru the opportunity to stand at a distance, view and comment on the overall construction of the piece.

Mari-Ruth Oda (UK)

Mari-Ruth Oda applies a gentle, subtle approach to clay that interacts with tones and colours. Her forms create depth, movement and shadows through their interaction with space, and when viewing her forms the curiosity to touch and experience the smooth surface is in many respects overwhelming. The Japanese-born maker, now based in Manchester, has created and worked on a variety of projects using natural inspiration as a key influence to develop and capture natural qualities on a wall's surface through the use of clay.

Mari-Ruth Oda has created a number of successful projects; her projects at Uplands and Brimble Hill Schools (*see* pp.38–39) demonstrate the successful evolution of an idea through to a finished piece with the Percentage for Arts Scheme. Commissioned by Swindon Council and Artpoint Public Arts agency to create 20 panels that respond to nature, Mari-Ruth had to reflect on the clay she was going to use as well as the inspiration, scale, backing material and the durability of the surface. The panels were to be sited in a primary and secondary school for children with special needs, and were intended as an opportunity for the children to interact with the surface and thereby the space, to help orientate themselves around the building through their sense of touch. So it was essential to consider if was going to be safe for children to touch and handle them on a daily basis. The positioning of the panels from floor to ceiling was therefore well considered to give the children scope for touch and interaction with the work. Oda did conduct several workshops with the children which led and influenced the inspiration: one child in particular was captivated by droplets of water, and Mari-Ruth could see this was one element she would be including in her work along with others: 'The key words I noted were relaxing, fun, lack of gravity, ease of movement, warm.'

The design reference originated from plants and cabbage leaves, as their textures and surfaces provided a good source of inspiration which the school children were able to understand and relate to. Oda sanded the ceramics after

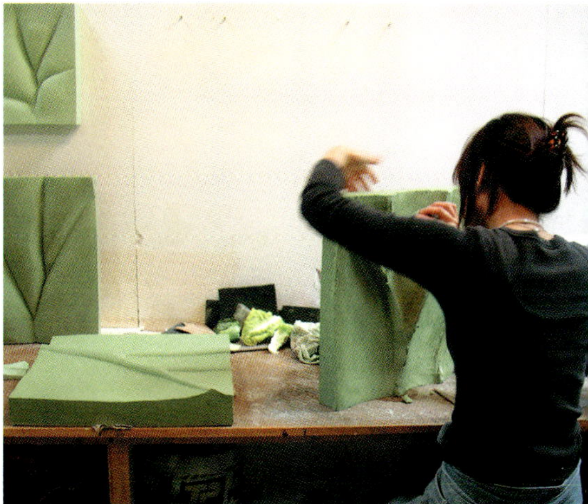

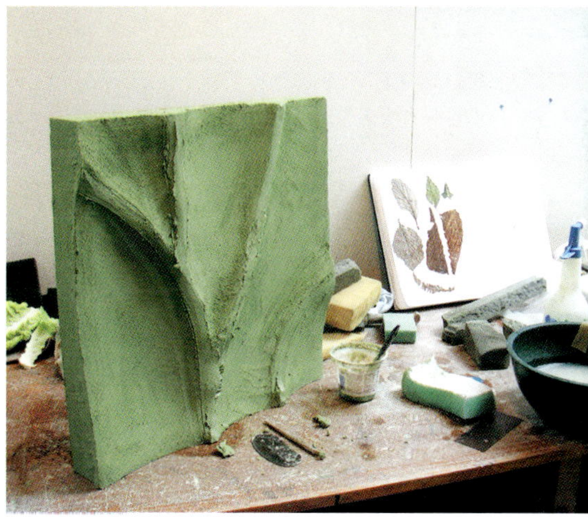

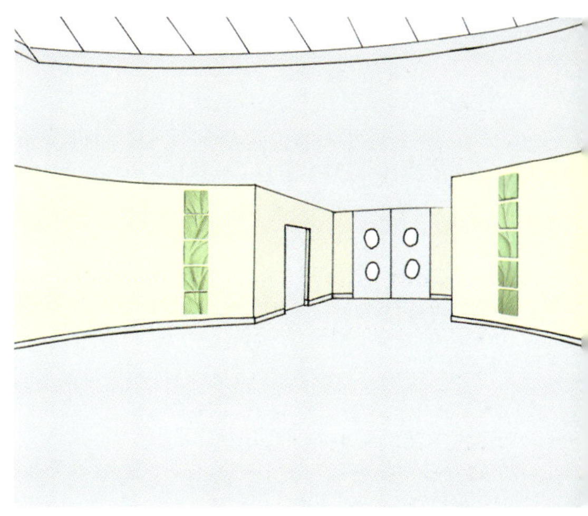

Uplands School, Swindon, project by Mari-Ruth Oda. Each square approx. 40 × 40 × 6 cm (15¾ × 15¾ × 2½ in.). Stoneware ceramics with body stain.

FROM TOP

Mari-Ruth in studio creating 'growth'.

Mari-Ruth working from sketchbook.

Final plan of main hall.
Photos by M. Oda.

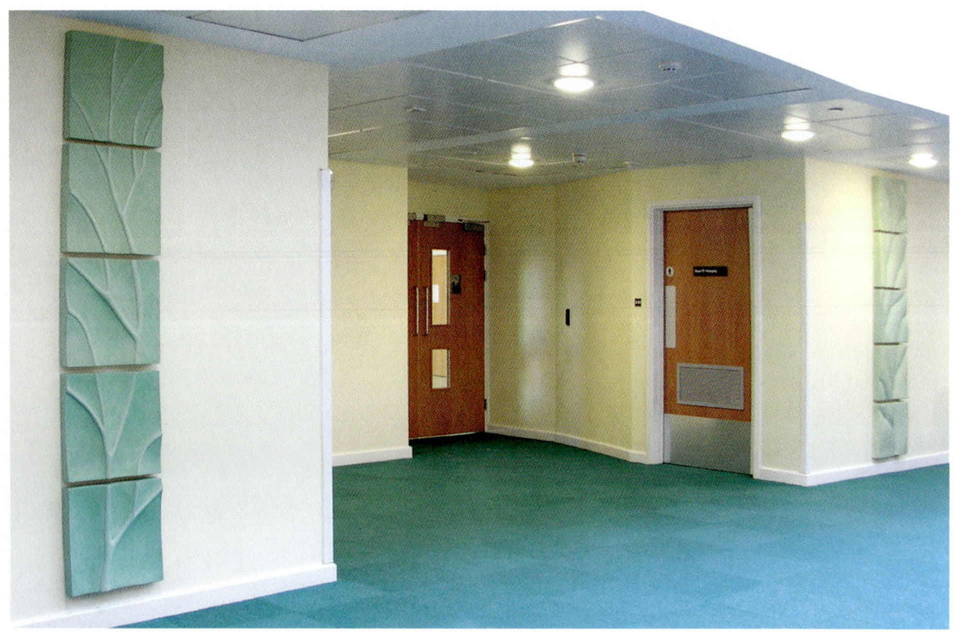

Uplands School, Swindon, project by Mari-Ruth Oda, 2008. Each approx. 40 x 40 x 6 cm (15¾ x 15¾ x 2½ in.). Stoneware ceramics with body stain. *Photo by M. Oda.*

the firing to ensure a smoother surface. The subtle green colour of the panels was achieved by working with stained (coloured) clay which was pugged with the main body (Scarva's Earthstone Handbuilding Material). Before Oda began the making for the final panels she made a maquette to give her the opportunity to play with scale and design.

The panels were installed by Oxford Exhibition Service. Mari-Ruth describes how the panels were created and hung: 'The panels are hollow and the back is open with an overhang lip, so from the back it looks a bit like a chunky picture-frame. The brackets are made of two thick strips of wood in L-shaped cross-section so the panels can hook onto this. The panels have two holes on the top side so they can be screwed onto the brackets (which are inside the panels when mounted) from above.'

Marie Bornet (Switzerland)

Rêverie, designed and made by the Swiss ceramicist Marie Bornet, was a piece 7.40 x 3 m (24 x 9 ft 10 in.). The location chosen for this piece was a corridor, which acted as a temporary location for this exhibition. With this piece it is interesting to see how a vision to transform a wall space can be realised. We often expect a wall piece to be placed on a central wall with the opportunity to move around the form, for example in a clean, clear space such as a gallery; but this is not always the ideal location. Marie Bornet refreshingly challenges these 'classical views of wall space', as a corridor can be an important wall space too, and we all need the chance to be visually stimulated while walking along these spaces. Over 1000 pieces of small slab-carved porcelain were used to express Marie's response to the impact of mountain ranges, in particular the Alps. The playful approach to scale in this piece relates to the original mountainous source.

The texture on each small piece of clay was created by dragging a tool across the slab's surface. Once the pieces were made they were placed on a kiln shelf to dry as they became too fragile to handle, and were then raw-fired at 1240–1260°C (2264– 2300°F). The assembling and installation of the work took about six days. The construction followed the designs and sketches created. Each piece was directly stuck on the wall with adhesive starting from the centre of the design and working outwards.

A Swiss Ceramicist's Rêverie by Marie Bornet, 2008. *Photos courtesy of the artist.*

FROM TOP

Sketches by Marie Bornet for *Rêverie*.

Installation.

Each piece 20 x 4 x 2 cm (8 x 1½ x ¾ in.), wall size: 7.40 m x 3 m (24 ft x 9 ft 10 in.). Porcelain clay, raw fired (oxidised) between 1240–1260°C (2264–2300°F). *Photo by David Freeman.*

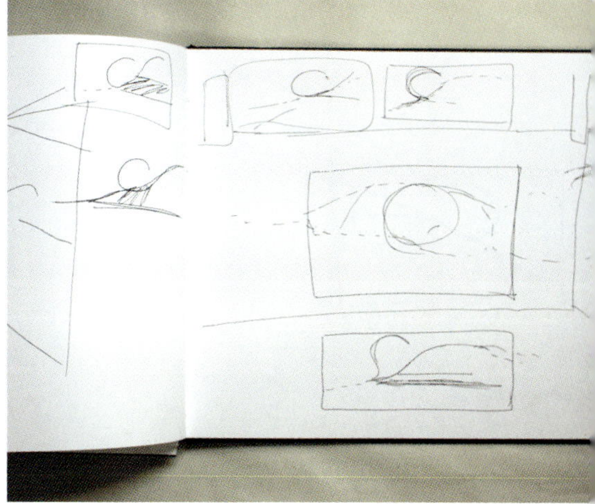

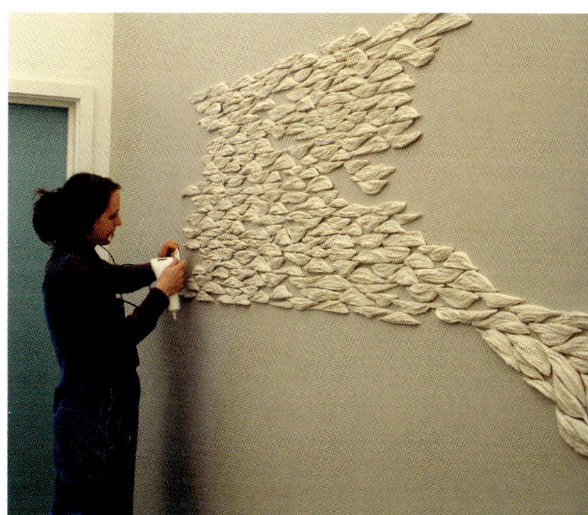

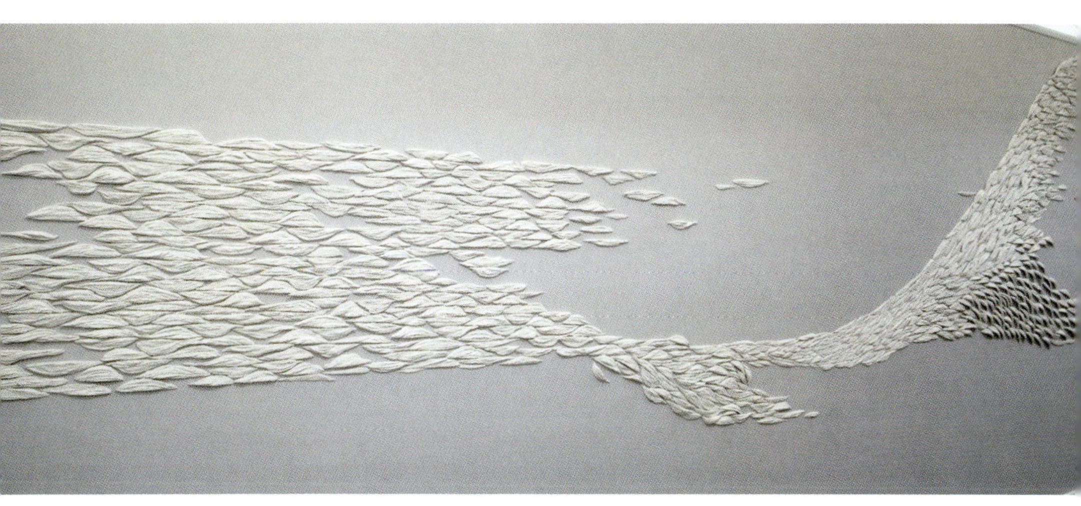

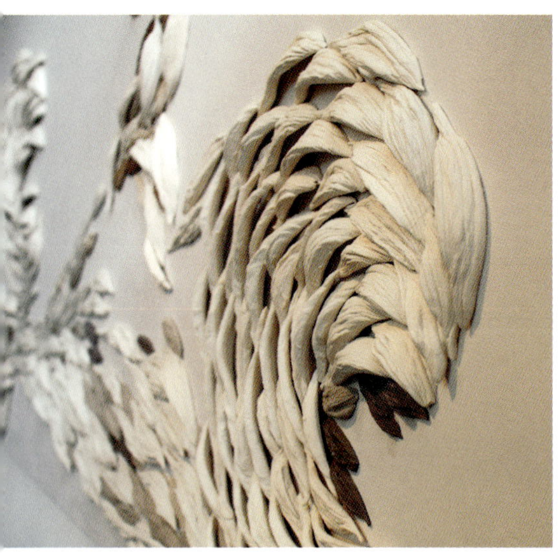

Detail of *Rêverie* by Marie Bornet, 2008. Each piece 20 x 4 x 2 cm (8 x 1½ x ¾ in.). *Photo by David Freeman.*

As this was a temporary exhibition it was important for Bornet to find an adhesive that would stick to surface, but at the same time would not damage the walls when the pieces had to be removed.

Dominique Bivar Segurado (UK)

Working from my studio in Norwich I have worked as a professional maker since graduating in ceramics from Harrow in 1999. The power and erosion of natural surfaces caused by the sea has always been a real fascination to me. Inspired by the erosion of rock and 'cliffscapes' my ceramic work is a constant journey of eroding clay, creating a reminder of the natural environment for contemporary locations. Working with materials such as glass and metal fittings has given me the opportunity to make innovative ceramic and glass wall pieces. The 'natural fragments' are created to remind the viewer of rocks and their ever-changing surface, slate in particular. Each fragment is three-dimensional and projects from the glass. Standing in front of the piece people have thought the ceramics were flat and embedded in the glass. It is only when viewed from the side that the fragments echo the structures and forms of mountains and eroded rock. The clay used to create the forms is Scarva's Earthstone Handbuilding Material. Once the clay has been formed and worked into through the process of handbuilding it is bisque-fired to 1015°C (1853°F) and then given several oxide washes and one glaze wash. After the pieces have dried they are then fired to stoneware temperatures of 1240–1250°C (2264–2282°F).

Natural Fragments, Horizontal drew its inspiration from a selection of drawings created while on a visit to Lyme Regis on the Jurassic coastline, Dorset. During the making process each piece is carved out deeply at the back to ensure the adhesive is hidden, but can stick on to the ceramic and glass successfully. The toughened glass is prepared by the supplier to the required size of 1 m x 75 cm (3.3 ft x 30 in.) and the drill holes are placed in the required location. As explained in chapter 3, once the ceramic pieces have been fired, the bases are then ground on silicon carbonate to ensure they are soft; it also ensures a flush surface between the glass, ceramic and glue. The design is placed under the glass to ensure each piece is positioned correctly and the sticking begins. After a couple of days for drying, the piece is then prepared for delivery and installation and is wrapped in several layers of bubble wrap, card and foam. When the pieces are shipped overseas a special crate is made.

In all the permanent, commissioned installations of wall pieces I have found

Natural Fragment by Dominique Bivar Segurado.

FROM TOP
Cutting into the clay fragment to create a textural surface.

Scooping out a well in the back of the clay fragment, in preparation for glue after firing.

Placing fired ceramic fragment with glue into position on the glass surface. The design drawn on graph paper can be seen underneath the fragment.

Photos by Mark Harvey.

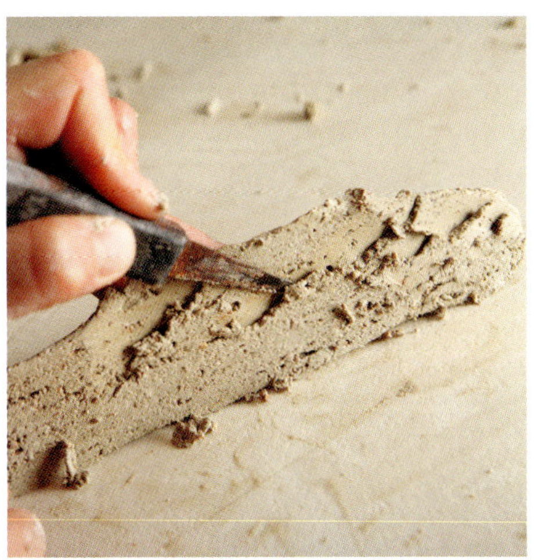

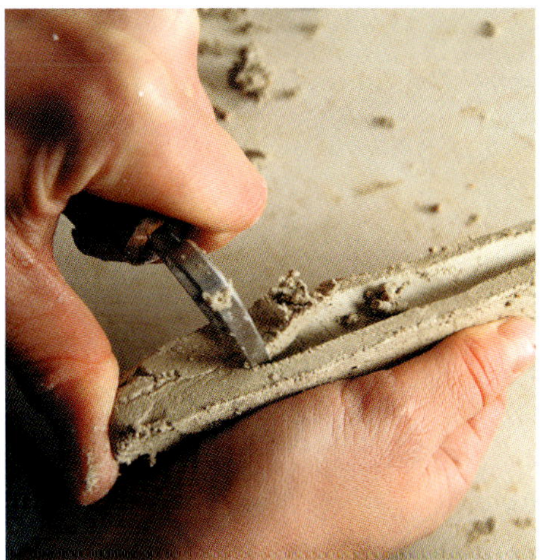

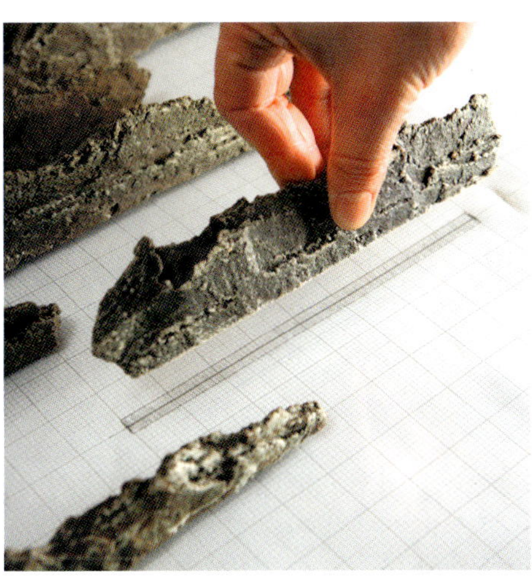

it wise to employ professional help as the glass is both heavy and fragile, and the fitting requires accurate installation. When Artmove was installing the piece it gave the client and me the opportunity to view the hanging, to ensure the correct positioning, a valuable opportunity to ensure that everyone was happy. When hanging the glass wall pieces, each hole's position is correctly measured and marked by holding the piece to the wall, the holes are then drilled and a rawlplug placed in each drilled hole. The fitting is then screwed into place and the glass placed onto the fittings, where the final part of the fitting is screwed into place to support the glass on the wall.

In 2006 I was commissioned to create two wall pieces and a sculpture for the Lowndes Hotel, London. This commission is a good example of creating for a limited size, and set design requirements. One wall piece, part of my *Natural Fragment* design, was to be set in a recess in the bar of the hotel and so the interior designer set the specific sizes of the wall pieces required: 120 x 80 cm (47 x 31 in.). A few confirmation

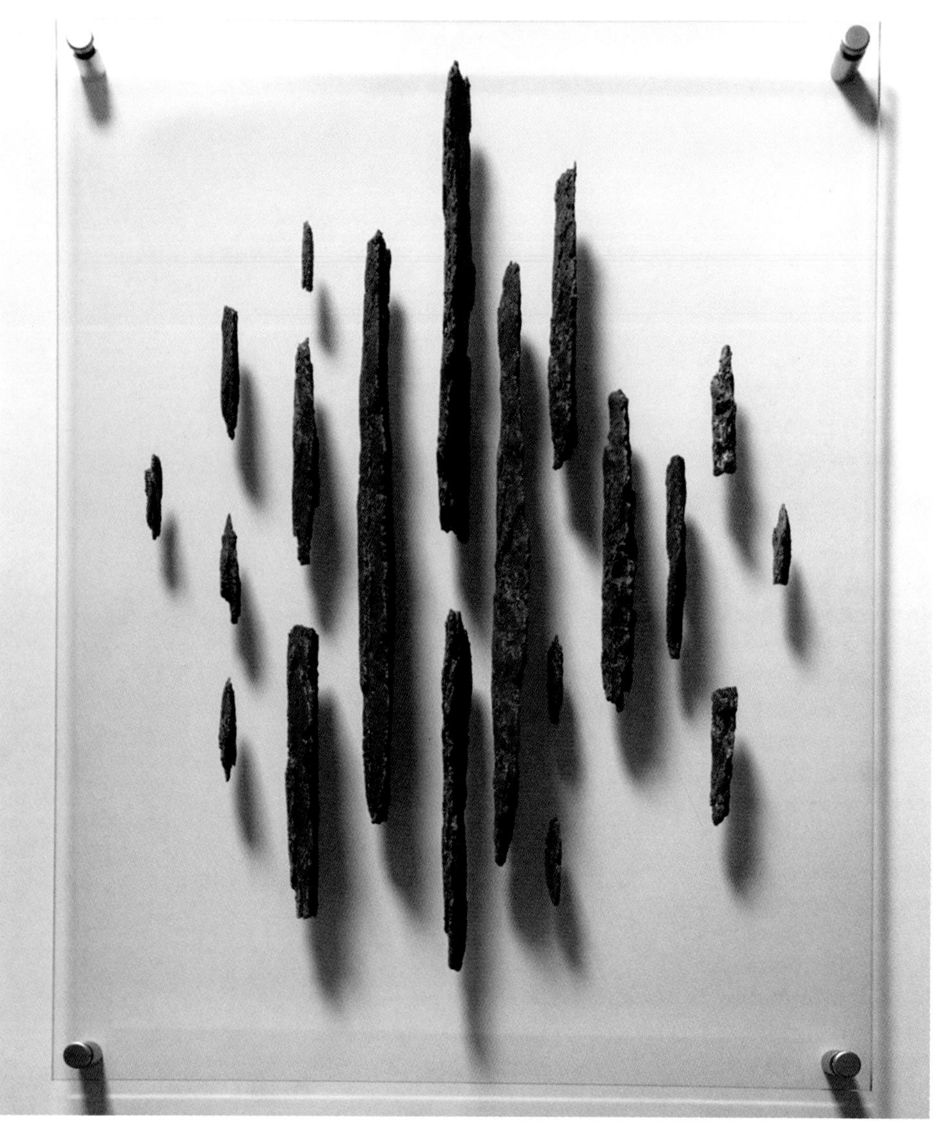

Ceramic fragments wall piece by Dominique Bivar Segurado, 2008. 1 × 0.75 m (39½ × 29½ in.). Stoneware clay with glaze washes fired between 1240–1250°C (2264–2282°F). *Photo by Mark Harvey.*

sketches and textural samples went to the interior designers, to ensure both parties were working on the same design ideas. The wall piece consisted of 20 pieces of shards of stoneware ceramics, each piece handmade and glazed.
The surface of the shards is rough and textured to touch, and in some of the fragments there are small holes, as if the rock has been weathered by the sea. Once the pieces were complete and delivered the hanging was handled by the commissioning agent.

Tulla Elieson (Norway)

Over the last 30 years Elieson's ceramics have presented a wave of exciting change and her most recent work continues to reflect this artist's knowledge and passion for clay.

For the past seven years her ceramics have been growing in scale due to the location of her current studio in a porcelain factory: Norsk Teknisk Porselensfabrikk (Norwegian Technical Porcelain Factory) in Fredrikstad.

One golden rule Elieson applies to her work is that the size should be limited by the length of her arms, and when viewing her work it is clear she must have a large arm span as the circular pieces range in diameter from 110 cm to 130 cm (43 in. to 51 in.).

Generation (*see* p.100) one of the larger porcelain circular pieces, sits on the wall with a real presence, as the ridges of clay create the strong outlines of shadows, cast as the light hits the dark black pieces. These ridges are similar to the ridges formed on the beach in the sand, and the folds of skin on the human body. It is only on the second viewing you notice the shadows of two, then three, then four, five

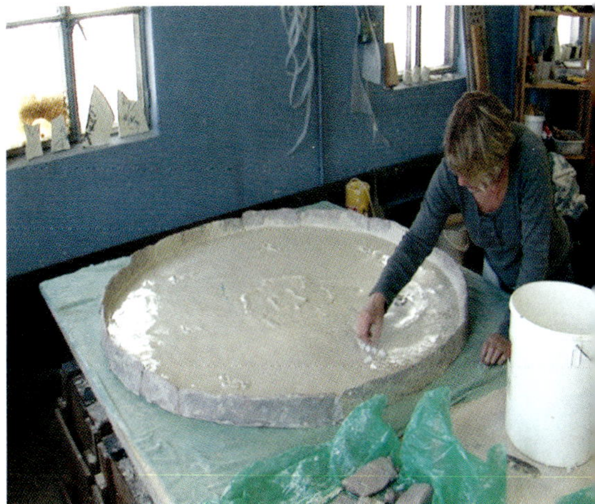

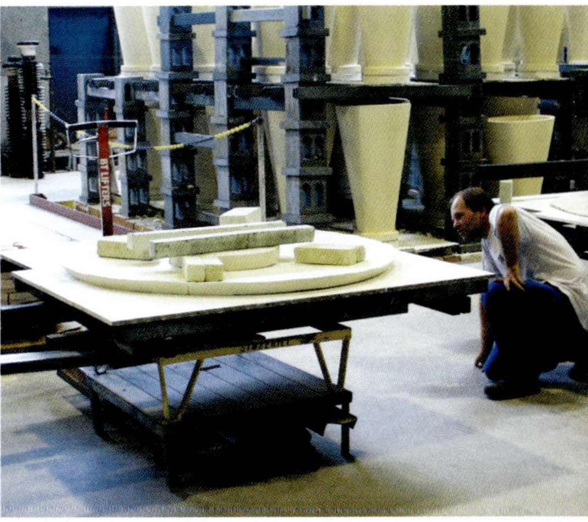

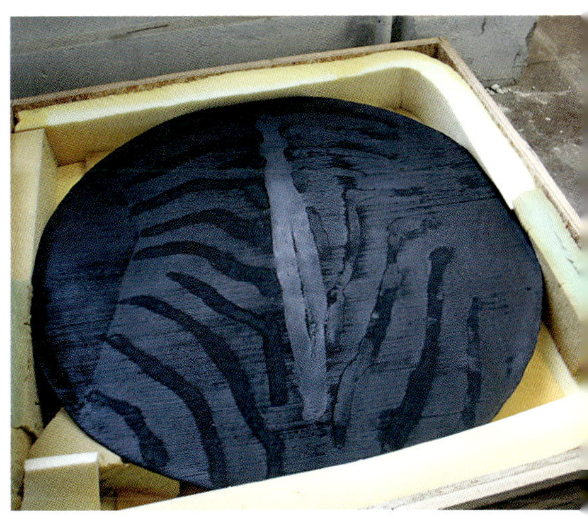

Spine by Tulla Elieson. 110 cm (45½ in.).

FROM TOP

Casting porcelain. Creating detail with chips of wax, casting porcelain has been poured onto textile surface.

The forks for the truck fit between the kiln bars, preparing and positioning the kiln shelf with the ceramics into the large-scale kiln for firing.

Spine is here, packed and ready to leave the studio in a shipping crate with foam.

Photos by Tiger Studios.

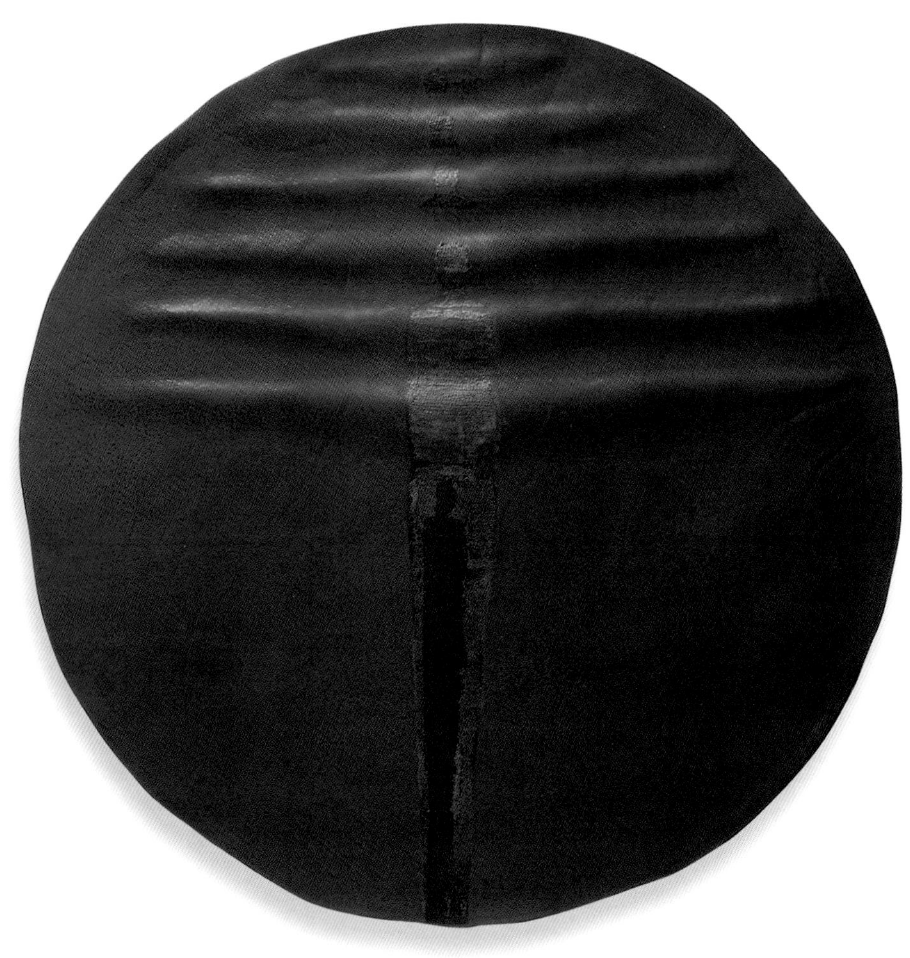

Generation by Tulla Elieson, 2003. 110 cm (45½ in.). Porcelain casting slip. *Photo by Studio Inge.*

and six human forms. The presence is faint, yet at the same time haunting. The dark black glaze on the surface absorbs the light, giving the eye an opportunity to read *Generation* from left to right across the whole piece. This piece does evoke thoughts of ritual, and the relationship we as people share with one another over time.

Tulia Elieson's approach is integral to the composition and success of her ceramics. Viewing her work it is apparent she is engaged in a dialogue between the subject, and the communication of her thoughts, feeling and ideas to the viewer. Elieson defines herself: 'I consider myself to be an artist of clay pictures more than a ceramic artist working on the surface decoration of the ceramic objects.'

Norsk Teknisk Porselensfabrikk gives Elieson the opportunity to create work that is technically demanding for the individual, studio-based ceramicist. Working in this environment has created a strong sense of collaboration in her ceramics, and she is an ideal example of how industry can support a maker's work successfully, to give a new dynamic to their creative practice. Access to the large kiln, machinery and casting slip has expanded her possibilities.

Once each piece is completed it is prepared for delivery, and in most cases a special crate has been made and lined with foam to ensure the wall piece is successfully supported while in transit.

On the back of each wall piece, high quality wooden board normally used for furniture is attached with a flexible glue. Wire hooks are screwed into the board enabling it to be hung on the wall.

Regina Heinz (UK)

The structural ceramics created by Regina Heinz are concerned with line, pattern and surface. Her wall pieces, created by slipcasting and slab-building, reflect an engagement with form. Heinz uses detailed incised lines in the clay which act as perfect receivers to retain the wiped-back lithium glaze, applied to the red terracotta once bisque-fired. Heinz's pieces can go through a minimum of three glaze firings to achieve the final desired effect.

Her work first began with using slab-building as the main construction process, which has developed into the use of slipcasting, giving the freedom to create the red terracotta multiples ideally suited to the wall. Although the pieces are relatively small, with a flat back and hole for hanging on the wall, each piece is taken through a detailed and lengthy glazing process which involves masking certain areas to ensure the coloured glazes can be applied successfully. This begins with the application of the lithium glaze and then the red oxide. After this the pieces are normally kiln-fired, so then the process can begin of applying the biscuit slips.

Created for the temporary Biennale exhibition in Gmunden, Austria, *Inverse* is a clear example of how ceramics with

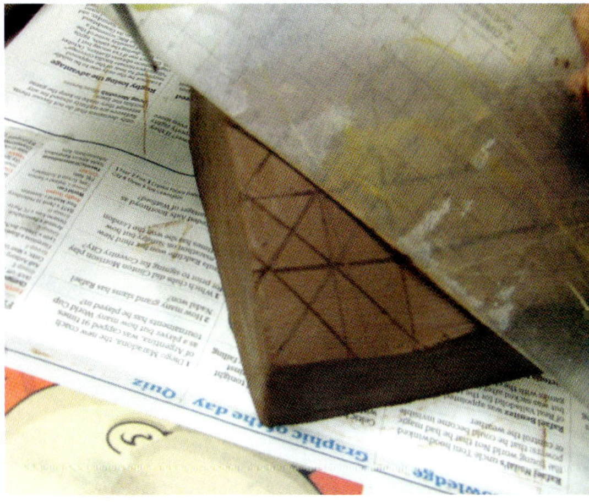

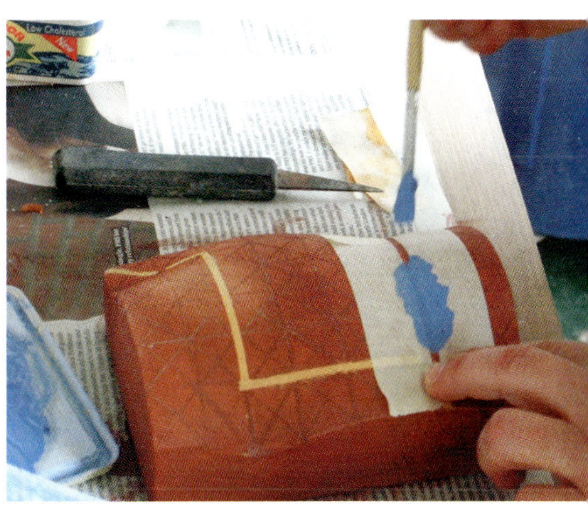

RIGHT, TOP Regina Heinz. Stoneware clay. A design is incised into the clay and fired on. *Photo by R. Heinz.*

RIGHT Regina Heinz. Lines are masked out and painted on in yellow and blue biscuit slip as part of the design. *Photo by R. Heinz.*

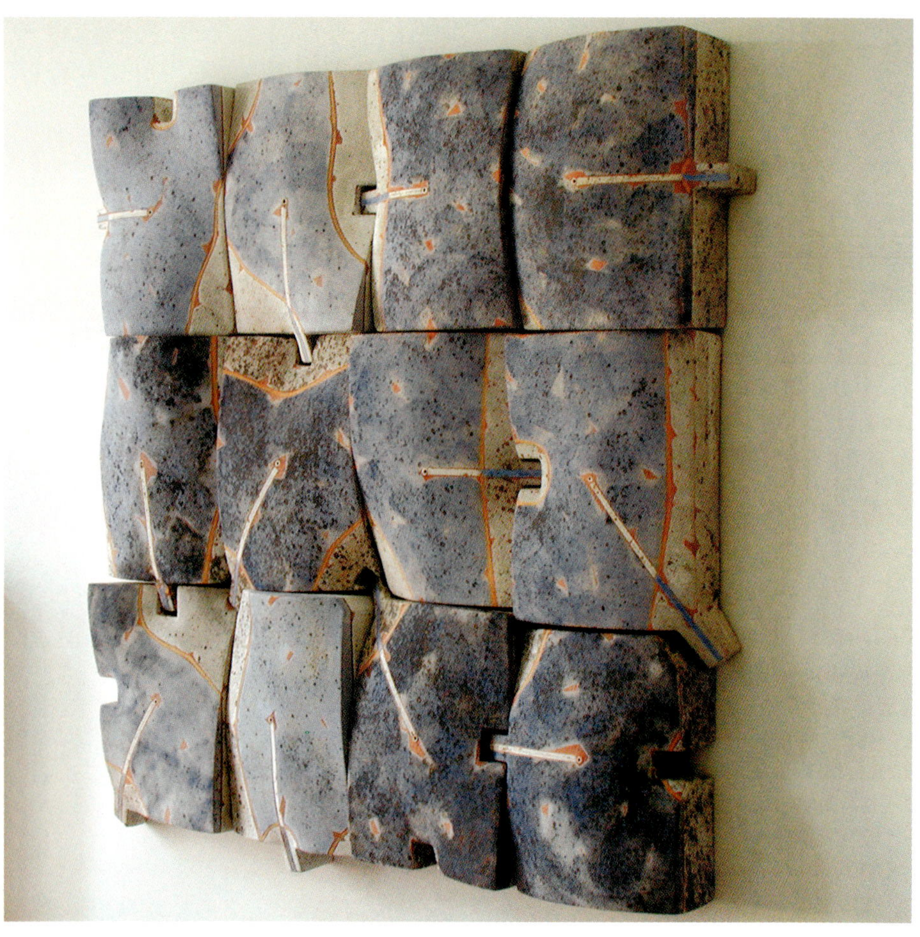

Inverse by Regina Heinz, 2006. 90 x 90 x 10 cm (35½ x 35½ x 4 in.). Stoneware clay, with oxides, glazes and lithium glaze, fired to 1035°C (1895°F). *Photo by A. Petri.*

an interesting surface can be successfully placed on a variety of wall surfaces. Similar works were displayed at the exhibition on a wall with the stone surface exposed, and the work also engaged with the landscape in the surrounding area.

Each of the 12 slabs are fixed on a wooden backing, which is then fixed on the wall with four screws. Each ceramic piece has a hole in the back and sits flush with the wooden surface to ensure it can be mounted on the board with a separate screw.

The design and consideration for the location of this piece were taken into account, and as this was a temporary show it was important to consider the transportation, installation and dismantling too. The use of the 12 slabs in the form of a puzzle ensured the piece could be successfully hung, transported and dismantled with ease in sections.

Victoria Ellis (UK)

Victoria Ellis has created a selection of detailed projects focused on interior spaces. Her works do merge the boundaries of wall pieces and tiles, but they do move beyond a simple definition of tiles as the pieces are intricate, hand-crafted and respond directly to the individual wall space. Ellis begins each project with a drawing, to give the opportunity to understand the scale and communicate her ideas successfully. The drawing will often show how the design is going to be divided into sections, as this helps to act as a plan for the making process and final installation. In many projects Victoria's ceramics might be limited to a certain scale, so it is essential for her to involve this in the planning stages. Scarva's Earthstone Handbuilding clay is used as the main clay, the slabs prepared using a slab roller with a thickness of 10 mm (1/2 in.). The clay gives a good strength and base colour which are ideal for the elaborate oxides and glazes painted on the surface. Ellis works with a finely detailed approach to the design on the surface, carving the clay away using a collection of old dentist's tools to achieve the fine, perfect marks in the clay. Finally the pieces are fired on a slow firing to 1260°C (2300°F).

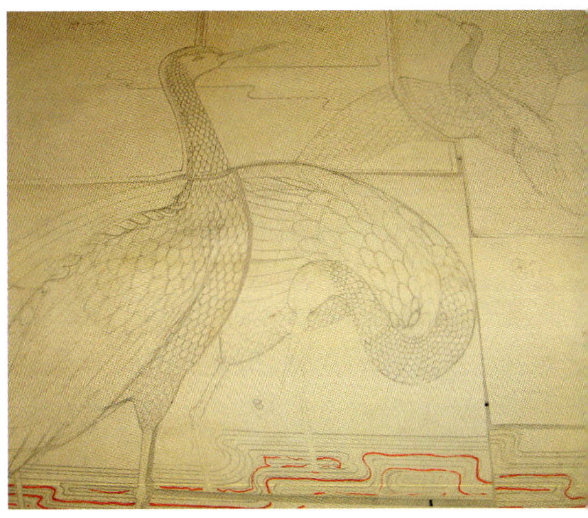

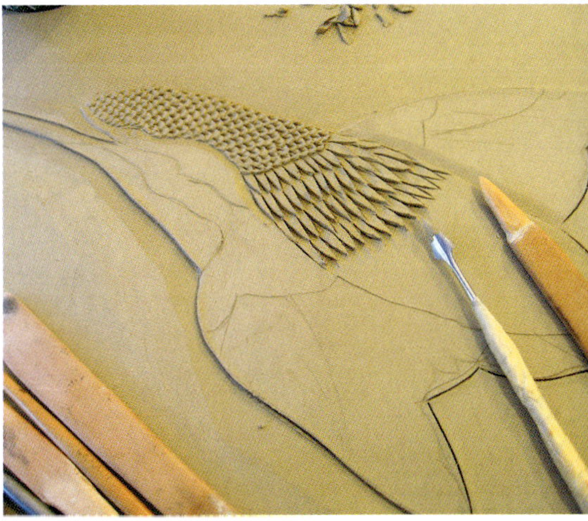

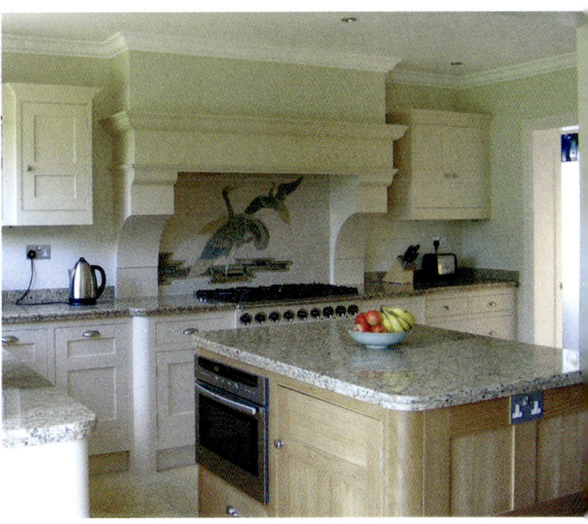

Wading Birds by Victoria Ellis, 2008. Scarva's Earthstone Original clay with under glazes and glaze fired between 1250–1260°C (2282–2300°F). *Photos courtesy of artist.*

FROM TOP

Close-up of template used for *Wading Birds* kitchen wall piece.

The design is drawn onto the slab and cut into the clay.

The panel was made for this kitchen to fit the space 145 x 125 cm (57 x 49 in.).

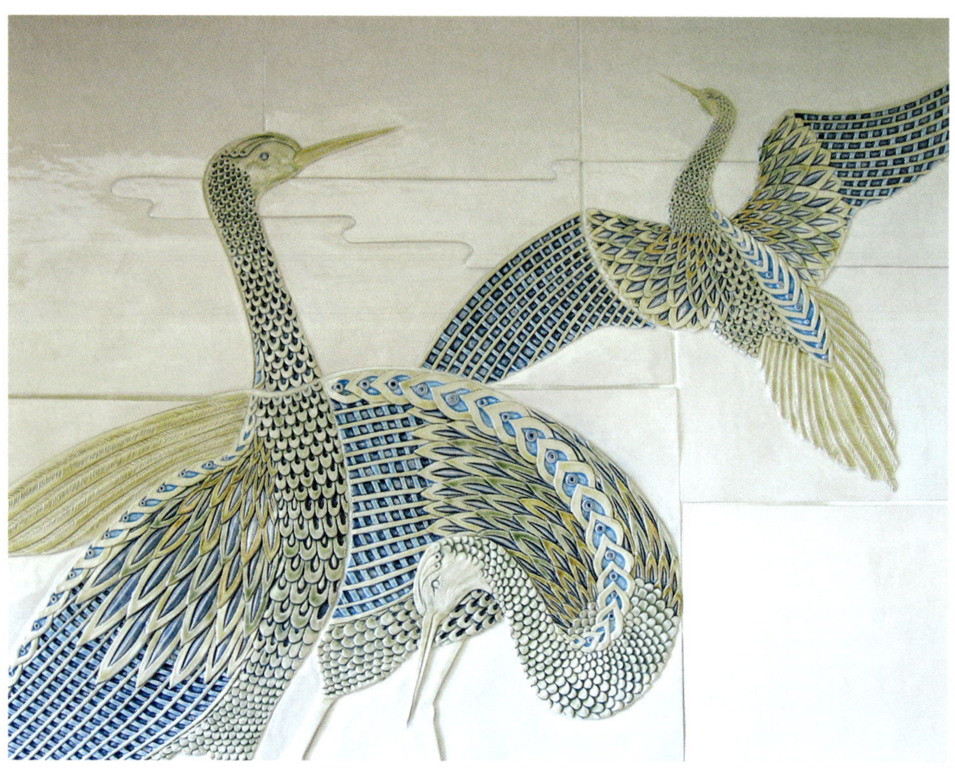

Wading Birds by Victoria Ellis, 2008. 145 x 125 cm (57 x 49 in.). Close-up of panel for the kitchen. Scarva's Earthstone Original clay with under glazes, glaze fired between 1250°C–1260°C (2282–2300°F). *Photo courtesy of artist.*

Once the tiles have been fired and prepared for transportation they are ready for installation. This is normally carried out by a professional tiler as Ellis finds this preferable, to ensure the tiles are successfully installed. Unless the project is large-scale and very complicated Ellis will not always oversee the installation of the project, but she makes sure a detailed plan accompanies the panel. This can include a set of detailed instructions, photographs of the layout and a design too, while the numbering on the back of the panels also helps to find the order for installation (these are added during the making process).

Valéria Nascimento (Brazil)

Valéria Nascimento often uses wood as a backing material to support and express her ideas. She has a sensitive and captivating approach to clay, with an understanding of space and the urban landscape from her experience as a qualified architect. Each piece of the porcelain is cut individually and formed from a thin textural slab. Once a selection of sizes is made and they have been through the kiln firing of 1260°C (2300°F), the wooden backing is cut to the required size and painted by a carpenter. Nascimento uses a variety of wood, from oak to MDF (if the surface needs to be painted). Everything is then prepared for the installation of the ceramics; a selection of sizes and lengths of galvanized flathead nails are gathered to support the pieces. Starting from the centre and working outwards, the longer nails are used in the centre and the smaller nails nearer to the outside. The flat heads of the nails provide a good surface to attach the ceramics to, and make it easy when hammering them into the wood. The varying height of the nails helps to add variety and depth to the whole piece. Once each nail is in the correct position, Nascimento begins to join the porcelain pieces, working from the centre outwards, using an adhesive to glue the ceramic gently into position on each nail head. As there are a large number of pieces, the wood backing acts as a clean and unobtrusive surface, allowing the viewer to focus only on the ceramics. The nails are hidden due to the height of the porcelain. The larger pieces of ceramics on the outer edges are stuck directly on to the wooden backing, and also help to disguise the nails.

Nascimento is mainly inspired by the natural world, conveying this through her interest in the elements of repetition, and the sequence the forms take using this approach. Her main interest is with

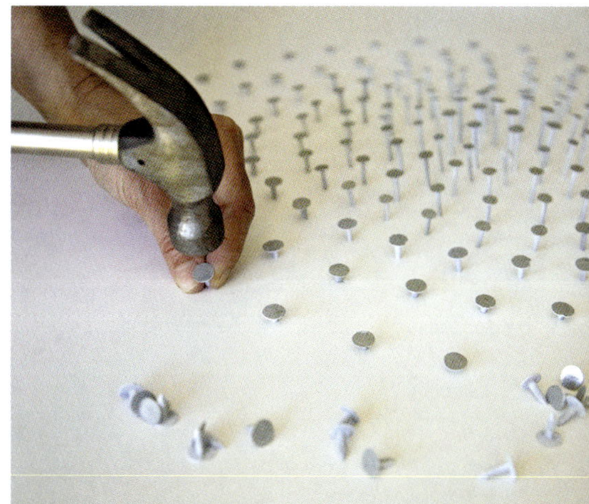

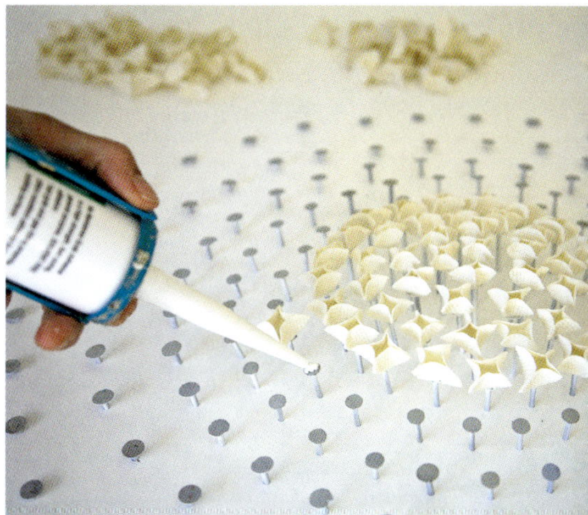

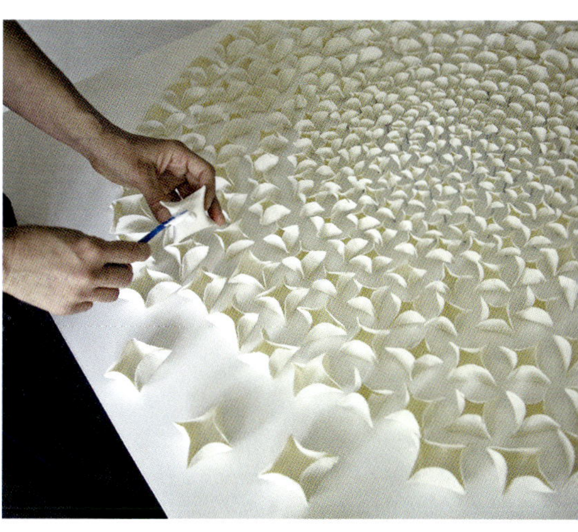

Flower, by Valéria Nascimento, 2008. Size: 100 x 100 cm (39½ x 39½ in.).

TOP TO BOTTOM

Hammering galvanized nails into position on the wooden backing.

Gluing fired porcelain ceramics into position, working from the centre outwards.

Gluing remaining larger fired porcelain ceramics into position, using a tool.

Photos by Christopher Pillitz.

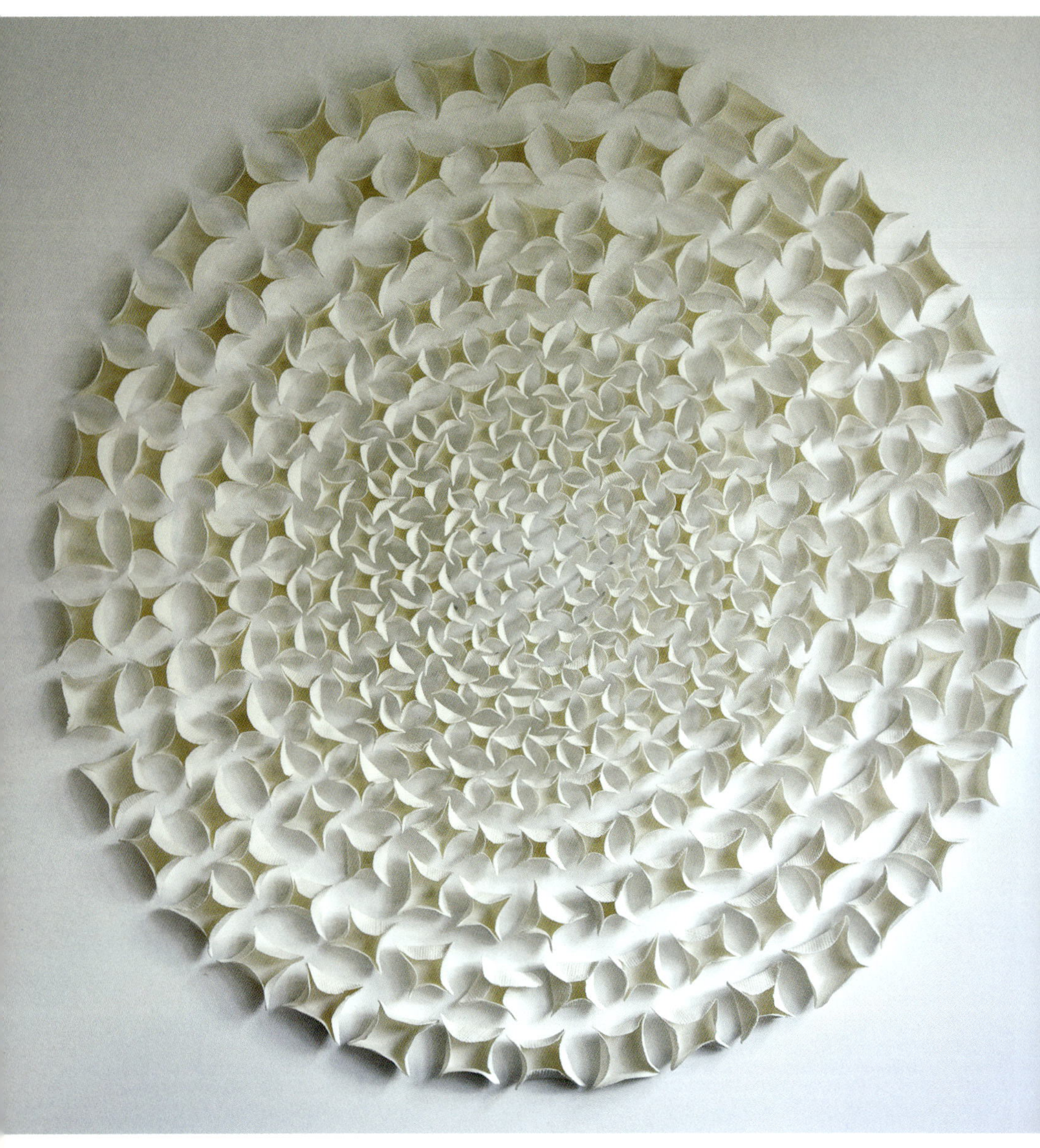

Flower, by Valéria Nascimento, 2008. Size: 100 × 100 cm (39½ × 39½ in.). Royal porcelain fired to 1260°C (2300°F), mounted on wooden backing. *Photo by Christopher Pillitz.*

larger-scale wall pieces and installations; as the scale increases the opportunity for echoing the visual concept grows too. Using the wooden backing is key to making the ideas a reality. In some of Nascismento's other wall pieces, such as *Roses* (*see* p.62) she has used wood as a backing and created a large circular recess within the wooden frame within which the ceramic pieces sit. The wooden recess creates a perfect frame effect which shows off the ceramics very successfully.

Brad Evan Taylor (USA)

Glaciated Mass is a breath-taking wall piece on an enormous scale. It involved a great deal of technical consideration and a team of assistants. A steel frame with a plywood membrane was used as an armature to support the weight of the ceramic pieces. Each steel structure was made with a calculated space of 41 cm (16 in.) to allow a person to fit inside the frame to secure the wood to the steel and the ceramics to the wood. Over 200 anchor bolts secured the frame to the concrete wall. *See also* pp.24–25, and p.108.

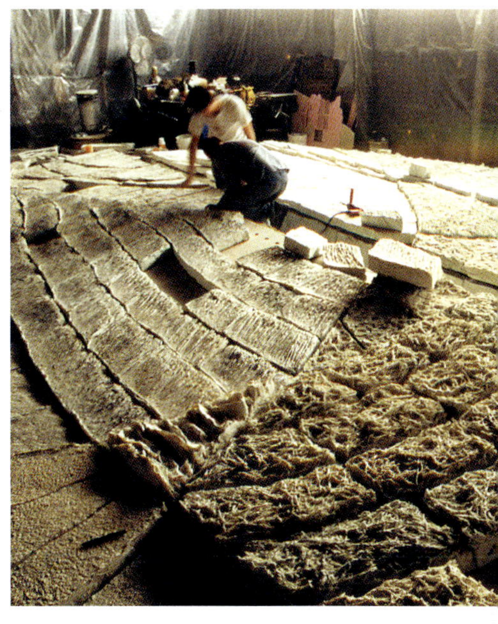

RIGHT AND BELOW *Glaciated Mass*, by Brad Evan Taylor. H: 10m (33ft), W: 8m (26ft), D: 1m (3ft 3in.), 2000–2003. Porcelain. Brad Taylor and Nolan Baumgartner fitting the sections of *Glaciated Mass* after firing. *Photo by Kerri Buxton.*

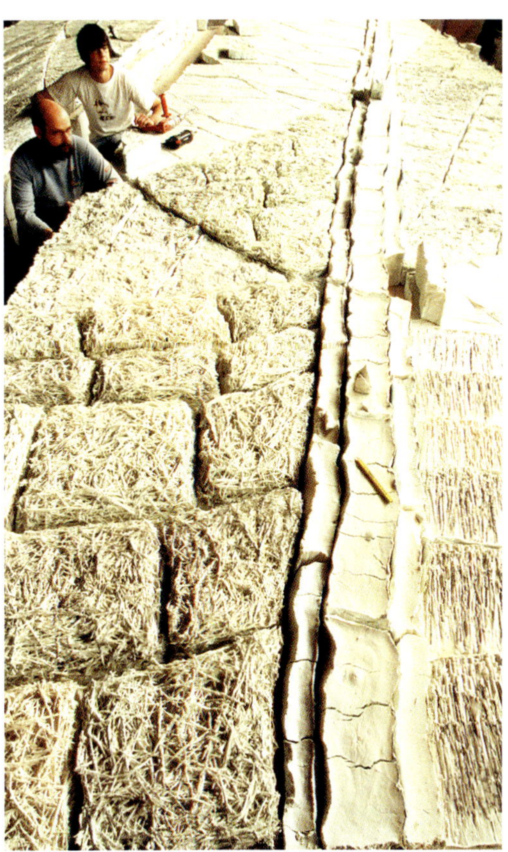

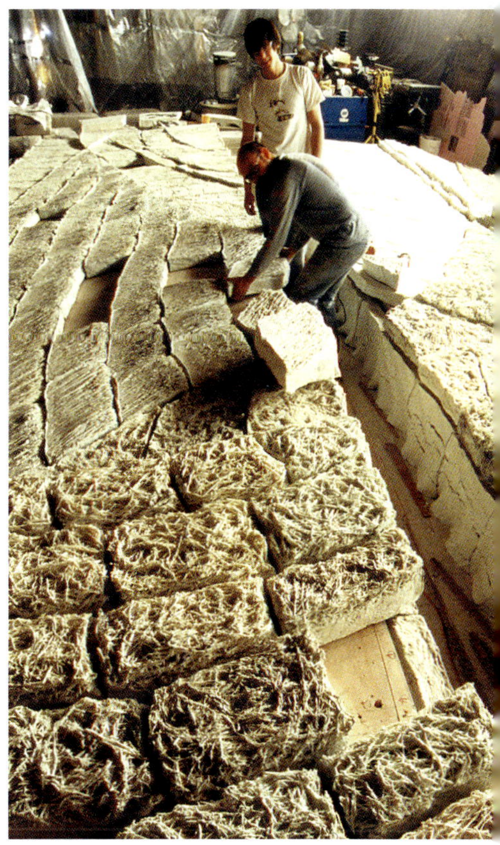

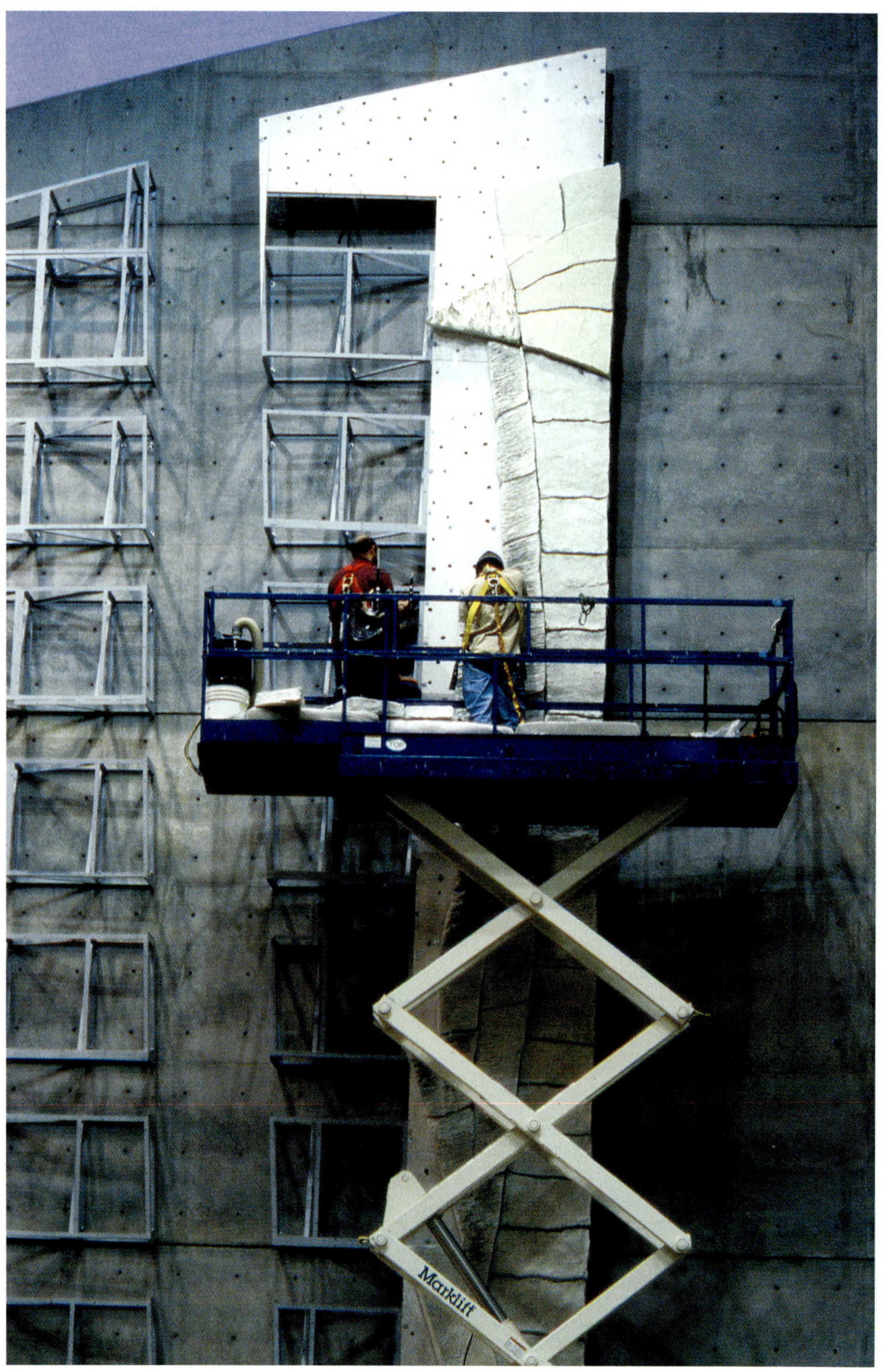
Marklift

LEFT Larry Wheeler (right) and Brad Taylor (left) installing the ceramic sections of *Glaciated Mass*. This image illustrates the underlying metal frame with the partially installed plywood skin and the overlaying porcelain blocks.

RIGHT Larry Wheeler (right) and Brad Taylor (left) bolting the ceramic sections of *Glaciated Mass* to the underlying metal frame and plywood skin.

BELOW, LEFT Detail of the central crevasse in *Glaciated Mass* illustrating the thickness of the individual porcelain blocks (8–30cm/ 3–12in.) and the overall relief (1m /3ft 3in.) of the piece.

RIGHT Larry Wheeler (above) and Brad Taylor (below) installing the final ceramic sections of *Glaciated Mass*.

Photos by Kerri Buxton.

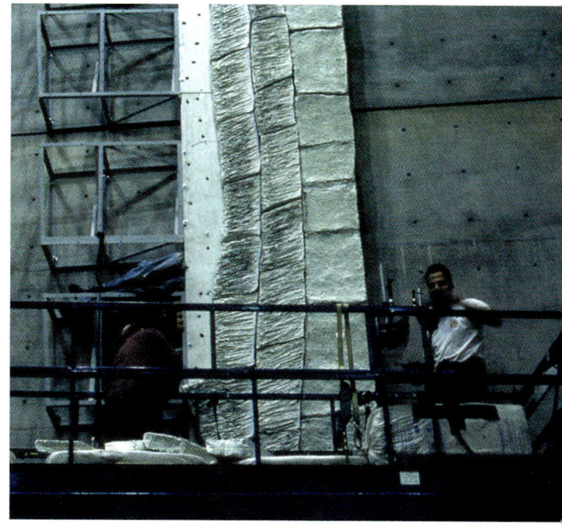

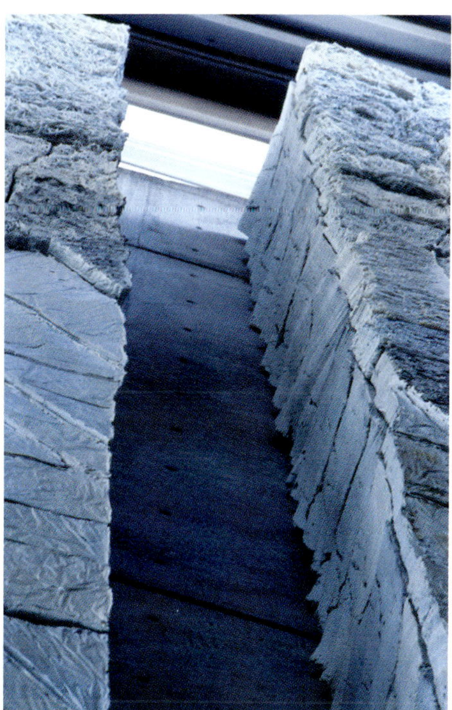

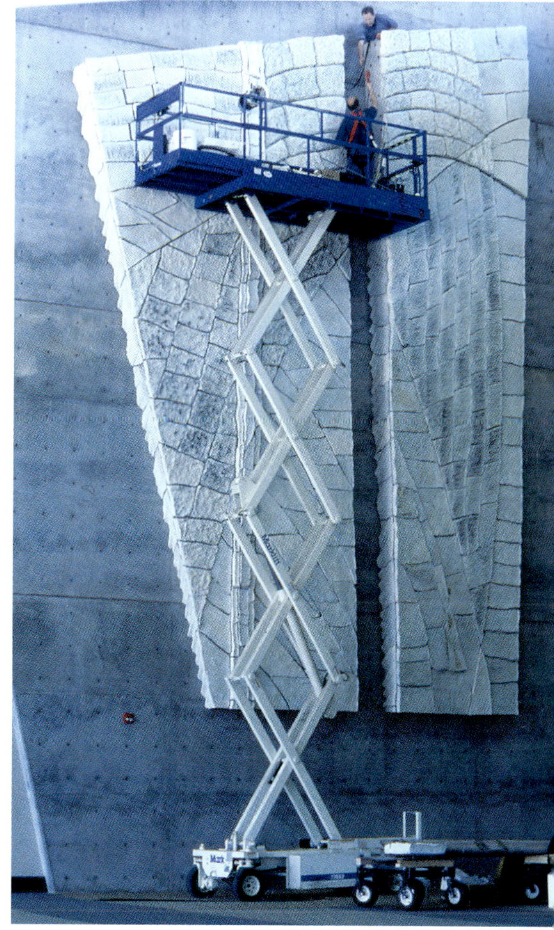

Chapter 5

Innovative wall pieces

Unlike the previous chapter this one does not focus on the making, or the practical aspects of installation, but on the ideas behind the ceramics, on the finished product and its interaction with the wall or space.

It is fascinating to see how the creative ideas of artists combined with their vision for the space as a whole have transformed an area or wall. Many of the makers featured here give a brief insight into their ideas and approaches to the concept of wall space. Although this is the last chapter there is no doubt that the evolution of the ceramic wall piece will continue to develop, and there are already many other projects which (due to space) were not included in this book.

This chapter offers a glimpse into the concepts and contemporary approaches these makers have towards wall space, and aims to demonstrate the wide variety. It is the ideas behind the work in these pieces which help to create an exciting use of space. Many of the projects discussed in this chapter introduce a new way of thinking about clay and its interaction with wall surfaces.

Ceramics can be perceived by some as a fragile material, and this questioning of the material is one aspect amongst many that some of the makers featured in this chapter have explored, amongst other things. This gives us an ideal opportunity to question this perception of clay, and encourage debate by presenting a material that is truly versatile, with at times both great strength as well as fragility.

The projects featured vary from public to private spaces, but nevertheless every project has left a personal mark on the buildings and clients involved with them. Whatever scale they are working on, all are combining 2D with 3D in interesting and exciting ways.

The projects discussed in this chapter are from all over the globe and highlight the diversity of approaches makers are using in contemporary ceramics. In many cases they have directly responded to the space and designed a piece specifically for the location; others have found a space and reacted to the space through their own creative vision. These projects offer an opportunity to extend personal boundaries and add a new dynamic to their creative practice. In some cases the projects discussed are collaborations between industry, fellow ceramicists or artists from different disciplines.

In many cases the success of the innovative wall pieces here is the result of the artist's personal dialogue with architecture and interiors, and an awareness of how to capture the viewer's attention for one moment of real reflection.

Chris Wight (UK)

Chris Wight's fascination with light, ceramics and space intrigued me when his work first came to my attention on a trip to Japan. His delicate use of casting, and the textural pattern impressed into

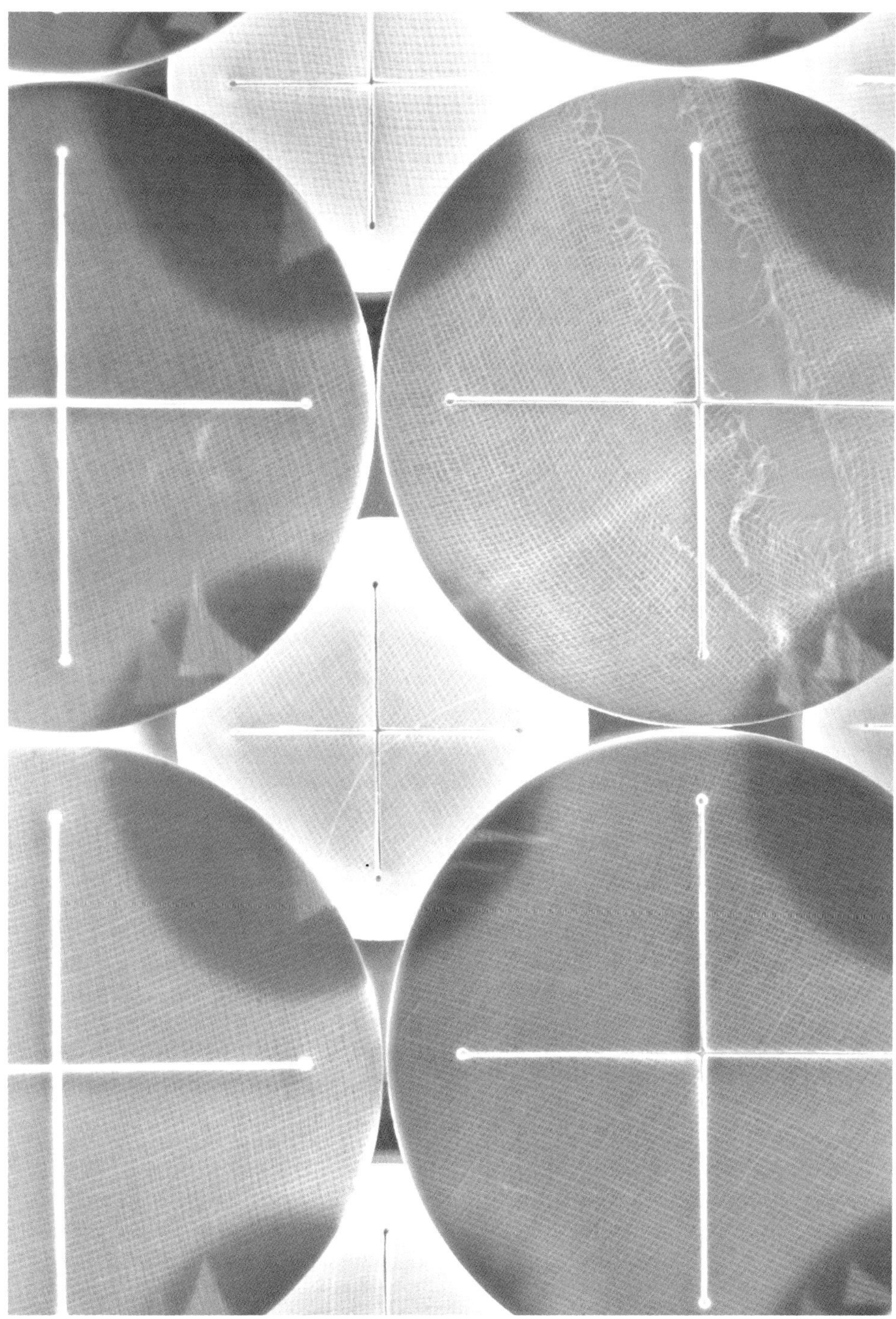

Detail of *Chapel Doors* by Chris Wight, 2008. Cross-hair bone china discs; toughened glass held within an aluminium framework. *Photo by C. Wight.*

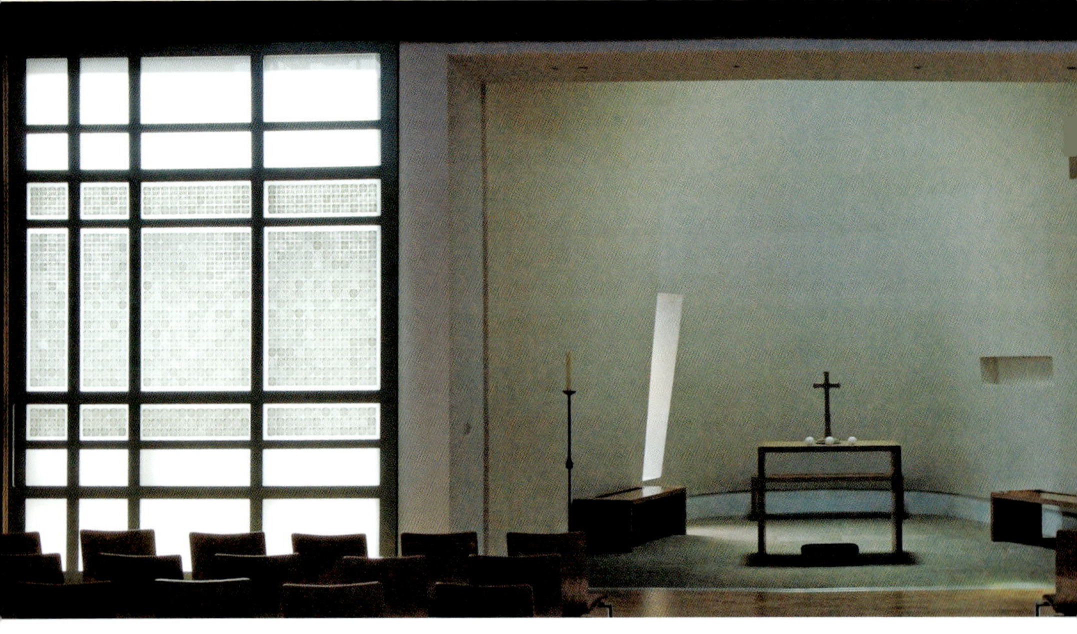

Chapel Doors by Chris Wight, 2008. Commissioned for The Minster School Southwell, Nottinghamshire. Each door: H: 4 m (13 ft); W: 3 m (9 ft 10 in.), Discs: 15.5 x 7 x 4.5 cm (6 x 2¾ x 1¾ in.). *Photo by C. Wight.*

the surface of the translucent bone china clay (high fired to 1250°C/2282°F) has been developed to display the beautiful qualities clay can reveal when sited in an architectural space. The interaction with materials such as glass, metal and lighting is a modern approach, showing how these materials can be combined effectively. A good example of this artist's understanding of the needs of an interior space, is the project at New Minster School, Chapel, Southwell England. In this piece Wight has designed and made a wall screen with a real sense of calm, the tranquil use of light giving you thought for reflection, all of which seems appropriate in the setting of the chapel. As the natural light filters through the sandblasted glass on to the ceramics panels encased within it, the minimal, pure forms of the circles also play they part. On closer inspection the viewer can also examine the surface and texture of the bone china.

Wight's inspired use of his bone china pieces, combined together with structural materials such as glass and metal create a contemporary but surprisingly natural feel to the wall, which divides the outside world from this inner sanctuary. The daylight has been cleverly integrated into the work, creating the aura of calm. It is eye-opening to see how the ceramics has become an architectural wall containing the space, not just as an attachment to an existing wall surface. It is not only decorative but functional too, concealing the outside view of the car park. Having the vision to transform and enhance this space has been very successful, and adds an element of privacy to it, as it is intended to be a place of quiet contemplation.

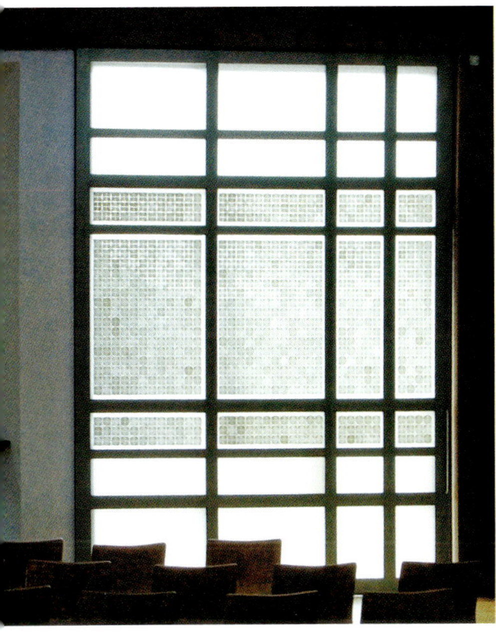

Henk Wolvers (Netherlands)

Henk Wolvers's ceramics has an intriguing use of line, evoking a certain fragility. When I first viewed his wall pieces at the Victoria and Albert Museum in London, it looked from a distance as if the artist had drawn the black square lines on the wall with a thin black pen, and each small square was creating an interesting composition in its own right. On closer viewing the pieces were so thin and delicate they could almost be likened to thin wire. It was a surprise that a maker could create such slender, slight structures through the technically difficult process of using porcelain clay.

BELOW Wall piece with carpet by Henk Wolvers, 2007. Wall: 190 x 90 cm (75 x 35.5 in.), Carpet: 200 x 300 cm (79 x 118 in.) Coloured black porcelain squares of thin lines, made by brush. The same design is transferred to the carpet, made of black and white wool.

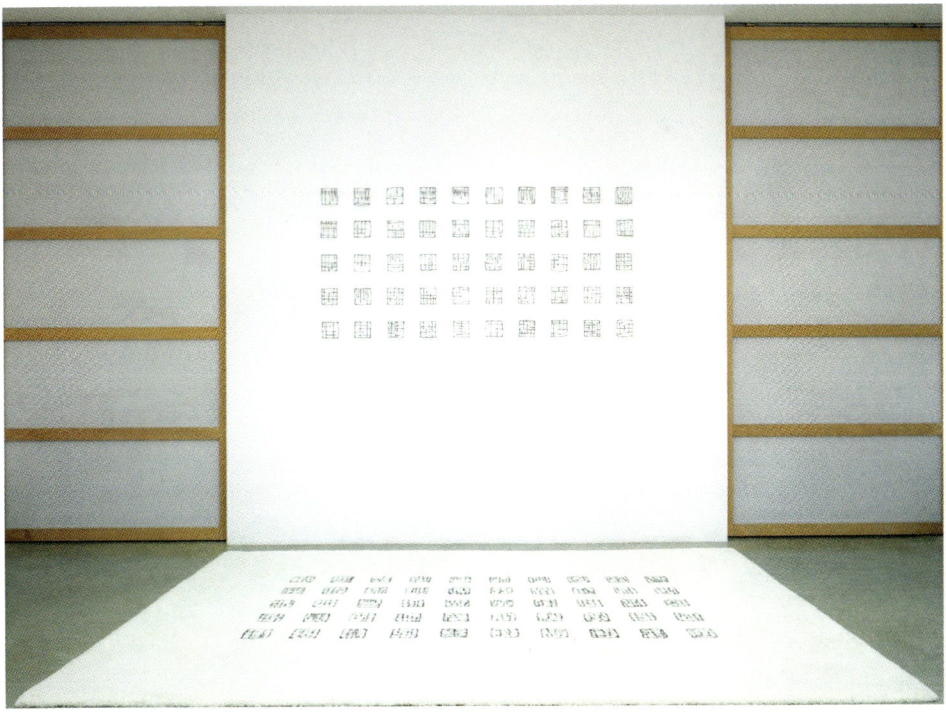

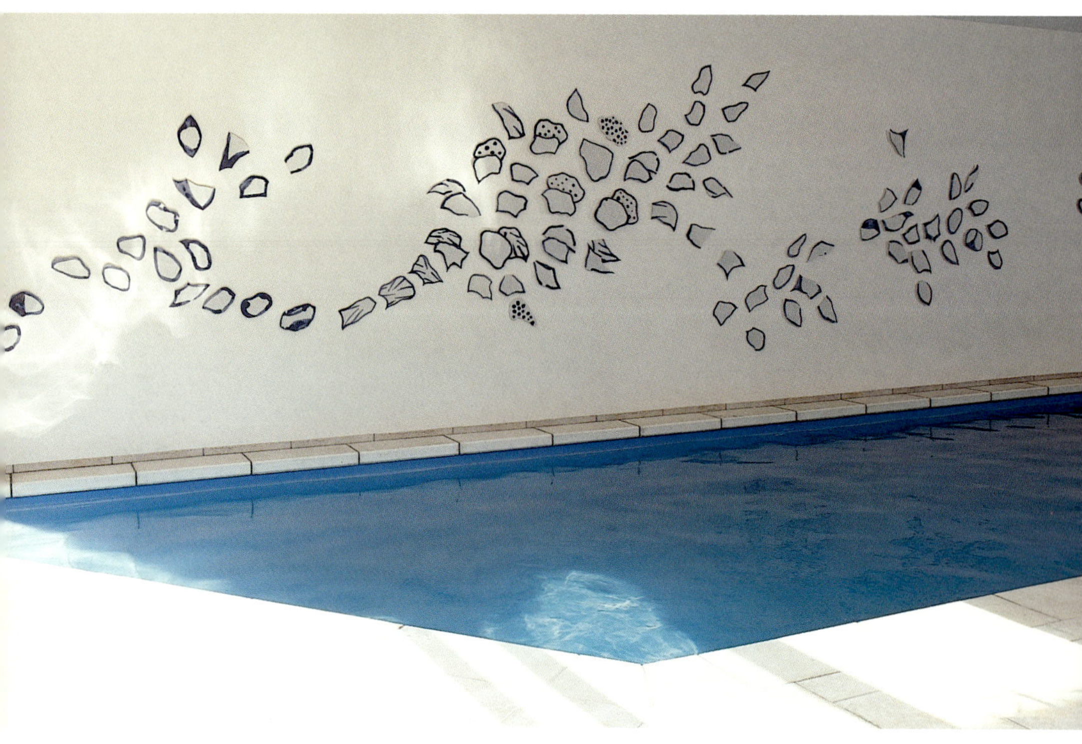

Swimming Pool by Henk Wolvers, 1998. Size: 8 x 2 m (26 x 6.5 ft). Limoges porcelain, fired at 1300°C (2372°F) in a gas reduction kiln. Thin slabs of porcelain, partly coloured with cobalt sulphate, are whirling on the wall like clouds in the sky and are reflected into the water of the pool. Steel pins were glued to the back of the porcelain slabs, holes drilled in the walls and plugs put into them. The pins were then pushed into the plugs. The slabs were hung a little bit off the wall – 5–7 cm (2–2¾ in.). *Photo by Ron Zijlstra.*

In 2007 Wolvers worked on an interesting new collaboration with Hester Onijs the textiles designer, to exchange ideas and create a hybrid of design and materials. Their collaboration, using a wall and carpet together, shows how this maker is able to transfer his use of delicate line to work with contemporary fabrics, techniques and interiors. Although the lines are subtle, the overall structure is positioned in a rectangle, giving you the illusion of lines set in an organised form, just as a painter would use the canvas to give the viewer a visual boundary.

The black porcelain squares set on the white wall remind you of the play with drawn line on the surface. Each small square was hung on the wall, and then its shadow and form echoed in the piece of textiles on the floor. The lines of the ceramic and position of each square was transferred onto the rug by weaving black wool into a rug. As the rug is positioned below the ceramic piece it gives the viewer the chance to experience the intricate attention to detail and successful communication of ideas between artists. This collaboration creates a direct link between wall and floor, making the whole piece approachable for all.

Henk Wolvers is a maker whose work is very varied, but still retains a strong sense of a focused, personal approach to clay. His *Swimming Pool* piece is a great example of this maker's flexibility and diversity when designing and creating for interiors. After exhibiting a smaller 'swimming pool' wall piece at the Singer Museum in Laren, Netherlands, Wolvers was approach by his client to create a larger piece for his swimming pool wall.

The piece not only heightens the feeling of movement but interacts with the water, wall and viewer as the pattern flows and dances across the wall's surface, almost as if the ceramics were the clouds in the sky. It also works by capturing reflections of the water, and creates its own shadows by being hung with a small clearance.

Using thin slabs of porcelain with a thin coating of cobalt sulphate, Wolvers made and installed 94 pieces of the ceramics, high-fired to 1300°C (2372°F). Each was individually installed with a backing of steel pins which were then glued to the ceramics backing.

Pieter Stockmans (Belgium)

Pieter Stockmans is undoubtedly a ceramicist who questions and pushes the boundaries of clay. His approach and understanding of space is truly inspirational, the in-depth thought given to his

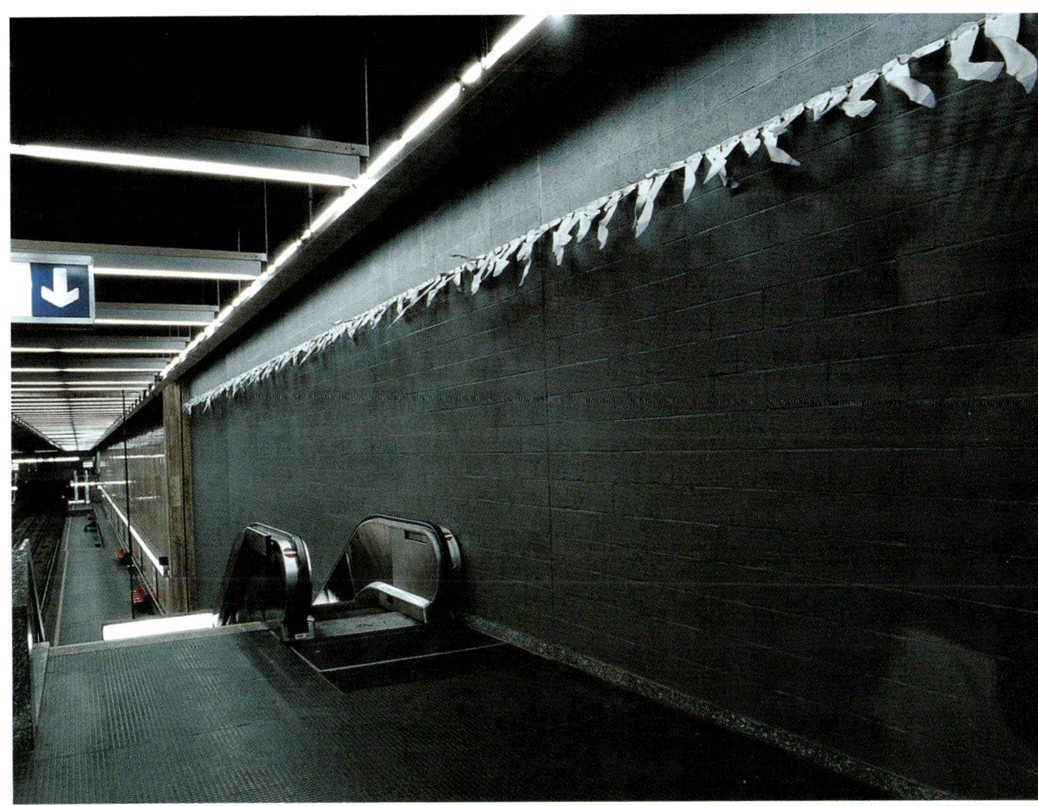

Brussels Subway by Pieter Stockmans, 1991. 4 separate sections, each over 25 m (82 ft.) in length. Installed in George-Henri Metro Station on the platform walls. Porcelain. *Photo courtesy of Pieter Stockmans Studio.*

work and concept shows the strength of his commitment to finding a successful conclusion for each piece. Many would define his work as installation art (but it *is* permanent). Pieter Stockmans' work is interesting because he continues to make objects at the same time as his 'installations', which clearly cross the boundaries from the crafted object. Nevertheless, his approach to space in many respects could be viewed as the vehicle for his changing ideas, and the continuing desire to interact with the wall space. He is also engaged with the action of reproduction and movement, that seem to drive his ideas further. Although Stockmans would argue it is the action of doing that inspires the pieces, it is clear these actions have had a profound effect on his thought processes and work over the years.

The scale of his work never seems to be an issue for this ceramicist. If anything, it is the scale of the wall, building or interior space that seems to encase and possibly restrict this maker. It is clear he has a vision for progressing our view of spaces through their marriage with ceramics. This could be due to his original training as a designer, and his need to transform our living environment for the better. In many respects his work is a subtle transformation of certain areas, making us stop and reconsider a location we might have passed before many times. As the work is not always hung at eye level, and is never small, his work does need to be viewed at a distance to appreciate both the scale, and the piece as a whole. The *Brussels Subway* is a good example of this: at over 25 m (82 ft) in length the piece becomes an echo of a journey we all experience in this environment. Though often made of many small pieces, the concept and end result is never small scale, and he is certainly one leading artist pushing the boundaries in this area.

Flock (UK)

Flock was created in 2003, after three months, 36 hours a week, 4000 pieces of glazed porcelain, and at a length of 14 m (46 ft). This installation was designed and made by four ceramicists: John Butler, Jonna Behrens, Anne Jamison and Debbie Metherell. *Flock* is an example of a successful collaboration between four makers who had one main thing in common when they were brought together to create this large-scale wall piece: all had previously studied for their ceramic degrees at the University of Westminster, Harrow, London. It is fascinating to see how bringing together four very different creative styles can result in such a strong, sensitive and exciting collaboration (*see also* p.34). This is an obvious outcome of a successful creative dialogue between the four makers.

Over 2000 students and staff have access to the University's main campus in central London, which was to be the location for the project. The courtyard is viewed from many areas as people walk from one end of the building to another, or just stop to rest. These considerations of the use of the space and location were important factors for the group to bear in mind when designing and making, as the aim of the piece was to turn this bleak stretch into an area of interest, which people would enjoy as they passed through.

The commission began with a two-day intense brainstorming session between the artists. This was a valuable experience for all involved, and helped to create a strong proposal. The needs of the space were carefully considered. With the grey background of the wall, the selection of colour was important, as the porcelain clay alone would have had a neutral tone and meant the space remained uninviting. Once they were happy with their design, the group's vision of the courtyard was presented to the Provost of the University through discussion and drawings.

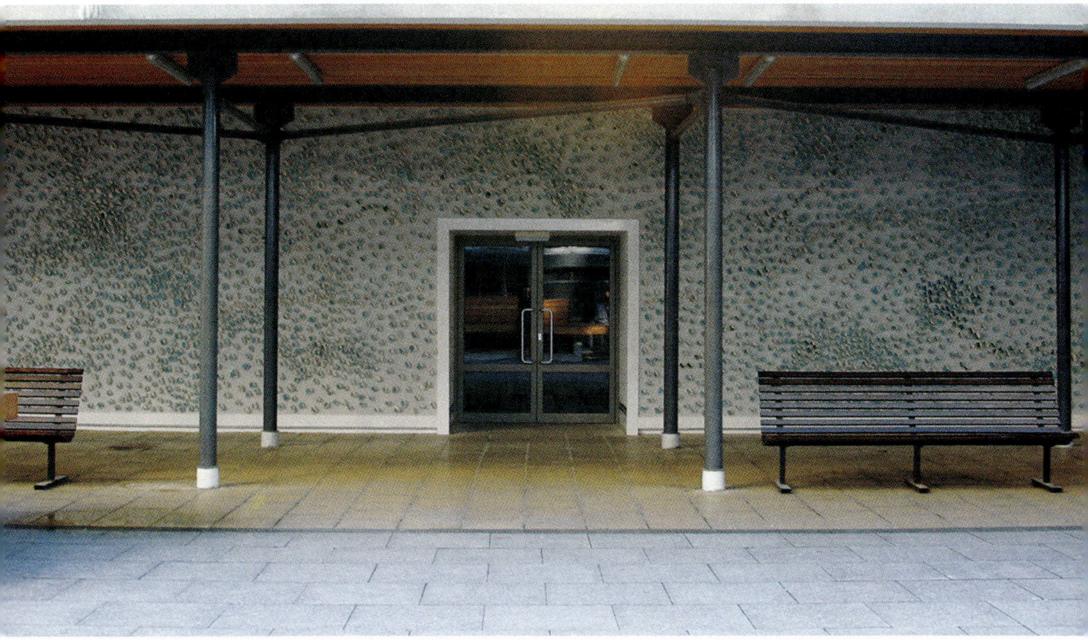

Flock is certainly a good example of successfully creating a new dynamic for a space. The variety and choice of blues has captured the light, the passer-by, and the viewer's attention. The tactile porcelain is inviting, and reminds the viewer of simple thumb marks made into soft clay. Although *Flock* is an abstract design, in many respects the clay forms seem to be growing and moving across the wall's surface. The title given to the piece also seems suitable, as 'flock' can refer to a shepherd's flock and/or a flock of birds, with connotations of nurturing, caring and guiding individuals to achieve and feel supported in this educational environment, and of moving forward together as a group.

Flock (detail below), by John Butler, Jonna Behrens, Anne Jamison, Debbie Metherell, 2003. Commissioned by University of Westminster, Regent Street Campus, London. Size: 40.21 m^2 (433 sq. ft). Valentine's Special Porcelain with glaze. *Photo by Andy Golding.*

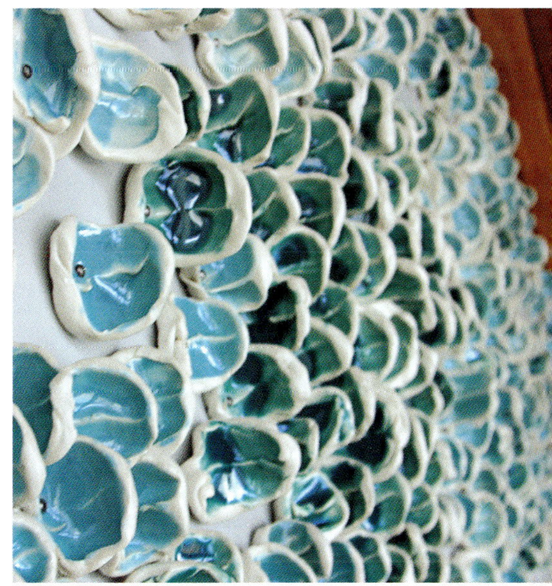

Stine Jespersen (Denmark)

Throughout Jespersen's work she communicates aspects of repetition by working in grid formations. One of her commissioned pieces, which is a good response to location and limited wall space, is one of her *Clay Knit* ceramic wall pieces created for the Cookbook Café, InterContinental Hotel, London. Mounted on the rich red background the dry white ceramics capture small squares of the rich red in a grid pattern, giving an intense focus on the wall. The wall enhances the contemporary and stylish environment of the restaurant.

Christie Brown (UK)

Inspired by elements of past ancient narrative, religion and forgotten cultures, Christie Brown's work responds to these themes by using the figure and human form as a vehicle for expression. In her work the body is a container conveying to the viewer reminders of past rituals and customs that have been long forgotten. The piece *Resource – Clay* was created as part of a solo show at Wapping hydraulic power station, London, and it seemed fitting for the organic red-brick pieces which hung on the wall to be placed in this setting. It is evident that this artist responded to the space and its

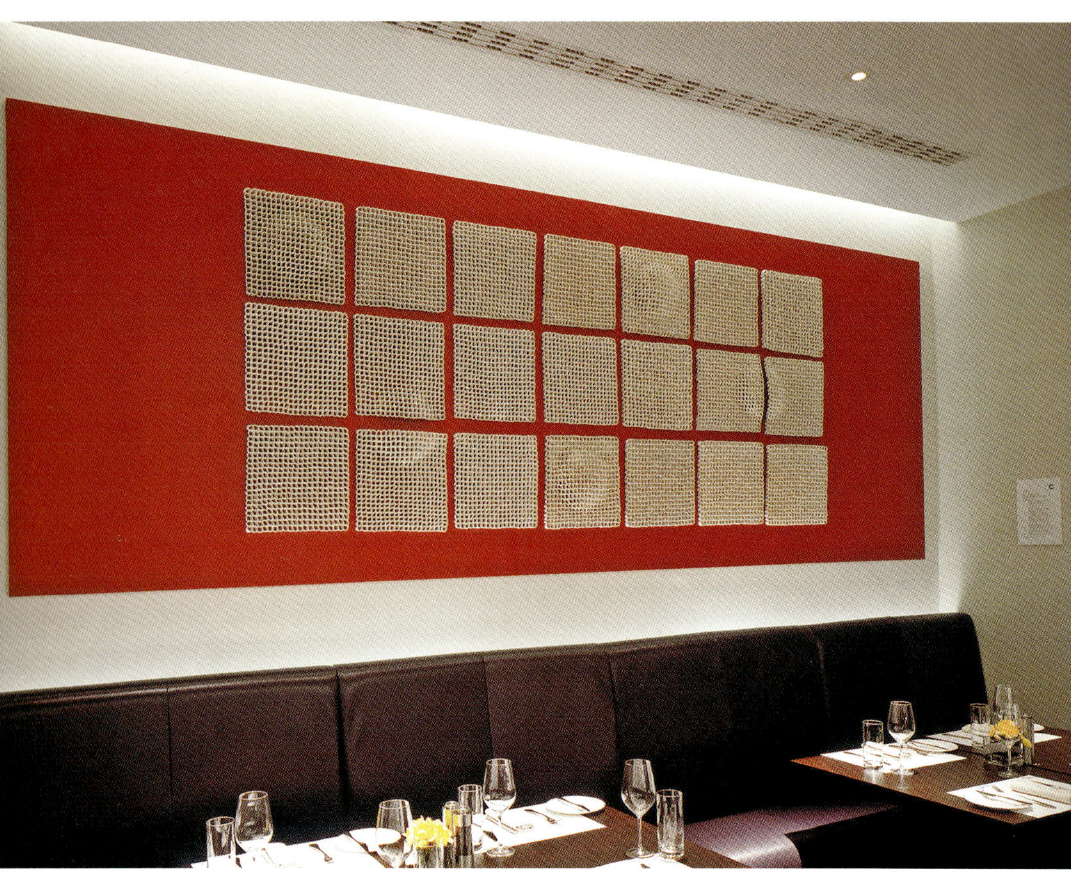

Clay Knit by Stine Jespersen, 2008. Size: 35 x 35 x 5 cm (14 x 14 x 2 in.). Ceramic wall-piece, white earthenware clay fired to 1080°C (1976°F). *Photo courtesy of the artist.*

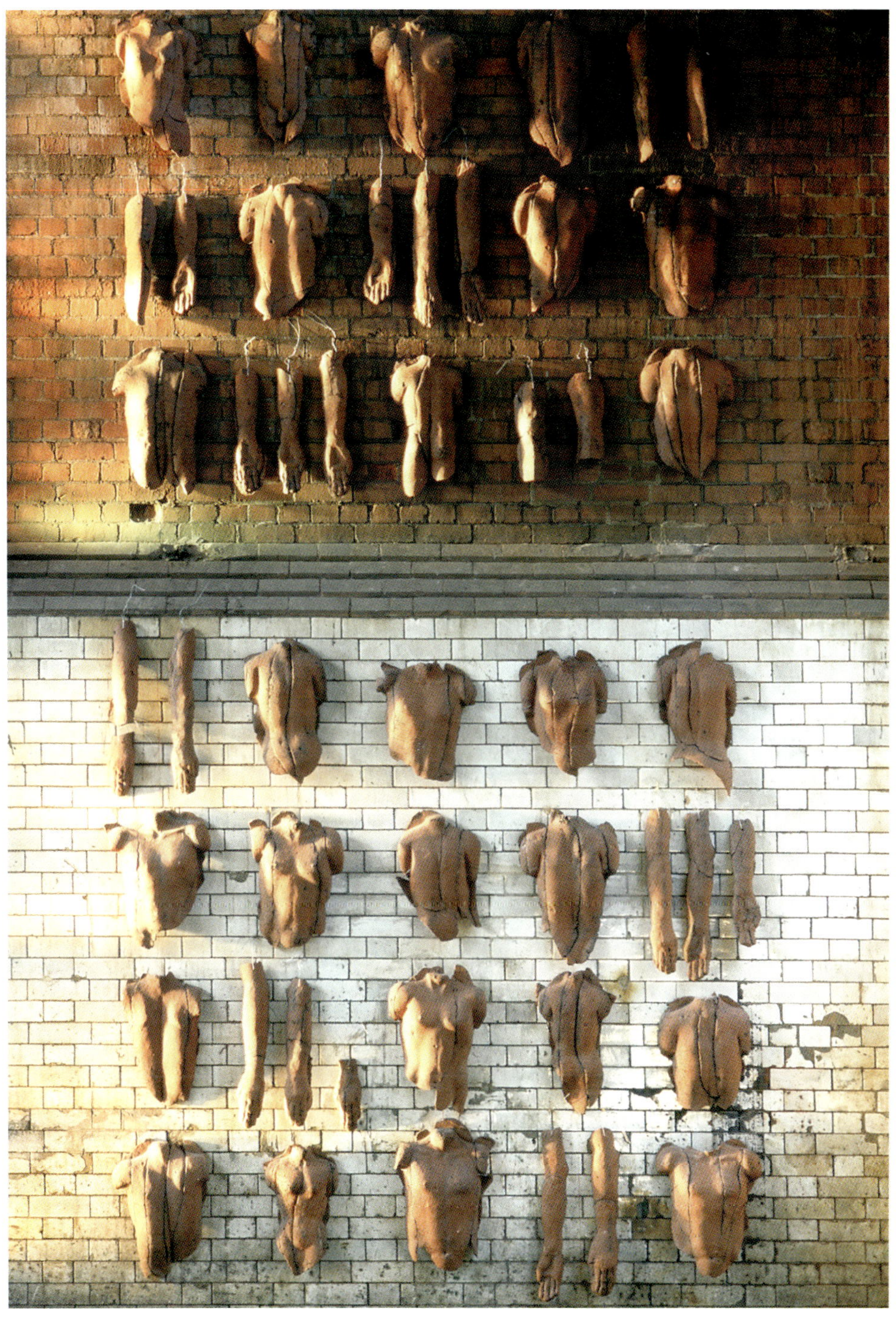

Resource – Clay by Christie Brown, 1999. Size: 2.60 × 4.90 × 0.30 m (8½ × 16 × 1 ft). Brick clay and spring steel. *Photo by Kate Forrest.*

past function as a power station, and in many ways the space created and developed a strong narrative with the work. There is something haunting about the limbs and torsos hung at this height against the eroded, white-tiled wall. Christie Brown explains her inspiration: '*Resource-Clay* paid homage to the workforce of the former power station who once contributed to the past life of the space. The work was also inspired by the practice of ex-votos. In ancient Etruscan and Roman cultures gifts were offered to the gods with prayer as a form of healing, a practice which still has a counterpart in some contemporary religions, where representations of an ailing body part demonstrate a belief in the healing power of mimesis.' The uneven joining of the red-brick clay slabs gives the impression of muscle and skin, and also creates interesting shadows across the forms.

Pekka Paikkari (Finland)

Pekka Paikkari's fascination with the surface, to rejoin cracked and broken ceramic forms, could be described as a passion to deconstruct and reconstruct one's own creative journey. Using his hands and feet as tools to work into the large sheet of clay placed on the studio floor, it is the action of their movement that creates the textured surface, which is later highlighted by oxides applied during the drying process. The broken shards are fired first to 1260°C (2300°F) in an industrial tunnel kiln at the Arabia Ceramic Factory, then finally fired in saggars filled with sawdust to create the deep varied colour surface. The expanse of his pieces and the feeling they create on the wall's surface is an ambition by the artist to remove the clean, bland wall space by reminding us of other, more alluring, landscapes.

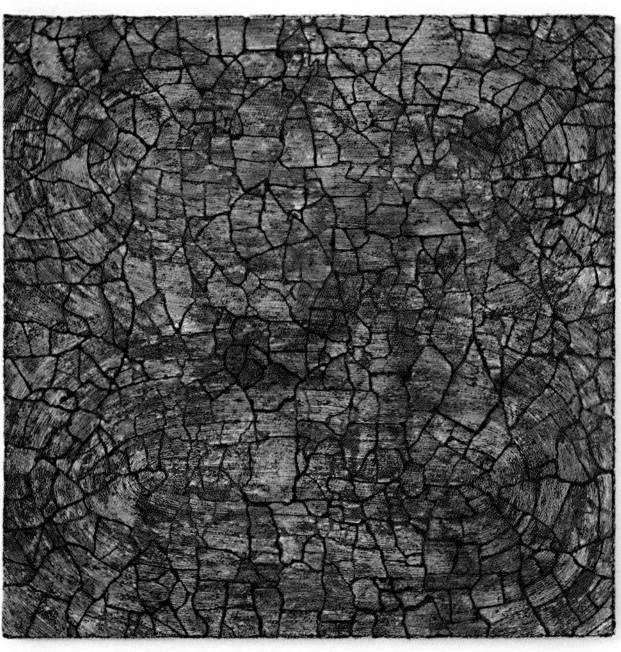

Follow the Path by Pekka Paikkari, 2008. 186 x 186 cm (73 x 73 in.). Stoneware clay fired to 1260°C (2300°F). *Photo by Tukka Paikkari.*

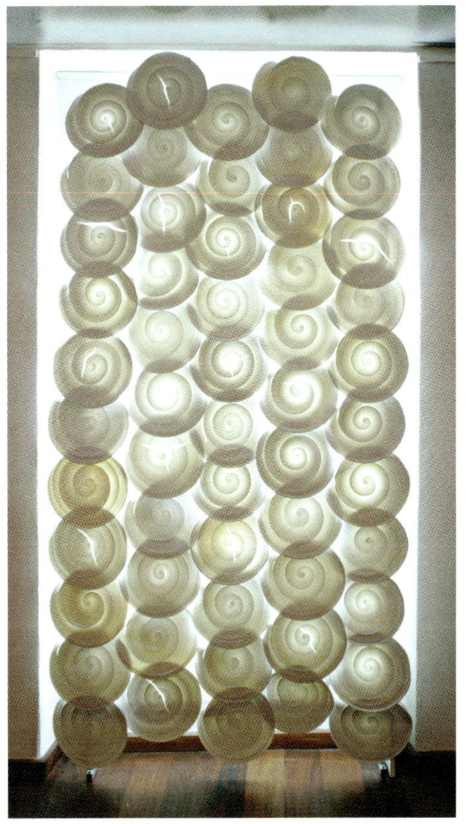

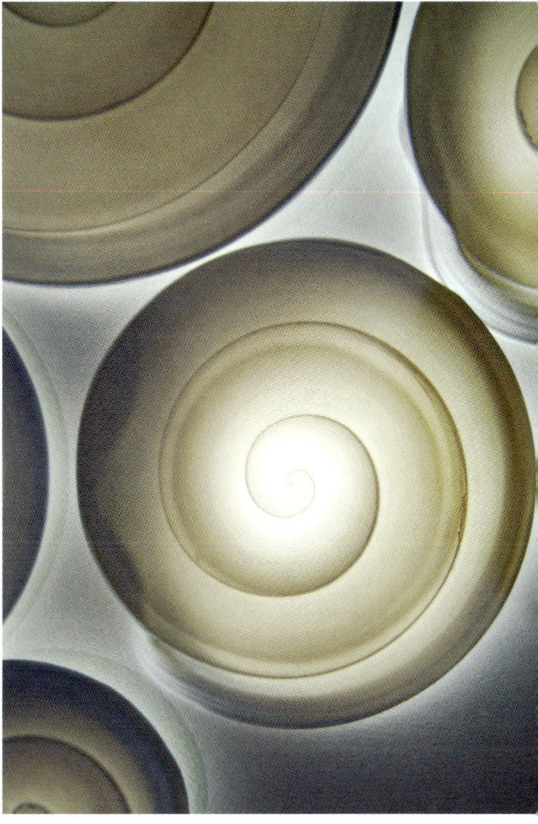

Thrown Discs by Margaret O'Rorke, (detail, right) 2002. Ht: 2.30 m (7½ ft); W: 1.12 m (3½ ft) Frame depth: 14 cm (5½ in.). Designed for an exhibition at Louis Poulsin Showroom, Copenhagen. Thrown porcelain discs, fired to 1300°C (2372°F). *Photo by B. Ryberg.*

Margaret O'Rorke (UK)

Margaret O'Rorke's work has continued over time to develop a strong dialogue between space, light and ceramics. Creating pieces that interact with a variety of locations and scales, she has continued to mix the translucent qualities of the thrown high-fired porcelain with the warm use of lighting. *Thrown Discs* is a good example of how this maker is sensitive to the essential requirements to transform a space. This piece was designed and made for an alcove space, and shows how a limited, dark space can be transformed by a wall piece and the use of lighting. Each thrown disc has been created and distorted to support a wire fixing, which in turn then joins onto a string of adjustable hooks. The whole piece is supported by an aluminium metal frame which the lighting is also attached to.

With their translucent quality the discs in the alcove are reminders of delicate shells you might find on the beach. It is also worth noting that the ceramics is hung all the way from ceiling to floor, all helping to create and contribute to the light bouncing around the space.

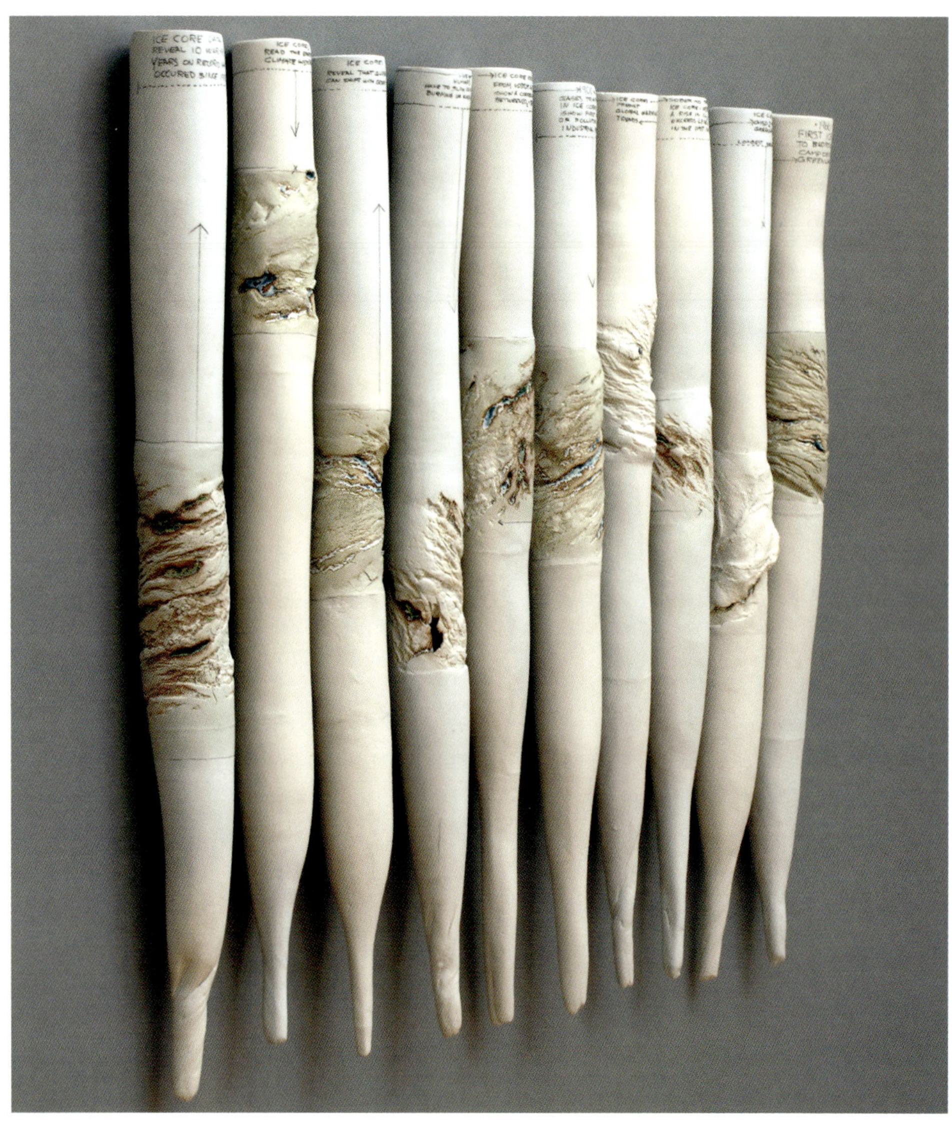

Ice Cores by Paula Winokur, 2004. 10 elements, each: Ht: 81 cm (32 in.); D: 7.5 cm (3 in.) Total: Ht: 81 cm (32 in.); W: 121 cm (48 in.). Porcelain clay/ceramic pencil/some glaze fired to 1300°C (2372°F). *Photo by John Carlano.*

Paula Winokur (USA)

Paula Winokur pieces are inspired by glacial landscapes, the geological erosion of the natural environment and how we as human beings are creating an impact on this beautiful, retreating landscape.

Her work communicates the need to rediscover our connection with this terrain. It is in many ways a surprise to discover that the piece *Ice Cores* is actually made from porcelain, as it is so evocative of the ice cores you would expect to see being drilled from ice sheets by scientists in field research, for example in the Antarctic. With this in mind, seeing these pieces hung on the wall you almost expect water to begin dripping from the cores, and the pieces to start to melt before your eyes. Winokur's choice of a deep grey to display these pieces against is extremely effective, and helps to focus the viewer on the beautiful details in the porcelain.

Rafa Perez (Spain)

Making his own clay, experimenting with surface and the expansion of form are all elements this Spanish ceramicist uses within his ceramics. Although his pieces are fired to 1150°C (2102°F) the element of risk, and control over the kiln firing is something that has developed his wall pieces. During the firing he is known to stop the kiln once the piece has reached its desired effect: this is done by looking into the kiln at high temperatures, no doubt an exciting process to watch!

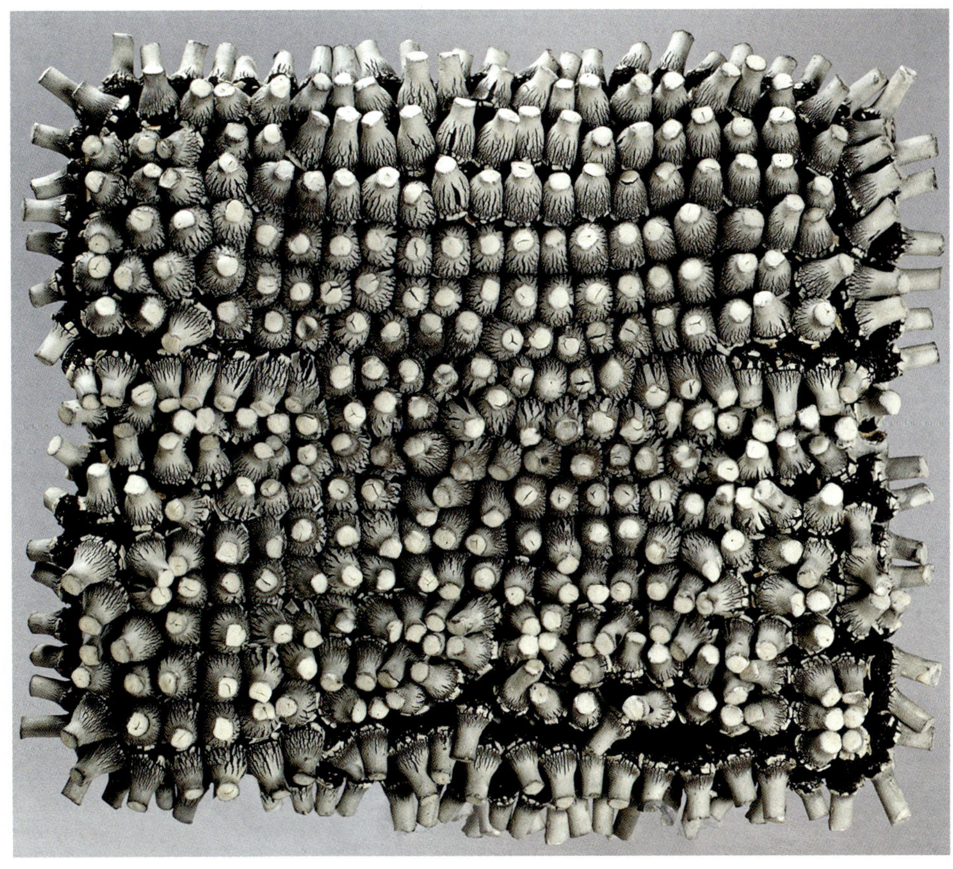

Untitled by Rafa Perez. 40 x 50 x 7 cm (16 x 20 x 2¾ in.). Fired clay to 1150°C (2102°F) using own clay. *Photo by Carlos Hermosilla.*

Bibliography

Bormand, M, Gaborit, R, *Les Della Robbia: Sculptures en Terre Cuite Émaillée de la Renaissance Italienne*, Réunions des Musées Nationaux, 2002.

Clayarch Gimhae Museum, *The Shin Sang Ho Exhibition*, exhibition catalogue, 2007.

Delbene, Giacomo (ed), *Public, Private, Ephemeral: Ceramics in Architecture*. Published by ASCER, Spanish Ceramic Tile Manufacturers' Association.

Hamer, Frank & Janet, *The Potters Dictionary*, 1997 (fourth edition), A&C Black, London.

Hamilton, David, *Architectural Ceramics*, Thames and Hudson, London, 1978.

Heeney, Gwen, *Brickworks*, A & C Black, London, 2003.

Herzog, Thomas, Lang, Werner, Krippner, Roland, *Façade Construction Manual*, PPUR Presses Polytechniques, 2007,

Higby, Wayne, *Earth Cloud*, Arnoldsche Art Publishers, Stuttgart, 2007.

Ceramics Art and Perception, issue 39, (Hoshino S & Tani A), 2000.

Maillard, Anne, *La Céramique Architecturale à Travers les Catalogues de Fabricants 1840-1940: Un Inventaire Raisonné de la Collection du Musée de la Céramique Architecturale à Auneuil*, Editions Septima, Paris, 1999.

Maillard, Anne, *La Céramique Architecturale, 1880-1930*, Paris, Normandie, Beauvaisis, Editions Septima, 1995.

Mansfield, Janet, *Ceramics in the Environment*, A& C Black, London/The American Ceramic Society, Ohio, 2005.

Moulding, Assembling, Designing: Ceramics in Architecture, Castellon, ASCER (Spanish Ceramic Tile Manufacturers' Association), 2006.

Peterson, Susan, *The Complete Potters Handbook. The Craft and Art of Clay*. Third edition, 1999, Laurence King Publishing, London.

Rauterberg, Hanno, *Talking Architecture*, Prestel Verlag, Munich, Berlin, London, New York, 2008. (See in particular the interviews of Cecil Balmond, Jacques Herzon & Pierre de Meuron, Peter Zumthor.)

Ritchie W, *Walter Ritchie Sculptures*. Date unknown, published by Walter Ritchie, Kenilworth, Warwickshire.

Robison, Jim, *Large-scale Ceramics*, 2005 (first printed 1997), A&C Black, London/The American Ceramic Society, Ohio.

Smithson, Pete, *Installing Exhibitions, A Practical Guide*, A&C Black, London, 2009.

Teutonico, Jeanne Marie (Ed.). *Architectural Ceramics: Their History, Manufacture and Conservation: A Joint Symposium of English Heritage and the United Kingdom Institute for Conservation, 22-25 September 1994*. London: James & James, 1996.

Tunick, Susan [et al], *Paris and the Legacy of French Architectural Ceramics*, Friends of Terra Cotta Press, New York, 1997.

Vallet, André, *Céramique Architecturale*, Dessain et Tolra, Paris, 1982.

Other Resources

Erven, René, 'Ceramics and Architecture', European Ceramic Work Center (www.ekwc.nl)

WOCEF (World Ceramic Exposition Foundation), South Korea (www.wocef.com)

List of suppliers

UK

Ceramic suppliers

Ceramatech suppliers
Unit 16 & 17
Frontier Works
33 Queen Street
London, N17 8JA
Tel: 020 8885 4492

Commercial Clay Ltd
Sandbach Road
Cobridge
Stoke-on-Trent, ST4 2DR
Tel: 01782 274448
Fax : 01782 206871
info@commercialclay.co.uk

Global Ceramic Materials Ltd
Milton Works
Diamond Crescent
Off Leek New Road, Milton
Stoke-on-Trent, ST2 7PX
Tel: +44 (0)1782 537297
www.globalcm.co.uk

Scarva Pottery Supplies
Unit 20
Scarva Road Industrial Estate,
Banbridge, Co. Down
Northern Ireland, BT32 3QD
Tel: 028 406 69699
Fax: 028 406 69700
david@scarvapottery.com

Valentine Clays Ltd.
The Sliphouse
18-20 Chell Street, Hanley
Stoke-on-Trent, ST1 6BA
Tel: 01782 271200
Fax : 01782 280008

Art installers

01 Art Services Ltd
Unit 2, Towcester Rd,
London, E3 3ND
Tel: 020 7515 7510

Art Move Ltd
Unit 3, The Arches,
Grant Road
London, SW11 2NU
Tel: 020 75851801
www.artmove.co.uk

Architectural, aluminium & glass installation

L2i Ltd
Unit 16, Lincoln Business Centre
Lincoln Road, Cressex Business Park
High Wycombe
Bucks, HP12 3RD
Tel: 01494 451545
www.l2iltd.co.uk

Peterlee Glass Company Ltd
28 Lister Rd
North West Industrial Estate
Peterlee
County Durham, SR8 2RB
Tel: 0191 586 4626.
www.peterleeglass.com/

Unit Glass Art
Armighall Close
Norwich
Norfolk, NR3 3UE
Tel: 01603 414557

Architects

Penoyre & Prasad LLP
28-42 Banner Street,
London EC1Y 8QE
Tel: 020 7250 3477
www.penoyre-prasad.net

Metalworks & lighting

Fairfields display and lighting
Head Office
127 Albert Street, Fleet
Hampshire GU51 3SN
Tel: 01252 812211
Fax: 01252 812123
info@fairfielddisplays.co.uk

Norwich Sheet Metal Co Ltd
11 Hurricane Way
Norwich, NR6 6EZ
Tel: 01603 416266?
Fax: 01603 419490?

Health & Safety

HSE Infoline
Caerphilly Business Park
Caerphilly, CF83 3GG
Tel: 0845 345 0055
www.hse.gov.uk/legislation/index.htm

Miscellaneous

(For museum gel & putty)
Milena Artworks
Tel: 020 8343 2003
www.milena-artworks.com

USA & Canada

Ceramic suppliers

American Art Clay Company
6060 Guion Road
Indianapolis, IN 46254
Tel: 800-374-1600
www.amaco.com

Axner Pottery Supply
490 Kane Court
Oviedo, FL 32765
Tel: 800-843-7057
www.axner.com

Continental Clay Company
1101 Stintson Blvd, NE
Minneapolis, MN 55413
Tel: 800-432-2529
www.continentalclay.com

Del-Val Ceramic Supply
1230 E. Mermaid Lane
Wyndmoor, PA 19038
Tel: 215-233-0655
www.delvalpotters.com

Laguna Clay Company
14400 Lomitas Avenue
City of Industry, CA 91746
Tel: 800-452-4862
www.lagunaclay.com

Mile Hi Ceramics
77 Lipan
Denver, CO 80223
Tel: 303-825-4570
www.milehiceramics.com

Tucker's Pottery Supplies Inc.,
Unit 7, 15 West Pearce Street
Richmond Hill
Ontario, Canada L4B 1H6
Tel: 905-889-7705
www.tuckerspottery.com

Glass suppliers

Bullseye Glass Co.
3722 SE 21st Avenue
Portland, OR 97202
www.bullseyeglass.com

Franciscan Glass Co. Inc
100 San Antonio Circle
Mountain View, CA 94040
www.franciscanglass.com

Hollander Glass Co. East
140 58th Street, Ste 1D
Brooklyn, NY 11220

SA Bendheim Co. Inc
61 Willet Street, Ste 6A
Passaic, NJ 07055
www.bendheimwall.com

Metal suppliers

XPress Metals
658 Ohio Street
Buffalo, NY 1420
Tel: 866-881-4326
www.xpressmetals.com

Mainline Metals Inc.
21 Bala Avenue
Bala Cynwyd, PA 19004
Tel: 610-668-0888
www.mainlinemetals.com

Alaska Steel Co.
1200 W. Dowling Road
Anchorage, AK 99518
Tel: 907-561-1188/800-770-0969
www.alaskasteel.com

Europe

Ceramic Suppliers

Solargil
89520 Moutiers-en-Puisaye
France
Tel: (00 33) 03 86 45 50 00
www.ceramique.com/solargil

Ceradel Socor
Z.I.N. 17 à 23 Rue Frédéric Bastiat
B.P. 1598
87022 Limoges Cedex 9
France
Tel: (00 33) 05 55 35 02 35

Metalworks & lighting

Fischerwerke GmbH & Co. KG
Weinhalde 14 - 18
72178 Waldachtal
Germany
Tel: +49 (0) 7443 12 0
Fax:: +49 (0) 7443 12 42 22

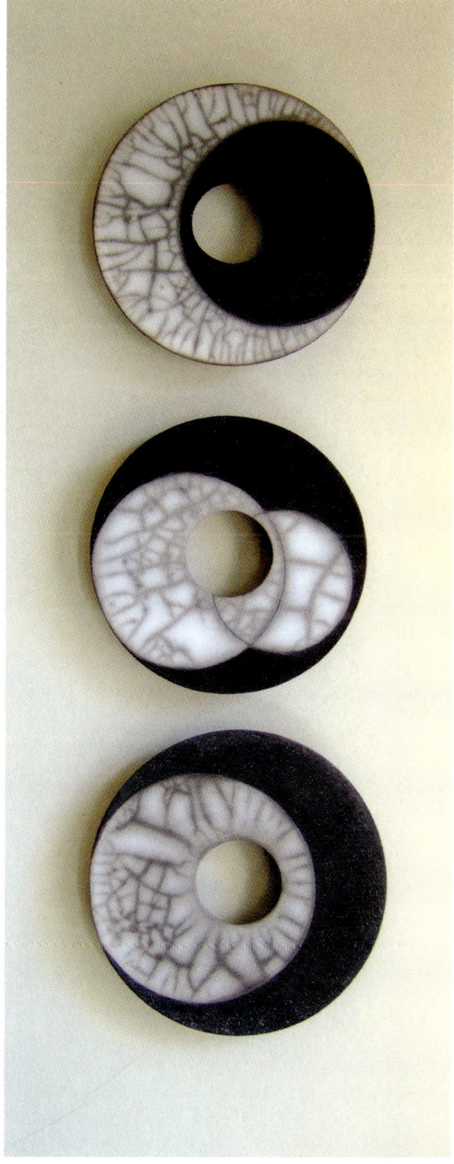

Wall pieces by Emma Johnstone. Raku-fired and mounted on wall individually. *Photo courtesy of the artist.*

Index